THE POLITICAL ECONOMY OF SENTIMENT

FINANCIAL HISTORY

Series Editor: Robert E. Wright

TITLES IN THIS SERIES

Slave Agriculture and Financial Markets in Antebellum America. The Bank of the United States in Mississippi, 1831–1852
Richard Holcombe Kilbourne, Jr

FORTHCOMING TITLES

Baring Brothers and the Birth of Global Finance
Peter E. Austin

Gambling on the American Dream: Atlantic City and the Casino Era
James R. Karmel

The Revenue Imperative: The Union's Financial Policies During the American Civil War
Jane Flaherty

Guilty Money: The City of London in Victorian and Edwardian Culture, 1815–1914
Ranald C. Mitchie

THE POLITICAL ECONOMY OF SENTIMENT:

PAPER CREDIT AND THE SCOTTISH ENLIGHTENMENT IN EARLY REPUBLIC BOSTON, 1780–1820

BY

Jose R. Torre

Routledge
Taylor & Francis Group

LONDON AND NEW YORK

First published 2007 by Pickering & Chatto (Publishers) Limited

Published 2016 by Routledge
2 Park Square, Milton Park, Abingdon, Oxfordshire OX14 4RN
711 Third Avenue, New York, NY 10017, USA

First issued in paperback 2015

Routledge is an imprint of the Taylor & Francis Group, an informa business

BRITISH LIBRARY CATALOGUING IN PUBLICATION DATA
Torre, Jose R.
The political economy of sentiment : paper credit and the Scottish Enlightenment in early republic Boston, 1780–1820. – (Financial history)
1. Paper money – History 2. Enlightenment 3. United States – Economic conditions – To 1865
I. Title
330.9'7304

ISBN 13 : 978-1-138-66521-7 (pbk)
ISBN-13: 978-1-85196-885-5 (hbk)

Typeset by Pickering & Chatto (Publishers) Limited

CONTENTS

ACKNOWLEDGMENTS

This book, as well as my education and training as a historian, is deeply indebted to my dissertation supervisors, Melvyn Dubofsky, Brendan McConville and Sarah Elbert. Their long support of my work has been invaluable. Over the years Carla Mulford of Pennsylvania State University, Jane Kamensky of Brandeis University and Naomi Zack of the University of Oregon also read parts of the project at various stages and warmly encouraged my ideas. A number of institutions supported my research for this book. The generous financial support of Binghamton University and the Binghamton University History Department was critical to the completion of this project. I undertook large parts of the research for this project at the Winterthur Library. Their financial support and the contributions of the faculty and students at Winterthur were important to the development of my ideas. Thanks go to Neville Thompson, Laura Simo, Sarah Fayen, Gretchen Buggeln and my Foulsham House-mates Lisa Strong, Benjamin Carp and Mary Beaudry. Special thanks go to the various libraries and librarians who contributed their time and efforts to assist my research. The staffs of the Binghamton University Inter-Library Loan department were especially patient and efficient. Eugene Zepp and his colleagues at the Boston Public Library created a comfortable environment for me to pore over the Town of Boston Tax Books. Likewise, Nicholas Graham and many others at the Massachusetts Historical Society took the time to fulfil my many haphazard requests. The series editor Robert Wright and his colleagues at Pickering & Chatto, Michael Middeke and Julie Wilson, have been encouraging and efficient. While the collegiality and helpful advice of these many colleagues has greatly improved the final book, any remaining errors are entirely my own.

Finally, my family deserves special acknowledgment. Our parents, Florencio and Josephine Torre and Michael and Lorna Hall, supported us emotionally and financially through graduate school, the birth of our two children and the creation of this book. Special thanks to Isabelle Magann, whose trust in us has made our privileged lives possible. Of course, I could never have completed this book without the full-time support and wise counsel of my wife, Melissa Hall. She read and reread numerous versions of my ideas even as she bore the brunt of our family responsibilities. Working on this project has been especially satisfying since the birth of our two wonderful children, AJ and Lenny. When I began *The Political Economy of Sentiment* Lenny was a distant egg and AJ used his fingers to stuff large overcooked broccoli flowers into his face from a highchair. Watching them grow up alongside this book has kept it all in perspective.

Este libro es para Manuel y Medardo,
no me he olvidado.

LIST OF CHARTS, TABLES AND FIGURES

INTRODUCTION: PROMETHEUS UNBOUND

Writing from Philadelphia to his 'gentle affectionate dove' for the second time that day, Massachusetts Senator Harrison Gray Otis begged his wife Sally to pay attention to Boston gossip. 'Please to be particular in notifying me what you hear respecting Craigie', he requested. Otis held Craigie's note of five thousand dollars, due in six months, and he feared the worst. Like many of Otis's friends and business partners, Craigie's finances teetered on the edge of disaster. Only three weeks prior he expressed to Sally his mortification at the imminent failure of another friend, 'H'. 'It is impossible for us not to feel a lively interest in the fate of such amiable friends', he wrote to her, 'especially reflecting upon the aggravations resulting from their high notions of life'. Indeed, he noted, Sally had been wise to remain in Boston. 'To witness trouble in that quarter would be fatal to your pleasure & happiness here, without alleviating the misfortunes of others.'[1] 'In short, such is the uncertainty of all men in business', he plaintively concluded the Craigie letter, 'that nothing can be called property which is not in one's own iron chest'.[2]

Otis's anxiety with regard to the fleeting nature of contemporary property was well warranted. The business world Otis mastered was new and full of exciting possibilities; it was also a world fraught with financial peril. Pick up a newspaper in Boston in August 1807 and in the classifieds was a 'Bank Thermometer!' – a regular feature from 1807 to 1809 in a number of newspapers in Boston and across Massachusetts. The 'Bank Thermometer!' listed the constantly fluctuating relative value of the numerous bank notes then circulating in Boston. Unlike sponsored listings from exchange dealers like *Cohen's Lottery and Note Exchange* or Boston's *Gilbert and Dean, Lottery and Commission Brokers*, the *Thermometer* was disinterested and provided a candid, disdainful and often humorous appraisal of the values, or lack thereof, of banks' notes. These listings and the services of stock 'jobbers' and money exchangers were vital to Early Republic Americans negotiating the paper storm then engulfing Boston and most other American cities. Bank notes issued by Boston banks, the 'country' banks located throughout Massachusetts, the other New England states – especially Vermont and Rhode Island – as well as the rest of the country, flooded the city. Bank notes even found their way to Boston in large volume (with a little help) from places as far away as the Michigan Territory. Add to this mix the private notes that merchants and retailers issued, the dividend cheques and other financial instruments that commonly traded as money, as well as British, Spanish and Portuguese specie, and you have a babble of currencies.[3] Fortunes were made and lost negotiating these instruments, one day trading at par, the next day negotiable only for surplus shoes and second-rate farm produce at fifteen cents on the dollar.

The number and variety of financial instruments circulating as currency was not the only source of financial anxiety and instability. The nature of the paper was also new and sufficiently novel as to have profound consequences. Bank notes in particular were a peculiar form of money. Between the Revolution and the Civil War, American banks issued private notes that circulated as money but were not, properly speaking, assets in the way that an ordinary person might think of 'money' as an asset. Bank notes were in fact liabilities – promises or debts, payable in specie. In theory, banks maintained sufficient specie reserves to service the day-to-day demands on their liabilities – a practice well understood as fractional reserve banking. In practice, however, banks issued notes far in excess of their specie reserves, stretching thin the veneer of solidity which specie provided the banking system. Furthermore, deposits – most often discounts (loans) negotiated with the bank and simply 'deposited' into borrowers' accounts – were also liabilities, a way of extending credit without printing notes, but often were not recognized as liabilities to be considered by the bank directors under the bank charter's legally prescribed limits. Furthermore, into the 1830s, restrictions on liabilities referred to the bank's capital, not its specie reserves. Thus as long as the directors could maintain confidence in the bank, there was little effective reason to limit their note issues or discounts – 'book money'.[4]

As opaque as these practices were, they nevertheless had clear consequences; banks never held anywhere near the sufficient amount of specie for redemption of all their liabilities and the value of their note issues fluctuated according to the confidence and trust that people had in the institution, its directors, and economic conditions in general. *Confidence* was in fact the 'commodity' that bankers depended on. They designed the banking system to use specie as a confidence-maintaining device, not an actual currency to redeem notes with. Bankers used specie reserves to satisfy the 'illusion of solidity' and maintain their notes in a state of perpetual circulation.[5]

The ambivalent nature of bank notes and the jumble of misunderstood practices and ideas associated with banking often resulted in counterintuitive situations and outcomes. Investors could, for example, purchase a bank, as Boston's Andrew Dexter did, with the bank's own assets by assuming the bank's liabilities. Bank notes were after all a liability; thus Dexter could assume the bank notes' explicit liabilities and use the debtor's notes held by the bank to buy the bank's stock from its 'investors' – often the very debtors whose notes were exchanged.

Likewise, banks during this period were, as a Committee of the Massachusetts General Court concluded, often founded not by those with money to lend but by those wishing to borrow. If you did not have access to credit, you could start a bank and print notes that were essentially credit on your own collateral. Indeed, it became common practice to go one step further and 'bank' on 'banks'. Investors petitioned for a bank charter, paid a portion of the original capital in specie or the bank paper of a competing institution, then granted themselves loans collateralized by the full value of the stock to pay the remaining debt with enough left over to invest in other securities. Thus, a bank director in a new institution could, for example, purchase $1,000 in stock in the bank with $500 in notes from the Bank of the United States, obtain a $1,000 discount from the bank collateralized by the stock, pay off the balance due on the stock with the bank's own notes, and walk away with $500 in the bank's paper, $1,000 in stock, and a debt to himself (more or less) of $1,000. Theoretically, an investor could do this several times, creating nests of debt – and increasing the amount of 'money' in circulation without ever committing a single dollar in specie. The little specie that was infrequently paid in to the banks gave the airy paper mountains a patina of 'solidity' and often sufficed to maintain the institutions in the imaginations of ordinary citizens who, awash in financial paper, accepted a financially polyglot economy.

The implications of these practices were both material and ideal. First, banks exponentially increased the money supply. Americans quickly took to heart the special powers of banks to, as David Hume put it, 'make liquid' their assets (and reputations) and competed lustily to charter as many banks as possible. The subsequent explosion of paper credit was, certainly inflationary and, given the specious nature of many of these institutions, volatile; but these new instruments also tapped the enormous potential of the Early Republic economy and greatly stimulated economic growth.[6] Second, bank notes transformed money, property and personality. Paper credit instruments ultimately became, as Janet Riesman has argued, an expression of the confidence people had in the nation and in themselves. Bank notes in particular came to be understood not as backed by specie *per se* but as a function of trust – a social web of confidence. Banks, as the bank supporter Erick Bollmann put it in 1810, were 'like a fleet, buoyed up by confidence and credit gliding down the spacious stream of trade and prosperity, each *just comfortably ballasted with specie*, and all of them *linked together* by a mighty chain of debtors and creditors, fastened to that ballast'. The banks were the basis for civilization; without them, he concluded, was 'stagnation, confusion, dissolution of the social bond, barbarism, and ruin'. Banks and other paper-emitting institutions of the day were, in the words of Boston's Samuel Blodget, the *'golden chains'* that held society together.[7]

The idea that paper credit instruments held society together is key to understanding Early Republic America. The new economic order – begun with the assumption and funding of the Revolutionary debt – was a 'venture'; an economic experiment 'floated' by the citizenry, not unlike the experiment of democracy. Creating and sustaining what critics called this immense 'fabric' required a new way of looking at value; it also both shaped and expressed new ideas and forms of property; ultimately, it both shaped and expressed changes in personality. To properly understand these developments, however, we must begin with J. G. A. Pocock.

'Property', Pocock declares, 'was both an extension and a prerequisite of personality'; and, he warns, 'we should be aware of the possibility that different modes of property may be seen as generating or encouraging different types of personality'.[8] Early modern political and social personality centred on real property, primarily land. In his capacity as property owner, the master dominated not only his family, but also the lives of his 'servants'. This property and household mastery, and the arms that he used to preserve them, allowed the idealized civic humanist or republican citizen independence and virtue; it was the basis for his political, economic and social personality.[9] Changes in the nature of personality, or alternately the construction of the modern personality, began, according to Pocock, with England's financial revolution and the rise of a new kind of property – credit.

The creation of the Bank of England and a national debt that generated a continuous and perpetual stream of income for investors was, according to Pocock, a new kind of property that existed only as an imagined entity in the mind of the investor. The government debt was a promise to pay into a future that would never arrive. The value of that debt thus reflected the perceived stability of the state; it was a function of confidence. Similarly, Pocock concludes, with the rise of a paper-credit economy, individual credit and debt relationships became immersed in the imagination of the investor. Furthermore, he might have added, 'deliberately organized issuing' banks functioning on a specie reserve ratio – a Bank of England innovation – further alienated money from its commodity value and seated that value in the subjective imagination of the holder.[10] And thus, 'property – the material foundation of both personality and government ... ceased to be real and has become not merely mobile but imaginary'.[11]

Pocock's conceptualization of this important point in human history is pregnant with meaning. The reconstruction of economic value as subjective and nominal unleashed an economic and cultural Prometheus. An economic order based on a perpetually expanding system of paper credit – a national debt or bank credits – broke the empiricist stranglehold on the economy and the mind. Economically, the mercantilist zero-sum game ended; one man or nation's gain need never be another's loss because the economy knew no bounds. The new economy, now conceptualized as an ever-expanding, self-regulating system limited only by confidence and the imagination, shattered the old world of 'real' values and limited economic growth. Subjective economic value also shattered 'real' values and fixed meaning in the realms of epistemology and personality. The 'conceptual basis of cognition' changed: knowledge and value became subjective, they came from inside. The transformation of money into an abstract idea based on subjective feelings represented a fundamental change in the 'constituent elements of the exchange abstraction' and ultimately shaped 'the conceptual elements of the cognitive faculty'.[12] Put another way, paper credit's rise changed the way human beings thought about value; it engendered an increased subjectivity that affected aesthetic and moral value, and transformed the ancient personality of the master into the modern, differentiated and subjective bourgeois.[13]

This new subjective bourgeois embraced and promoted a new world order; he had lost his ancient republican virtue. A society founded on credit and exchange mechanisms was fundamentally different from a land-based social order. Credit changed the relationship of the people to the state; through the national debt they were now its patrons, not its clients. Credit also changed the relationship of people to each other, who were now bound in an interdependent economic order, ultimately maintained by their confidence in that system. A new sociable and refined interdependence replaced the master's stoic republican and martial independence. Nevertheless, the master turned bourgeois was more than compensated for these losses, Pocock argues, through manners and a new relationship with things, or with people, through things.[14] The new bourgeois also understood his world through a new epistemology or world-view, best expressed by the eighteenth-century Scottish Moral Sense philosophers and political economists.[15]

Writing in an eighteenth-century Scotland dominated by imaginary forms of economic value, the Scottish Moral Sense philosophers and political economists developed an emotive epistemology and commercial humanism that shaped and reflected the new Anglo-American polite commercial society into the nineteenth century. At the centre of their new epistemology lay human feelings and emotions – sentiments – that operated in economics, morality and aesthetics. These men (and they were exclusively men) both promoted and gave shape and logic to the radical social, cultural and psychological changes that the rise of paper credit engendered. Francis Hutcheson, David Hume, Adam Smith and, of course, many others, were extremely important in the creation of political economy. They also wrote at length about the nature of society and personality. The common thread in all of their texts, however, is subjectivity. Their economic, moral and aesthetic values all derive from a new and uncharted subjectivity central to the modern personality. Widely read and influential in Britain and on the Continent, they were also, of course, influential in British North America, and what became the United States. Their efforts to map out the logic of modern society resonated with Americans during the Early Republic, when the architects of the Revolution turned their efforts to just such a radical enlightenment project.

This book traces the material and ideal elements of these changes as they developed in Harrison Gray Otis's Boston. It is an attempt to provide a 'unified conceptual framework' with which to understand the tremendous social, cultural, economic and psychological changes in Early Republic America.[16] The first two chapters examine the early-modern British background for these changes.

Chapter 1 details the early modern relationship between intrinsic value in silver, empiricism and theological voluntarism. It argues that we can best understand John Locke's bullionist position during the English recoinage debates of the 1690s through a reading of his epistemological treatise, *An Essay Concerning Human Understanding* (1690). In this influential text Locke argued that the true nature of 'matter' substances was external to human beings. Following Locke's logic, this meant that man could not question or replace intrinsic value in silver-as-money. This position was consistent with his *tabula rasa* sensational psychology and his empiricism, both derived from his theological voluntarism and orthodox Calvinism: an all-powerful Calvinist deity demanded an 'empty' humanity that absorbed all value knowledge at his will. Intrinsic value in silver was thus the economic correlate of empiricism, *tabula rasa* and orthodox Calvinism's theological beliefs; this was a complete epistemic system – a way of understanding the world that encompassed economic, moral and aesthetic value systems.

Chapter 2 explores the challenge to this world-view, and to Locke's empiricist and Calvinist formulation of humanity in particular, developed by the third Earl of Shaftesbury and the Scottish Moral Sense philosophers. The challenge to Lockean empiricism began with Shaftesbury's repudiation of Locke's *tabula rasa* assertion. According to Shaftesbury man was not born empty and selfish. Instead, God created man with an inner knowledge of wrong and right, beauty and deformity, harmony and dissonance. Shaftesbury's Neo-Platonic vision undermined Locke's sensational psychology, empiricism and theological voluntarism.

The Scottish Moral Sense philosophers transformed Shaftesbury's innate ideas into a moral sense that instinctively or intuitively recognized moral good and beauty. Francis Hutcheson, David Hume, Adam Smith, Dugald Stewart and others developed a 'theory of moral sentiments' that positioned a benevolent humanity as intimately associated with the *summum bonum*. An innate sympathy, derived through the imagination, marked human relationships and dominated human morality. Moral and aesthetic beauty, the Scots argued, derived from within; it was grounded in feelings. These Scottish ideas of man and his role in the cosmos challenged Calvinist formulations of a depraved and damned humanity (indeed, they were largely written in the midst of the conflict between Moderate (liberal) and Popular (Calvinist) religion in Scotland).

The Scots also constructed a synthetic political economy that connected the 'trichotomy of economic, aesthetic, and moral value'.[17] They put human institutions, instruments, everyday needs, and emotions at the centre of their moral, aesthetic and economic value systems. Their theory of money and the economy was completely at odds with Locke's bullionist mercantilism. For the Scottish political economists, money was not a store of value or wealth, but an exchange medium; money did not need intrinsic or commodity value; it was not a 'natural' entity created by the deity, but a human instrument. Paper credit or other confidence-based instruments thus best served as a circulating medium. The Scots' definition of the purpose and nature of the economy also reflected these changes. Wealth was in no way measured by specie or the accumulation of precious metals; it was a function of consumption and the satisfaction of individual desire. Furthermore, human desire drove the economy and spontaneously generated a socially-benevolent economic order. Hence, individual interests could not conflict with social interests – the pursuit of individual gain benefited all. Overall, Scottish political economy imagined a profoundly anthropocentric and individualistic economic order driven by the emotional needs of human beings and fuelled by self-created and confidence-based exchange instruments and institutions. These changes represented a radical new way of looking at the economy, and they were also part of a new way of looking at the world; part of a new emotive epistemology that also transformed morality and aesthetics.

The remaining five chapters look at changes in economic, moral and aesthetic value in Early Republic America overall, and Boston in particular. Chapter 3 develops the conflict between objective (silver) and subjective (paper credit) theories of money as expressed in the United States during the Early Republic. Engulfed in an economic and financial revolution, Early Republic theorists debated the nature of money and the purpose of the economy. Echoing the monetary debates of the Recoinage Crisis, some nascent American political economists explicitly argued that money needed intrinsic value to function as an exchange medium; you could not trade things for signs. For these thinkers, subjective theories of money, founded on a different epistemological basis than metallism, undermined the objective reality of a purposefully guided economy and social order. Supporters of paper credit followed Scottish political economy and increasingly emphasized the exchange value of monetary instruments, defined wealth as consumption and expressed confidence in the self-generating tendencies of human activity – as well as the epistemological platform for these ideas.[18]

Chapter 4 examines the rise of paper credit instruments in Boston from the 1780s into the 1820s and provides the material context for the cultural changes discussed in the following chapters. Over this period, banks, bank notes and paper-credit instruments of all sorts dominated economic life in Boston. Bostonians not only invested greatly in paper credit, they used these instruments on a daily basis. Further, banks and the language of speculation saturated Boston's public sphere. The vitality of this new economic system depended on its acceptance by Bostonians; banks and bankers relied absolutely on the confidence ordinary Americans had in the new economic system they 'floated'; they had to believe in it in order for it to work. Overall, though bankers sorely tested this 'web of confidence', the proliferation of banks and the various paper-credit instruments associated with this new system provide *de facto* acknowledgment of the accept-ance of this new economic order.

Chapter 5 ties Boston's Unitarian controversy to the larger changes in the nature of property and personality. During this period Anglo-Americans hotly disputed Calvinist notions of innate depravity, predestination and free will. Overall, over the time period under discussion, liberal or latitudinarian notions of a benevolent humanity undermined Calvin's damned and depraved sinners. More importantly, however, the conflict between these different value structures derived from different ways of looking at the world – from different epistemolo-gies. Orthodox Calvinist values derived from without; they expressed a received, external and authoritarian moral knowledge. Liberal or Unitarian religion ulti-mately found the source of moral virtue within; moral knowledge was the law writ in the hearts of men; it was a sentiment. Driven by Scottish Moral Sense phi-losophy and epistemology, especially the ideas of Francis Hutcheson, Unitarian religion emphasized a subjective and internal moral law based on human feelings and emotions. It was the moral and religious expression of the changes in political economy and money.

Chapter 6 explores the epistemological debates surrounding the novel and other forms of sentimental literature. Critics characterized novels and novel read-ing as pernicious – untrue to 'nature' and corrosive of 'real' human morals. They were not, to use the language of the pseudonymous Corneille, 'of *sterling worth*'.[19] For these readers, moral standards derived from the pulpit or through hierarchical authority; they were real and objectively verifiable. Supporters of novels con-firmed the new age's epistemology – feelings counted. Novels and other heartfelt narratives constructed new social bonds based not on early modern domestic and social hierarchies or Calvinist notions of an all-powerful God, but on Scottish heart-based emotions. Americans comfortable with the new emotional episte-mology defended and avidly devoured the romantic tales, sentimental fragments and seduction novels of the period. Furthermore, they perceived the consump-tion of these sentimental narratives as the production of society. Once again, these debates expressed the larger changes in morality and political economy and used the language and logic of Scottish Moral Sense.

Chapter 7 situates changes in Anglo-American aesthetic theory in the context of the epistemological conflict between empiricism and emotions. Theories on the nature of beauty dominated the aesthetic debates of the eighteenth and early nine-teenth centuries. These debates echoed the discussions on the nature of money: was beauty/value intrinsic in the object or a function of the subject? Again the divide was between empiricism and subjectivity – between a 'real' and objectively knowable beauty derived from certain characteristics in the object; and beauty as a private system, a function of the subject's imagination. Using aesthetic treatises in books and Boston magazines, this chapter first traces the development of these ideas in the Anglo-American world. Overwhelmingly, the shift during this period was from the mimetic empiricism of someone like the early Sir Joshua Reynolds or Thomas Reid to the Scottish Moderate party minister Archibald Alison and his imagination-driven aesthetics. Under Alison's aesthetic ideal, subjects created beauty – it was an affair of the heart; an emotional response that relied, in large part, on the epistemology of Scottish Moral Sense.

Second, using art and material culture, the final chapter traces the rise of an imagination-driven aesthetic. The discussion of material objects draws on a variety of approaches and sources: the early romantic aesthetic at the centre of Washington Allston's and Joshua Shaw's paintings; popular prints (plates) in Boston magazines that expressed Alison's aesthetic ideas and often tied visual narratives to sentimental narratives *vis-à-vis* the imagination; and finally, household furnishings that, like the popular prints and the sentimental narratives, increasingly relied on the imagination for the greater part of their aesthetic (and emotional) value.

These ideas came together in consumption and the world of goods. The larger cultural shift from Lockean Calvinism to Scottish commercial humanism involved, as Charles Taylor argues, a 'Celebration of Everyday Life'. Thus Archibald Alison argued that God's designs included beauty and utility; they gave us pleasure in goods, spurred consumption and production, and celebrated humanity. Bostonian Washington Allston also saw sentiment, material goods, and moral and aesthetic beauty as intimately connected. The providential order included the emotions generated by sentimental novels, household furnishings and art – internalized and reconstructed in the 'fancy' of the subject – which were expressed through desire and consumption. These changes represented a massive shift in the locus of human value and in the nature of the social order: value – be it economic, moral or aesthetic – was created; it was a human and subjective idea. Feelings, for centuries denigrated as the sources of disorder, suddenly developed as the well springs of life – the source of the *summum bonum* and the key to economic, aesthetic and moral value.

1 'THINGS WITHOUT HIM': LOCKE AND THE LOGIC OF METALLISM

Writing in the midst of the 1690s English Recoinage Crisis, John Locke vigorously refuted the efforts of contemporary political economists to alter the mint ratio and recoin the money supply at a reduced silver content. Silver was money was silver, Locke argued, it was impossible for money to have a value that differed from its precious metal weight. Silver, Locke concluded, '... is the Instrument and Measure of Commerce in all the Civilized and Trading Parts of the World. It is the Instrument of Commerce by intrinsick value ... Silver is the Measure of commerce by its quantity.'[20]

Locke's insistence on silver's intrinsic 'natural' value as money has puzzled and fascinated scholars ever since.[21] Many of Locke's contemporaries had long abandoned a strict metallism (money as precious metals by weight) and merchants knew full well that their exchanges did not depend on the intrinsic value of silver[22] Indeed, elsewhere, in his *Two Treatises of Government* (1690), for example, Locke seemed to suggest as much, pointing to money as a function of the 'fancy'.[23] In his *Further Considerations Considering the Value of Money* (1695), however, he inexplicably insisted that silver was money and promoted a metallist monetary policy that eventually spelled disaster for England's economy.[24]

While Locke's monetary theories were not always current or consistent, the metallism he expressed during the Recoinage Crisis was consistent with his empiricism and theological voluntarism.[25] Following the empiricist and voluntarist epistemology Locke outlined in *An Essay Concerning Human Understanding* (1690), money *had* to have a '*natural*' value ordained by the deity. God ordained all value upon a *tabula rasa* humanity; it behoved man to accept value as revealed by God and 'sit down in a quiet ignorance of those Things, which, upon examination, are found to be beyond the reach of our Capacities'.[26] The '*natural*' value of silver as money was, for Locke, part of this system of received values and was consistent with Locke's notions of morality and purpose. Furthermore, deviation from this empiricist definition of economic value implicitly threatened all other value structures: if economic value in money was not a 'real' objectively knowable standard dictated by the supreme deity, was moral value also arbitrary – a function of men's beliefs? And if value itself was but an accumulated opinion or feeling, a function, as David Hume later argued, of men's habits, manners and sentiments, then what kept men from the quagmire of relativism?[27] Locke's refutation of nominal value in money was consistent with his rejection of 'any conception of the causal processes of human belief as a self-subsistent locus of value'.[28] In Locke's mind, subjective human values threatened to usurp God's design for man yet could not establish social consensus, cohesion and order, or even individual purpose.

In this way the long historical argument about the nature of value in money touched on the mainsprings of human life. The question was not just where value in money lay – in gold and silver, or in law and confidence; the question was from whence did all value and knowledge derive? Were values part of an external, received, objectively knowable and divinely-ordained structure or system? Or were values subjective human creations or ideas? For Locke, the answer was obvious. The very idea that human action, institutions, ideas and feelings could spontaneously generate values that engendered social order, harmony and human purpose challenged his Calvinist deity. It was precisely this vision of a social order 'attained through institutional design and the causal mechanisms of human belief and human passion' that Locke 'prophylactically' established himself against.[29]

The Recoinage Crisis

Numerous scholars have pointed to the importance of the English Recoinage Crisis in the development of modern economic theory and practice.[30] Put briefly, in the 1690s a series of monetary crises rocked the English economy. For nearly half a century Englishmen had clipped coins and melted down the silver into bullion. Others took advantage of differences in the English mint's silver and gold ratios and international silver and gold prices and melted down whole silver coins into bullion for export.[31] Milled coins with unclippable edges provided some relief against clipping, but the Treasury minted the new milled coins at the standard weight, ignoring both the continued circulation of clipped coins and international fluctuations in bullion prices. These 'heavy' coins immediately disappeared – melted and exported or hoarded. While these practices plagued England throughout the seventeenth century, the financial crises associated with the War of the Grand Alliance that culminated in the creation of the Bank of England in 1694 forced the king's ministers to address the issue.[32] The immediate question was whether to recall all the coin, change the mint ratio and recoin at a lower silver content, thus giving *de jure* legitimacy to the *de facto* devaluation of clipped English silver coins; or recall and recoin the nation's silver money supply at the established mint rate (increasing the silver content), thus taking coins out of circulation. Recoinage at the established mint rate threatened to tighten the money supply by perhaps as much as £2.5 million.[33] Furthermore, it did not address the discrepancy between the mint prices for gold and silver and international bullion prices. The potential economic dislocation of maintaining the established rate was severe.

Faced with recoining the nation's money supply, King William's anxious Privy Council called for Secretary of the Treasury William Lowndes's opinion. In his *Report*, Lowndes carefully examined English monetary policy over four hundred years and found an overwhelming number of instances in which the Crown had changed the precious metal content of coins (the mint ratio) to suit particular circumstances.[34] This was, in his opinion, *de facto* proof that money was a sign of value and need not be a commodity in and of itself. Lowndes thus recommended a 20 per cent reduction in coins' silver content.[35] This measure, Lowndes argued, would stop the haemorrhage of silver coin to bullion and would avoid the massive loss entailed in recoining at the old standard. Furthermore, it would disassociate the idea of silver and money. The Privy Council did not, however, accept his report calling for devaluation, and requested the opinion of the highly popular and important philosopher, John Locke.

In the 1690s Locke's intellectual peers and patrons respected his political and epistemological theories. He maintained some following as a political economist in part as a result of his contributions to a series of debates surrounding the interest rate.[36] He was also deeply immersed in the political controversies surrounding the Exclusion Crisis and the Glorious Revolution.[37] Furthermore, he played a formative role in the creation of the mercantilist Board of Trade.[38] Thus, in the 1690s, his ideas on money were intellectually out of season but not out of political favour.

The Logic of Metallism

Locke responded to the Privy Council's request and Lowndes's *Report* with a series of pamphlets that invigorated the 'metallist' position. Echoing Nicole Oresme's medieval arguments denying the sovereign the right to alter the mint ratio – arguments he was surely familiar with – Locke argued that silver had 'intrinsic' value and the State did not have the power to increase or diminish the silver content in coins.[39] Oresme emphasized the sovereign's theocratic responsibility to maintain this standard: 'If the prince, then, despite this inscription [of sacred formulae] should change the material or the weight', Oresme argued, 'he would seem to be silently lying and forswearing himself and bearing false witness, and also transgressing the commandment which says: "Thou shalt not take the name of the Lord thy God in vain"'.[40] Locke, however, emphasized what he perceived to be the 'unnatural' consequences of nominal value in money. Were there any discrepancy between the nominal value of the coin and its silver weight, Locke pointed out, you could trade one quantity of silver affixed with the sovereign's stamp for a lesser or greater quantity of silver with no stamp. Yet who would trade one quantity of silver for a lesser quantity? Silver could purchase only equal amounts of silver and the mark of the sovereign had no influence whatsoever on that transaction. 'This, common Sense, as well as the Market, teaches us', Locke concluded. 'For Silver being all of the same nature and goodness, having all the same qualities, 'tis impossible but it should in the same *quantity* have the same value. For if a less *quantity* of any Commodity were allowed to be equal in value to a greater *quantity* of the same sort of Commodity, it must be for some good quality it has which the other wants. But Silver to Silver has no such difference.' 'An equal quantity of silver', Locke plaintively pleaded, 'is always of equal value to an equal quantity of silver'.[41] For Locke, the sovereign's stamp could not create or 'add' economic value; money value in silver and gold was a '*natural*' reality.

Locke's metallist tracts touched on notions of wealth, consumption and the purpose of economic activity. For Locke, the logic of metallism and mercantilism denigrated consumption.[42] A nation, like a household, he argued, grew wealthier by spending less, especially on luxuries, and saving more. Money was the measure of wealth, and 'Money is brought into England by nothing but spending here less of Foreign Commodities, than what we carry to market can pay for; Nor can Debts we owe to foreigners be paid by Bills of Exchange ... For nothing will pay Debts but Money or Moneys worth, which three or four Lines writ in Paper cannot be.'[43] Merchants, he argued, entered into and fulfilled contracts in specie, the value determined by weight. Foreign exchange was, to be sure, affected by the relative demand for a nation's goods (and thus the national coin).[44] Nevertheless, at the end of the day, for Locke, the standard was weight.[45] These ideas corresponded with his vision of economic and social purpose. Wealth was not a personal measure but a national goal; power, not pleasure, was its purpose.

Locke's pamphleteering did not completely lack sophistication in its analysis of money. He subscribed to the increasingly popular quantity theory of money, arguably first developed by Jean Bodin in his explanation of the sixteenth century's 'Great Price Wave'.[46] As a physician Locke was key in modifying the quantity theory through the application of physician William Harvey's blood circulation theories.[47] These ideas led many men to think that the nation's money supply was, not unlike the body's blood supply, in perpetual circulation. Thus, though the balance of goods to money determined price, velocity of circulation was key to economic activity. Nevertheless, though his circulation theories emphasized exchange, Locke could not leave the intrinsic theory baggage behind. Money in circulation contradicted money as accumulated wealth, yet he promoted both ideas. Furthermore, his version of the quantity theory of money, true to its metallic base, espoused finite quantities of money and finite quantities of goods and maintained a zero-sum economy, and thus the mercantilism common to European nations during the early modern period.[48] Finally, Locke's quantity theory of money denigrated human agency and feelings. It was a 'hydraulic' explanation of price equilibrium that relied on factors exogenous to demand. 'Thus the Quantity Theory', G. L. S. Shackle concludes, 'puts money beyond the control of thought and feeling, making it something inhuman, automatic and quite alien to that Theory of Value which explains the exchange ratios of "real" goods for one another'.[49] Overall, Locke's theory of objective 'natural' economic value in the precious metals and stubborn mercantilism denied the power of individual human choices and desires to establish social and economic harmony.

Locke's stalwart defence of the mint ratio and 'intrinsick' value in silver called forth responses from numerous critics. Overall these essayists pointed out that confidence in the authority and legitimacy of the state and the demand for the currency determined the value of a nation's money. The demand for a nation's products affected the demand for its money and thus the price of its money, or the exchange rate. Furthermore, clipped coins had long circulated at face value regardless of their silver weight – an irrefutable empirical observation that ordinary Englishmen did not wholly equate money with silver. Finally, these critics denigrated Locke's organic vision of economic value and activity and pointed to a new social order based on desire.

Nicholas Barbon and the Wants of the Mind

One of the more celebrated of these respondents, Nicholas Barbon, in a well-circulated pamphlet written in 1690, prior to the crisis, constructed a vision of the economy and society completely at odds with Locke's ideas. 'Mony', Barbon argued, 'is a Value made by a Law; And the Difference of its Value is known by the Stamp, and Size of the Piece'. Gold and silver proved useful to make money because of the difficulty in making the alloy and stamp upon them. Furthermore, their scarcity maintained a high commodity value that further discouraged counterfeiting. They did not, however, possess any 'Intrinsick Vertue'. In fact, useful metals such as iron had, at present, much more intrinsic value than gold. For Barbon, utility determined value. Money had utility as a measure of value and to facilitate exchange. Overall, however, 'Nothing in it self hath a certain Value; One thing is as much worth as another: And it is time, and place, that give a difference to the Value of all things'.[50] Barbon thus espoused a relativist theory of value: men's needs and desires determined value and thus price. 'Natural' or intrinsic value did not exist in any substance.

In a second pamphlet published after the crisis broke, Barbon answered Locke directly. Locke's argument, Barbon noted, insisted that gold and silver had intrinsic value and therefore that 'Gold and Silver are the only riches'.[51] From this position, Barbon argued, Locke followed balance-of-trade economic ideas

('Money is brought into England by nothing but spending here less of Foreign Commodities, than what we carry to market can pay for ...'), and the erroneous notion, in Barbon's opinion, that the quantity of money set the prices of goods and the interest rate. For Barbon, desire (demand) created and fixed the value (price) of all goods. Furthermore, wealth was in goods and consumption; the aggregate of individual wealth, measured in goods, constituted national wealth. 'By *Riches*', Barbon concluded, 'is meant all such Things as are of great Value. By *Value*, is to be understood the Price of Things; that is what any thing is worth to be sold ... The Value of all Things, arise from their Use.' Overall, for Barbon, things had two general uses: 'They are either useful to supply the Wants of the Body, or the Wants of the Mind'. The body expressed wants by hunger; the mind expressed wants by desire. Of these, the wants of the mind were the most numerous. These goods had an 'Imaginary or Artificial Value which depends only on opinion, and change their Values according to the Humor and Fancy of the persons that use them'.[52]

These ideas formed the core of a different vision of the economy and ultimately of the social order. The nation and the person were, according to Barbon, different entities. The national economy and the household economy were not analogous. 'For the Stock of a Nation is vastly different from that of a private person', Barbon declared. 'The one of infinite, the other finite ... But if we consider a Nation as consisting of a Body of people, the Inhabitants may be made richer or poorer; but it is not by consuming the Stock of the Nation, but for want of improving the Stock. It is not by Trading, but for want of Trade. That Nation is accounted rich, when the greatest number of the Inhabitants are rich.'[53] The balance of trade (and thus the balance of bullion) did not measure wealth or poverty. Consumption and trade did not impoverish the nation – to the contrary, it was only in consumption and trade that men satisfied their desires and thus increased their riches.

Lowndes's and Barbon's ideas on money, the economy and the social order differed from and opposed Locke's. Lowndes and Barbon saw money as an instrument created by men for their benefit. Locke saw money as a natural reality. Lowndes and Barbon argued for an expansive economy based on the consumption of goods – in Barbon's words, 'the wants of the mind', or 'plenitude'.[54] Locke imagined a fixed and limited mercantilist economy based on the national accumulation of precious metals.[55] Lowndes and Barbon imagined an atomistic social order based on individual human choices and driven by desire. Locke's organic society existed as an external structure or system that men followed.

Locke's insistence on silver's intrinsic value puzzled contemporary theorists such as Barbon and contemporary merchants who knew full well that the nature of their exchange did not rely on the intrinsic value of silver, as well as generations of modern scholars.[56] This confusion is due in no small part to the numerous contradictions in Locke's multiple money narratives. For example, in his *Two*

Treatises of Government, Locke saw all money as a function of the 'fancy' – and thus, seemingly, a completely human invention.[57] In the same text, however, he also argued that this 'fanciful' human invention played an uncharacteristically important role in the definition and/or creation of property and allowed for the development of civilization and political society.[58] In *Further Reflections* he clearly argued that money as silver had an 'intrinsick' value, yet he also paradoxically based that value on 'common consent'.[59] Though the tensions inherent in Locke's money narratives are difficult to resolve, his ideas on money as expressed during the Recoinage Crisis are consistent with his empiricism and theological voluntarism.[60] Locke seated the '*natural*' value of silver as money in a 'natural law' narrative. But Locke's 'natural law' was a theistic and voluntarist structure that provided the logic of the natural and social order. Put simply, for Locke, the 'natural law was part of the Divine law'.[61] Men discovered the 'natural law', and thus God's will, through 'the operation of reason upon sense experience', but it existed outside of them as an external system. Locke's 'natural law' was a binding system – an objective value structure that kept at bay the chaos of subjectivity. Without this external 'law of nature', John Dunn concludes, Locke feared that each man would be 'the utterly free and supreme arbiter of his own actions'.[62] The '*natural*' value of the precious metals as money was thus part of the larger God-ordained social order – a '*natural*' and theocratic 'law' of money – an objective reality that could not be undermined without questioning all other objective realities, including men's notions of morality, religion and their place in the cosmos. Mankind, in Locke's view, lived in a world fixed and bound by the deity – limited in choices, in bounty and in the power to create value or knowledge, including economic value in signs. Locke best defined these limitations in his explication of empiricism, *An Essay Concerning Human Understanding*.[63]

An Essay Concerning Human Understanding

Modern scholars have long praised Locke's contribution to the Enlightenment.[64] His theory of human knowledge, however, might more properly have been styled *An Essay on the Limitations of Human Understanding*. Locke sets out in the text not to plumb the depths of the human capacity to know but rather to detail the limitations of all our queries and to prescribe caution in our efforts to expand these limits.[65] The *Essay* is in many ways a challenge to free inquiry. Locke makes this clear in the introduction to the text and in the book's structure. 'If by this Enquiry into the Nature of the Understanding, I can Discover the Powers thereof; *how far* they reach; to what things they are in any degree Proportionate; and where they fail us', Locke begins, 'I suppose it may be of use, to prevail with the busy Mind of Man, to be more cautious in meddling with things exceeding its comprehension; to stop when it is at the outmost Extent of its Tether; and to sit down in a quiet ignorance of those Things, which, upon examination, are found to be beyond the reach of our Capacities'.[66] Locke's limit-setting agenda embraced epistemological and theological ideas. Why study what cannot be verified, or known with certainty – what is not objectively knowable and thus what does not, for society, exist? Or, put another way, why question God's logic and generosity in his revelation? Speculation was not only fruitless, it was pernicious and corrosive to the social order. God knew best. Men needed only to *discover* his generosity. 'Men have Reason to be well satisfied with what God hath thought fit for them', Locke concluded, 'since he has given them, (as S. *Peter* says ...), Whatsoever is necessary for the Conveniences of Life, and Information of Vertue; and has put within the reach of their Discovery the comfortable Provision for this Life and the way that leads to a better'.[67]

Locke followed up his introduction with a refutation of innate ideas titled '*No innate Principles in the Mind*'. Locke's assault on innate principles followed earlier empiricists' challenges. Francis Bacon originally questioned the validity of *a priori* ideas and/or speculation, particularly as expressed by the Cambridge Neo-Platonists.[68] For Locke and Bacon, innate principles were both theologically and epistemologically dangerous and unnecessary. Innate ideas called into question the logic of God's grand design as revealed to man's senses.[69] Why did God create faculties, Locke insisted, if colours and other ideas are imprinted upon the mind? 'For I imagine any one will easily grant', he concluded, 'That it would be impertinent to suppose, the *Ideas* of Colors innate in a Creature, to whom God had given Sight, and a Power to receive them by the Eyes from external Objects'.[70] Furthermore, innate ideas held God to certain truths, in effect, divined by man and imposed on God's sovereign power. Men deemed it best and thus attributed it to God. This was clearly outside of a voluntarist Calvinist and/or Lockean point of view.[71] 'But it *seems to me a little too much Confidence of our own Wisdom*', Locke argued, '*to say, I think it best and therefore God hath made it so*'. God furnished mankind with faculties to discover all that he needed in the world, and it was superfluous to suppose that this was for naught; an unnecessary exercise, since men already possessed all vital knowledge imprinted on their mind. 'I think I am fully persuaded', Locke concluded, 'that the infinitely Wise GOD made all Things in perfect Wisdom, cannot satisfy my self, why he should be supposed to print upon the minds of Men, some universal *Principles*; whereof those that are pretended, and *concern Speculation, are of no great use; and those that concern Practice, not self-evident; and neither of them distinguishable from some other truths not allowed to be innate*'.[72]

Having discounted innate ideas on both the ground of reason and deference to God, Locke then set out to explain how God revealed knowledge and/or value to mankind. For Locke, all knowledge was a function of '*Experience*': 'Our Observation employ'd either about *external, sensible Objects; or about the internal Operations of our Minds, perceived and reflected on by our selves is that which sup-*

plies our *Understandings with all the materials of thinking*'.[73] In other words, ideas came to man through the senses and reflection. What Locke called 'simple' ideas devolved directly from the senses and perception. 'Complex' ideas were 'formed by the voluntary mental union of simple ideas'.[74] A candle burning, to use Locke's example, was a complex idea perceived as a series of simple ideas – wax hot and soft to the touch, light and colour to the eye, etc.

Locke categorized all ideas as either 'adequate' or 'inadequate'. All simple ideas were adequate – they were 'Powers in Things, fitted and ordained by GOD'.[75] 'All complex ideas of *Modes*, being voluntary Collections of simple *Ideas*, which the mind puts together without reference to any real Archetypes, or standing Patterns, existing any where, *are*, and cannot but be *adequate ideas.*' A triangle, for example, was a complete and thus adequate idea. There was no archetypal triangle of which the idea of a triangle was a copy. Overall, what Locke called '*Mixed Modes*' and '*Relations*' were 'Archetypes without Patterns, and so having nothing to represent but themselves, cannot but be adequate, everything being so to itself'.[76] Ideas of substances were, however, according to Locke, 'ectype' ideas that referred to archetypes in nature – they referred to a natural reality and were 'dependent on that reality for their truth value'.[77] These ideas were clearly 'inadequate'. In Locke's epistemology the essence of substances was ultimately unknowable to men. Men could not make, and therefore could not know, substances. Only God could know his own workmanship – his own property.[78]

In discussing the opaque nature of substances, Locke used gold as an example. Men, according to Locke, described gold as a series of simple ideas. 'Its peculiar Colour, Weight, Hardness, Fusibility, Fixedness, and change of Colour upon a slight touch of Mercury, etc.' were the simple ideas, knowable to the senses, which 'Adam and his friends' agreed upon to describe the ectype idea or substance of gold.[79] They could not, and did not, however, speak to the real essence of gold. 'Whosoever first light on that parcel of that sort of Substance, we denote by the word *Gold*', Locke concluded, 'could not rationally take the Bulk and Figure he observed in that lump, to depend on its real essence or internal constitution'.[80] By God's design, the essence of gold – indeed the essence of all substances – remained unknowable to mankind. 'The infinite wise contriver of us and all things about us', Locke postulated,

> has fitted our Senses, Faculties and Organs, to the conveniences of Life and the Business we have to do here. We are able, by our Senses, to know and distinguish things; and to examine them so far, as to apply them to our Uses, and several ways to accommodate the Exigencies of this Life. We have insight enough into their admirable Contrivances, and wonderful Effects, to admire, and magnify the Wisdom, Power and Goodness of their Author ... But it appears not that God intended, we should have a perfect, clear and adequate Knowledge of them: that perhaps is not in the comprehension of any finite Being.[81]

Thus, according to Locke, men could have no knowledge of the real essence of gold and silver (or any other substance). They could and did reach some agreement as to the common attributes of substances. Men agreed, for example, on the common attributes of the precious metals – their 'peculiar Colour, Weight, Hardness, Fusibility, Fixedness, and change of Colour upon a slight touch of Mercury, etc.'. More importantly, however, they could know the 'admirable contrivances and wonderful effects' of substances, including the precious metals; all substances, in Locke's view, had 'intrinsic' and thus 'natural' utility and value – a gift from 'their Author' to his human creations.[82] Thus, though men were strangers to the inner essence or truth-value of gold and silver, they could nevertheless know their 'natural' function as money – clearly, for Locke, part of God's design.

In many of these ideas Locke seems to once again look backwards, this time to the sixteenth-century 'doctrine of signatures', according to which God left clues for human beings to indicate which of his substances suited their needs. External characteristics – 'signs' – corresponded to 'internal qualities'. 'It is not God's will that all He has created for the benefit of man and has given him as his own should remain hidden', the sixteenth-century physician Paracelsus argued. '[God] left nothing unmarked, but provided all things with outward, visible marks, with special traits … We men discover everything that lies hidden in the mountains by external signs and correspondences, and thus also do we find the properties of herbs and everything that is in stones. There is nothing in the depths of the seas, nothing on the heights of the firmament', Paracelsus concluded, 'that man is unable to discover.'[83]

Locke's notions of substances were also consistent with his ideas on agency. Locke's fixed world-view did not cease with man's inability to understand the inner essence of God's creations beyond the 'admirable Contrivances' of substances. Indeed, as Andrea Finkelstein and W. Stark both point out, according to Locke's *Essay*, God limited mankind's freedom by design.[84] Man, Locke argued, acted on the basis of pain and pleasure both on the physical and moral level. Put another way, God created man's reason to be directed by hedonism. Man was thus physically or materially happy insofar as he avoided pain and consumed pleasure. Ethical behaviour also followed this pattern. Ethical or moral behaviour brought about ultimate happiness; unethical behaviour brought about ultimate despair. Man in this world acted – but he could make only two choices: the right choice and the wrong choice. According to Locke:

> A man is at liberty to lift up his hand to his head, or to let it rest quiet; he is perfectly indifferent in either; and it would be an imperfection in him if he were deprived of that power, if he were deprived of that indifferency. But it would be as great an imperfection if he had the same indifferency, whether he would prefer the lifting up his hand, or its remaining in rest, when it would save his head or eyes from a blow he sees coming: it is as much a perfection, that desire, or the power of preferring, should be determined by good, as that the power of acting should be determined by the will; and the certainer such determination is, the greater is the perfection. Nay,

were we determined by any thing but the last result of our own minds, judging of the good or evil of any action, we were not free: the very end of our freedom being that we may attain the good we choose. And therefore every man is put under a necessity by his constitution, as an intelligent being, to be determined in willing by his own thought and judgment what is best for him to do.[85]

A man should not fret over the apparent lack of freedom to do 'what is worst for him', Locke argued. 'If to break loose from the conduct of reason, and to want that restraint of examination and judgment, which keeps us from choosing or doing the worse, be liberty, true liberty, madmen and fools are the only freemen: but yet, I think', he concluded, 'nobody would choose to be mad for the sake of such liberty, but he that is mad already'. Locke even postulated that God, in his absolute fiat, might be determined by what is best: 'And if it were fit for such poor finite creatures as we are', he concluded, 'to pronounce what infinite wisdom and goodness could do, I think we might say, that God himself cannot choose what is not good; the freedom of the Almighty hinders not his being determined by what is best'.[86]

Thus, in Locke's theocratic epistemology, the natural law was God's law which was the natural order, and which asserted, James Tully has argued, 'the existence of an order of value'.[87] Men discovered but did not shape or create this natural and fixed order of value. 'Nature', Locke argued in the *Essays on the Law of Nature*, 'has provided a certain profusion of goods for the use and convenience of men, and the things provided have been bestowed in a definite way and in a predetermined quantity; they have not been fortuitously produced nor are they increasing in proportion with what men need or covet'.[88] The intrinsic value and utility of precious metals as money was, for Locke, clearly part of this natural order of value. God 'bestowed' silver as money for the 'use and convenience' of men; it was part of the 'definite way' of God's creation. To deride, ignore or substitute the 'natural' function or 'definite way' of his creation was to 'choose' wrongly. Men had limited power within Locke's theocratic system; God implored them to conform to the reality that he created for them. 'What liberty *Adam* had at first to make any complex *Ideas* of mixed Modes, by no other pattern but his own Thoughts, the same have all Men ever since had', Locke concluded in the *Essay*. 'And the same necessity of conforming his *Ideas* of Substances to *Things without him*, as to *Archetypes* made by Nature, that *Adam* was under, if he would not wilfully impose upon himself, the same are all Men ever since under too'.[89] Men were not at liberty to speculate on or modify the nature, use or value of substances: these were received and external to man, or in Locke's words, '*Things without him*'.

Locke's metallism was the economic expression of his empiricism and part of a larger social, religious and epistemological debate current through the seventeenth and eighteenth centuries. Empiricism, as Charles Taylor and others have noted, derived from theological voluntarism: a series of assumptions about

God, the universe and the nature of the social order. Bacon was the first of the seventeenth-century thinkers to usher in an empiricist world-view through his voluntarist beliefs.[90] Bacon's tremendous challenge was first and foremost to *a priori* ideas. Observation drove human intellectual exploration, not metaphysical speculation. Science was concerned with 'real' phenomena that could be measured, weighed or otherwise observed and known objectively to man through sense experience. Locke continued this project and argued that human beings were in fact void of ideas or knowledge – they were, in his phrase, *tabula rasa*. This was consistent with the theological voluntarism of Calvinism. All *a priori* speculation implied inner knowledge. If men had access to inner truths, was not God then obligated to live by these formulations? Theological voluntarism, M. B. Foster notes, 'attributes to God an activity of will not wholly determined by reason'. 'Thus', Edward Davis concludes, 'the products of God's creative activity are not necessary, but contingent. Since our minds cannot have demonstrative *a priori* knowledge of a contingent reality, the created world can only be known empirically.'[91] For Bacon and Locke, God revealed all knowledge to man. and ultimately knowledge and value were contingent on God's will. That 'things' worked through a system of knowable laws was further evidence of his design. In this regard, John Dunn notes, 'natural science' was 'not so much a form of knowledge (as Locke understood this) but, rather, a peculiarly complicated and cunning form of belief – a matter of judgment (or guessing), not of direct vision'.[92] The logic of this divinely-ordained system gave man purpose and was the basis for social order; conversely, to step outside this system invited relativism and chaos. For Locke, Dunn concludes, 'Once we have lost the religious guarantee that reason, 'the candle of the Lord,' shines bright enough for all our purposes, we have no conclusive reason to expect it to shine bright enough for any. And once we can no longer see our purposes *as authoritatively assigned to us from outside our selves*, it becomes very hard to judge just which purposes we have good reason to consider as (or to make) our own.'[93] Anthropocentric definitions of economic value and purpose substituted human feelings and design for God's 'natural law' of money value in the precious metals – 'assigned to us from outside our selves'. Nominal value in money undermined the logic of Locke's empiricism and threatened his vision of a theocratically-determined social order.

Locke won the recoinage debate, with disastrous results for the English economy.[94] In the long run, however, he lost the argument. Locke's metallism in *Further Considerations*, like his *tabula rasa* empiricism and theistic natural law, was a self-conscious 'refusal of the future as it was to come to be'.[95] Through the eighteenth century, however, the third Earl of Shaftesbury and the Scottish Moral Sense philosophers undermined Locke's vision of a theocratic social order with their sociological values and liberal political economy.[96] They reconstructed humanity precisely so that the sources of value and knowledge were not 'without us' but within us.

2 SHAFTESBURY AND SCOTTISH MORAL SENSE COMMERCIAL HUMANISM: INCLINATIONS IMPLANTED IN THE SUBJECT

'Tis impossible to suppose a mere sensible Creature originally so ill-constituted and unnatural, as that from the moment he comes to be try'd by sensible Objects, he shou'd have no one good Passion towards his Kind, no foundation either of Pity, Love, Kindness, or social Affection. 'Tis full as impossible to conceive, that a rational Creature coming first to be try'd by rational Objects, and receiving into his Mind the Images or representations of Justice, Generosity, gratitude, or other Virtue, shou'd have no *Liking* of these, or *Dislike* of their contrarys; but be found absolutely indifferent toward whatsoever is presented to him of this sort. A Soul, indeed, may as well be without *Sense*, as without admiration in the Things of which it has any knowledge.

    Anthony Ashley Cooper, third Earl of Shaftesbury, *Characteristicks of Men, Manners, Opinions, Times*, 3 vols (1711; Farnborough: Gregg, 1968), vol. 2: *An Inquiry Concerning Virtue and Merit*, book 1, part 3, section 1, p. 43.

Following the third Earl of Shaftesbury, Anthony Ashley Cooper, and writing in Scotland's 'age of improvement', the Scottish Moral Sense philosophers, Francis Hutcheson, David Hume and Adam Smith, constructed an anthropocentric emotive epistemology in opposition to Locke's Calvinist empiricism. Locke had insisted on the extrinsic and objective nature of the world, including value knowledge; God created the earth and the value structures by which it 'worked' for men's discovery and utility. Human beings were, in this vision, fundamentally alienated from the good, and had little true agency. Human powerlessness corresponded to divine omnipotence and Locke's Calvinist deity demanded absolute and arbitrary fiat. The Scots followed Shaftesbury and rebelled against this peevish Calvinist deity, envisioning a social order created by human beings. At the centre of this vision was a new subjectivity – an emphasis on feelings that dominated all value structures; moral, economic and aesthetic. Moral value derived from the heart – it was, to paraphrase Hume, a matter more properly felt than judged of.[97] Aesthetic value derived from the subject or spectator's imagination. Economic value too was subjective, derived from and dependent upon the abstract notions of trust and confidence. Furthermore, human needs, desires and institutions drove the economy and 'spontaneously' generated a harmonious and beneficent economic and social order. Men's 'wants' were good; they were part of God's plan, driving innovation, employment and human fulfilment. Thus the Scottish Moral Sense philosophers envisioned a society marked by anthropocentric and internalized moral, aesthetic and economic value structures based on feelings. Paper-credit instruments were central to this new world; they were both the catalyst to and the economic expression of ideas and acts that spanned moral, aesthetic and political domains. This was a radical departure from Locke and his theocratic, empiricist universe.

Shaftesbury

Scottish Moral Sense properly begins with an English Whig thinker, Anthony Ashley Cooper, the third Earl of Shaftesbury. The grandson of the first Earl of Shaftesbury, the great Whig politician and patron of John Locke, the third Earl grew up in the midst of his grandfather's involvement in Whig politics during Restoration monarchy. The first Earl delegated his grandson's education to John Locke, his household physician, and the person who delivered the third Earl into the world. Throughout their lives Shaftesbury and Locke maintained a correspondence that touched both on intellectual and family matters. This did not, however, stop Shaftesbury from constructing a view of the world that completely contradicted Locke's philosophy.

Shaftesbury's opposition to Locke hinged on Locke's empiricism and theological voluntarism. Empiricism, as described above, legitimated a vision of man disengaged from the sources of value. Human beings were 'empty' receptacles to be filled by divine purpose and knowledge. This was a central tenet of theological voluntarism. As Charles Taylor notes, under a voluntarist belief system, 'God's law is what he decides it is, and God's law determines the good. God cannot be seen as bound by a good which would be already implicit in the bent of the nature he has created.'[98] Men could have no knowledge of God's designs or intent; they could have no implicit 'bent'. God had to have an arbitrarious capacity – or else he was bound by principles known to men. Thus, according to Locke, man was empty, or *tabula rasa* – void of any innate qualities that might hold God to some principle and thus limit his power.[99] Reason upon sense experience revealed an all-mighty God who chose to exercise his powers through his rational design – the natural law – though he was not limited to that capacity; indeed reason itself was a function of God's arbitrarious will – he defined it.[100]

Shaftesbury developed his opposition to these doctrines through his reading of the Cambridge Platonists, Henry More, Ralph Cudworth, Benjamin Whichcote and John Smith. These thinkers fought against an arbitrarious and '*peevish*' Calvinist God. Calvin, according to these Neo-Platonic thinkers, described a tyrannical deity, 'entic'd' by flattery, and obsessed with power. These attributes described not the deity, they argued, but the limitations of the men who created him. Religious worship was not a form of tyranny, but a celebration of life and God's love. In the words of John Smith:[101]

> The spirit of true Religion is of a more free, noble, ingenious and generous nature ... It [divine love] thaws all those frozen affections which a Slavish fear had congealed and lock'd up, and makes the Soul most chearfull, free and nobly resolved in all its motions after God.

Love was central to these ideas; human beings were part of the deity's grand universal circle of love.[102]

Shaftesbury fashioned from these thinkers a vision of man and God in the universe distinctly at odds with that of his tutor. For Shaftesbury, God's law, natural law, value and moral knowledge were not received or external ideas. Nor were they entities to be discovered. All value and moral knowledge – the order of the universe – everything was internalized; it was part of humanity's endowment. The natural harmony of the universe, including that of the plant, animal and insect world, corresponded to the inner knowledge and harmony of man. The universe was thus 'a single entity', and to understand and feel this was to get closer to God. Furthermore, the idea that man's goodness or benevolence was triggered by the hedonistic principle of self-love (and pleasure and pain) was the antithesis of Shaftesbury's principles. Human beings were innately good and part of the *summum bonum*. Goodness came 'spontaneously from our being'. Ironically, this pushed Shaftesbury to espouse a less arbitrary (if more subjective) theory of value than Locke. For Locke, Shaftesbury argued, 'all actions are naturally indifferent ... they have not note or character of good or ill in themselves; but are distinguished by mere fashion, law, or arbitrary decree'. They are, in other words, a function of God's arbitrariness. In his opposition to these ideas Shaftesbury again followed the Cambridge Platonists. 'If it should be supposed that God should plant such a religion in the Soul that had no affinity or alliance with [the bent of nature]', John Smith argued, 'it would grow there but as a strange slip. But God when he gives his Laws to men, does not by virtue of his Absolute dominion dictate anything at randome, and in such as arbitrarious way as some imagine.'[103] Instead, Shaftesbury argued, 'good and ill' are real creations of God, known to men in the bent of their nature, and in harmony with a universal good.

A priori or innate ideas, the antitheses of Locke's *tabula rasa*, were central to these formulations. Human beings, according to Shaftesbury, did not discover moral value through reason and sense-experience in objects or ideas; nor did God's vengeful power arbitrarily create or dictate value; rather, its source was man's affection – 'certain inclinations implanted in the subject'. Human beings were, in

Shaftesbury's opinion, intrinsically attuned to God's word and God's works.[104] 'A Soul, indeed, may as well be without *Sense*', Shaftesbury concluded, 'as without admiration in the Things of which it has any knowledge'.[105] Thus Shaftesbury internalized, or 'subjectified' the 'teleological ethic of nature' and associated the 'ethic of order, harmony and equilibrium' with an 'ethic of benevolence'. There was a 'natural affection' for the good of the whole implanted in the breast of mankind, and in accord with the universal good.[106]

Shaftesbury internalized ideas about moral knowledge but did not deny an objective reality of morality, virtue or beauty. Nevertheless, he placed a great deal of power in the human imagination:

> Coming therefore to a capacity of seeing and admiring in this new way, [the mind] must needs find a Beauty and a Deformity as well in Actions, Minds, and Tempers, as in Figures, Sounds or Colours. If there be no *real* Amiableness or Deformity in moral acts, there is at least an *imaginary one* of full force. Tho Perhaps the thing itself shou'd not be allow'd in Nature, the imagination or fancy of it must be allowed to be from Nature alone.[107]

Imaginary or *real*, 'things' were parts of a larger universal organic whole – a whole that included mankind. They existed out there as part of God's grand design, which included man's innate knowledge of, and affection, for the good.

Shaftesbury constructed this vision of humanity in opposition to Locke's Calvinist epistemology: his external morality or value structure, and the idea of innate human depravity. Human beings were not born *tabula rasa*. They were full of value knowledge; they were also innately good. Furthermore, their goodness was part of the order and beauty of the universe. His ideas were the first step in the modern internalization of the universal order. The Scottish Moral Sense philosophers further developed and articulated Shaftesbury's ideas into the theory of moral sentiments. This was, in effect, an effort to construct a new moral order based on feelings.

Scottish Moral Sense Commercial Humanism

The Scottish Moral Sense philosophers followed Shaftesbury and delineated a heartfelt value system, or theory of moral sentiments. Francis Hutcheson, David Hume, Adam Smith and others constructed a new commercial humanism that combined Shaftesbury's epistemology and sociology with many of Locke's ideas, though, as one scholar has put it, they used Locke to very un-Lockean ends.[108] These philosophers envisioned a social and moral order based on the intrinsic benevolence of the heart in opposition to the early modern logos based on reason, sense experience and self-interest. They continued Shaftesbury's ideas and further legitimized the relationship between emotions, the providential and the human order – and introduced the previously sullied world of commerce and the activities associated with everyday life into the language of virtue.

These ideas had tremendous implications for political economy and are key to understanding the self-centred society constructed by the middling bourgeois common to the Atlantic world through the late eighteenth century. The legitimization of sentiment and desire was critical to the new subjectivity that permeated economic and social life. Property, justice and morality all derived, the Scots argued, not from reason but feeling. Men were, according to these Scottish philosophers, best understood outside of their politically or divinely-ordained identities – they were first and foremost *homo economicus*: 'doers, demanders and possessors', deeply immersed in their everyday travails, driven by their inner thoughts in both moral and economic matters. Put another way, desire and sentiments – feelings – drove and directed both men and the economy.

Francis Hutcheson

Francis Hutcheson was, of course, the first and arguably the most prominent and powerful of these thinkers. Born in 1694 in Armagh, Ireland, Hutcheson attended the University of Glasgow where he studied under John Simson and Gershom Carmichael. These scholars exposed Hutcheson to liberal religion. Carmichael in particular promoted religious beliefs that brought him into conflict with Presbyterian Calvinism. He also introduced Hutcheson to the natural law theorists Grotius, Pufendorf and Cumberland.

Hutcheson made two important contributions to eighteenth-century philosophy. First, he constructed the Moral Sense. Second, he applied the Moral Sense to natural law and natural rights ideas. This second move tied natural law ideas of property, usually based on reason, to emotions and legitimized the world of commerce and labour.

Hutcheson's first volume, *An Inquiry into the Original of our Ideas of Beauty and Virtue* (1726), was a refutation of the explicit egotism expressed in the philosophies of Bernard Mandeville and John Locke. Selfish impulses, according to these thinkers, guided humanity. Mandeville had explicitly attacked Shaftesbury's ideas on benevolence in his *Fable of the Bees* (2nd ed, 1723). All men, he argued, seek their advantage – even in apparently selfless acts men follow their vanity, not benevolence. Locating virtue in the passions was folly, Mandeville argued. Virtue, according to Mandeville, depended on the restraint of the passions. Thus mankind had to practice a high degree of denial in order to attain virtue – something Mandeville did not think humanity was naturally capable of (or interested in). Human efforts at virtue, he concluded, were a purchase – a calculated manipulation.[109]

Locke's position was more ambivalent. As discussed above, Locke argued that God designed the human experience with a rational egotism as the logic of existence. It was in effect a natural law that man should seek out what is best for him and thus indirectly benefit all of mankind. God designed this system in a rational fashion – but clearly, in the logic of Calvinist theological voluntarism, he need not have done so. For Locke, it was within God's arbitrarious power to design a malevolent world. This was part of an extrinsic theory of morality that Locke shared with Hobbes. 'According to this view', concludes Charles Taylor, 'nothing is good or bad, admirable or contemptible intrinsically, but only in relation to some law or rule under which it is made to fall, backed by penalties'.[110]

Hutcheson strongly refuted this position. Humanity, Hutcheson argued following Shaftesbury, to whom he dedicated his first treatise, shared an instinctive goodness. Mankind was naturally benevolent and sympathy not self-interest provided the social bonds between men; sympathy was the basis for society. Directly addressing Mandeville's ideas, Hutcheson argued that not all love was self-referential. Our love for family and friends and for their approval spoke to more than just self-advantage. Furthermore, Mandeville's ideas depended on a tension between virtue and passion. For Hutcheson there was no dichotomy between virtue and the passions – mankind was naturally benevolent – virtue stemmed from the passions. This natural benevolence derived from a Moral Sense. The Moral Sense allowed for a spontaneous and disinterested sociability:

> [T]he author of *Nature* has determin'd us to receive by our *external Senses*, pleasant or disagreeable Ideas or Objects, according as they are useful or hurtful to our Bodys; and to receive from *uniform Objects* the Pleasures of *Beauty* and *Harmony*, to excite us to the pursuit of knowledge, and to reward us for it; or to be an argument to us of his *Goodness*, as the *Uniformity* it self proves his *Existence*, whether we had a *Sense of Beauty* in *Uniformity* or not: in the same manner he has given us a Moral Sense, to direct our Actions, and to give us still *nobler pleasures*; so that while we are only intending the *Good* of others, we undesignedly promote our own greatest private *Good*.[111]

Deeply indebted to the language of Lockean sensational psychology, Hutcheson nevertheless argued for a 'disposition to goodness' and an 'instinctive benevolence' that struck the heartfelt innate principles of Shaftesbury's humanism.[112] His Moral Sense continued the internalization of the providential order begun by Shaftesbury. 'How clearly does the Order of our Nature point us to our true Happiness and Perfection, and lead us as naturally as the several Powers of the Earth, the Sun, and Air, bring Plants to their Growth, and the Perfection of their Kinds?', he asked rhetorically.[113] Human feelings and sentiments naturally constituted man's 'happiness and perfection'. Indeed, human benevolence was central to the order of the universe.[114] Furthermore, all of these phenomena were the instruments and/or effects of God's grand design.

These ideas were, in the early eighteenth century, revolutionary. Hutcheson proposed that the passions – for generations of theologians and philosophers the bane of mankind – were in fact the source of virtue.[115] The Renaissance Humanists extolled the perfectibility of humanity as the result of the control or sublimation of the passions by reason. Hutcheson found this unacceptable; virtue derived from feeling and sentiment. More specifically, however, Hutcheson aimed his Moral Sense at the Locke-Bacon-Newton Puritan or Calvinist nexus of empiricism, innate depravity, sense experience and reason. Not only was humanity bent to the good in the universe, the linchpin of this system was man's feelings. Moral Sense theory, Richard Teichgraeber concludes, 'redefined the issue of virtue in terms of observing moral judgments as an internal process abandoning the view that virtue was the goal of rational decisions meant to shape man according to a predetermined ideal vision of what he ought to be'.[116]

Hutcheson also made commerce a central part of his ideas and set the stage for Hume and Smith's construction of a liberal economic order. Hutcheson saw property and commercial activity as part of the larger natural rights endowment of humanity. 'Whenever it appears to us', he argued, 'that a *Faculty of doing, demanding or possessing any thing, universally allow'd in certain circumstances, would in the whole tend to the general Good,* we say that any Person in such Circumstances, has *a right to do, posses, or demand that Thing*'.[117] In this spirit, Hutcheson delineated, among others, men's 'rights to the fruits of his own innocent Labour', and an exclusive right to Commerce and exchange: 'The Labour of each Man cannot furnish him with all the Necessarys, tho it may furnish him with a needless Plenty of one sort: Hence the *Right* of *Commerce*, and *alienating* our Gods; and also the *Rights* from *Contracts* and *Promises*, either to the *Goods* acquir'd by others, or to their *Labours*',[118] These ideas were not totally revolutionary; the natural law thinkers Grotius and Pufendorf both made commercial activity a central part of their natural rights narratives. Where he differed from other natural law thinkers was, however, in his application of the Moral Sense to these ideas.

Grotius, Pufendorf and Locke postulated that property was at the centre of human activity. Property arose when humans used what had once been in common. If nature's bounty was available to all then the consumption or exclusive use of that bounty directly created private property.[119] For Grotius this was an exclusive right not limited by other people's rights. Pufendorf developed a more sociable vision of property, limiting rights to goods and property, insofar as they contributed to the common good. Locke took a different tack and argued that property was *made* by human action. The clearing and tilling of a certain area made it property and limited the benefits of that area for the tiller – this was a natural right created by God to 'excite' men to industry and improvements, and thus improve the quality of life.

Hutcheson revised Locke's ideas and ground property in the Moral Sense. Property was created not by some imaginative transference derived solely from action. Property was instinctive and emotional. Heartfelt emotions told man that to take the sustenance or the product of another's labour was wrong. Furthermore, property in itself was not some ingenious egotistically-driven, God-created spur to human activity and improvement. Humans improved land for their families and friends as well as their own benefit. 'For the strengthening therefore our motives to *Industry*, we have the strongest attractions of *Blood*, of *Friendship*, of *Gratitude*, and the additional motives of *Honour*, and even *external Interest*. *Self-love* is really as necessary to the *Good* of the *Whole*, as *benevolence*; as that *Attraction* which causes the Cohesion of the Parts, is as necessary to the *regular State* of the *Whole*, as *Gravitation*.'[120] Property and other natural rights were embedded in the moral sense; they were based on affections and feelings, not reason. Further, these feelings were as natural a part of the divine order as gravity.[121]

Hutcheson's ideas on property blended a reason-based Grotian natural law ideal with his instinct-based Moral Sense. Hume and Smith developed these ideas further and redefined man's everyday activities in terms of sentiments and desire. The Scottish reconceptualization of humanity described a social and economic order based on desire and emotions instead of reason; it described a new subjectivity.

David Hume

Born and educated in Edinburgh, David Hume early on set out to create a new philosophy. Hypothetical ideas about the nature of humanity obsessed the philosophers he studied. Not one, according to Hume, based his ideas on the true nature of man – on man as he existed. Thus he set out to create a science of man based on humanity as it lived and died. In this project he borrowed extensively from Hutcheson. In particular he emphasized sentiment and emotions – the passions – as the basis for human morality and economic activity.[122]

For Hume, mankind was driven exclusively by passions and sentiments – not reason. Hume went further than Hutcheson in that he derived this moral order without the Providence of God. Coming of intellectual maturity slightly later than Hutcheson, he belonged to a radical Enlightenment generation that critiqued the providential-order ideas espoused by Shaftesbury and Hutcheson. Voltaire's *Candide* is perhaps the most scathing of these criticisms, destroying, in its own way, the idea of a benevolent and providential organic social and/or universal order and man's place within it.[123] Hume, however, did not buy into these ideas completely and maintained a close connection to Hutcheson's thought, albeit without a deity. Hume in effect constructed a 'complete account of moral obligation ... without reference to a divine legislator.'[124] 'Morality', he wrote to Hutcheson, 'according to your opinion as well as mine is determin'd merely by sentiment, it regards only human nature & human life. This has been often urg'd against you & the consequences are very momentous.'[125] Thus, for Hume, sentiment and the passions were even more important than they were for Hutcheson. The human order was mankind's creation. It was, in his own language, not 'unnatural', but 'artificial' – and thus all the more necessary and important.[126]

Hume's exclusive focus on sentiment was important for the development of a liberal political economy in a number of ways. First, Hume developed his closely intertwined ideas of justice and property on the basis of this naturalist psychology. Second, Hume turned his 'system of human liberty' to an attack on mercantilism, first as a matter of economic policy, and second as contrary to human nature.

Hume began his reconstruction of property with the idea that all rules based on reason must have support in the passions. Reason, he argued, has no dominion over the passions; ideas about ethics, justice, morality and property can be developed using reason, but human beings would never follow rules that contradicted their inner feelings. Concepts such as justice and property thus arose only with the support of the passions. In a world dominated by economic instability and contrary interests, Hume argued, continued insecurity in terms of possessions (property) gave rise to a series of 'conventions'. Indeed, society itself was a 'convention enter'd into by all members of the society to bestow stability in the possession of external goods'. Property and justice were not part of a conscious reason-based formulation dictated to the heart, but the development of a 'common sense of interest' which brought about a modification of behaviour. 'In sum', Richard Teichgraeber concludes, 'Hume understood justice [and thus possession of property] as a specific "habit of mind" that controlled self-interested passion by an "alteration of its direction" rather than the dictates of right reason'.[127]

Second, Hume brought this naturalist psychology to his understanding of economic activity and government policy. Mercantilism, Hume argued, with its focus on state power, necessarily limited men's freedom and slowed the development of the citizen and society; it identified a citizen in political terms, and tried to shape his or her desires towards political goals. This, Hume argued, was not only ineffective, it was unnatural. Part of the divide between Hume and the mercantilists derived from a different vision of national and world economies. Mercantilists saw the economy fundamentally as a national 'weapon' designed to strengthen one society at the expense of another. Hume took a much more cosmopolitan tack and envisioned an interdependent world order in which an increase in French or Spanish or any other nation's wealth was not a diminution of British wealth. In this vision, the work of the merchant transcended national boundaries and was impaired by the rules and regulations that mercantilists created from their mistaken notions of the purpose of the economy. On another level, Hume again argued that all rules must be based on the passions. Thus any attempt by the state to shape the consumption or production patterns of individuals was 'unnatural' and counterproductive. Individual as well as national happiness suffered from these efforts. Hume's attack on mercantilism was thus directly based on his confidence in the human propensity and necessity to feel, think, and want – and on the power of those feelings and desires to create a harmonious and beneficent social order. Mercantilist restraints on human activity contradicted his system of natural liberty.

Hume's other economic ideas are less clear. His ideas on money, for example, are confusing and have been often misunderstood.[128] 'Money', Hume began his essay 'Of Money', 'is not, properly speaking one of the subjects of commerce; but only the instrument which men have agreed upon to facilitate the exchange of one commodity for another. It is none of the wheels of trade: It is the oil which renders the motion of the wheels more smooth and easy'. Later in the same essay he concluded, 'money is nothing but the representative of labour and commodities, and serves only as a method of rating or estimating them'.[129] In keeping with these ideas, he argued against efforts to control the flow of precious metals and, by and large, saw money as a facilitator of economic activity.[130] Thus it appears that Hume espoused ideas radically different from Locke's bullionism and consistent with his emotive epistemology and his criticism of mercantilism elsewhere. In other writings, however, he clearly protested paper currencies – and was, as S. G. Checkland notes, 'equivocal about a developed banking system'. Indeed, Hume argued that 'banks, funds and paper credit ... render paper equivalent to money, circulate it throughout the whole state, make it supply the place of gold and silver, raise proportionably the price of labour and commodities, and by that means either banish a great part of those precious metals, or prevent their farther encrease'.[131] Nevertheless, he also paradoxically argued for free entry into banking and the free issue of notes.[132] In part these contradictions derive from Hume's devaluation of money as critical to economic prosperity. More important than money, Hume argued, were 'manners' and the industriousness of the people. To assume that money held back or promoted prosperity independent of the 'manners and customs of the people', was to mistake, as Hume put it – 'a collateral effect for a cause'.[133] Thus Hume could discount paper money as unproductive, and diminish the importance of the precious metals, based on his ideas of human behaviour.[134]

Overall, Hume subscribed to the Hutchesonian theory of moral sentiments and developed more fully than did Hutcheson a moral and economic system centred on the 'passions'. This was a particularly organic vision of humanity that conflated or synthesized all aspects of human existence. All of these ideas were, however, more fully developed by Adam Smith. Smith reconstructed ideas about humanity that reflected the interdependent moral and commercial society he championed.

Adam Smith

Born in Kirkcaldy, Scotland, in 1723 and educated at the University of Glasgow under Francis Hutcheson, Adam Smith followed Hutcheson and Hume and mapped the nature of sympathy and sentiments and their role in social relationships. For Smith, sympathy, or moral approbation, was clearly an internalized function derived through an act of the imagination. 'The source of our fellow-feeling', Smith argued, derived from changing places 'in fancy' with the sufferer.[135] In fact, for Smith, all moral and social approbation derived from an internalized 'impartial spectator'. Adam Smith's impartial spectator, Charles Griswold notes, 'exemplifies sympathetic understanding at its best, a stance of caring for the other, of caring to understand the truth of the matter and the reasons for which the people in question have acted as they have. This sympathetic care is at the core of morality and sociability; it holds us mutually responsible to each other, drawing us together in the exercise of responsiveness and perceptive judgment.'[136] With the impartial spectator Smith completed the internalization of the providential order that Shaftesbury and Hutcheson began. He articulated a self-conscious, reflective morality derived in part from the sociability and interdependence inherent in a commercial world.[137] Furthermore, Smith argued that 'sympathy', a personal moral standard, constructed the larger moral fibre or law through the accumulated instances of individual sympathetic emotive responses. For Smith, moral approval or disapproval derived from the accumulated wisdom of numerous encounters – 'the unanticipated product of a multiplicity of moral judgments'.[138] Human morality derived from human agency; it was an aggregate of sentiments.

The impartial spectator was not, however, limited to moral value structures. It also played a central role in many of Smith's economic and political ideas. For example, following Hutcheson, Smith argued that men did not respect 'property by occupation' out of some abstract notion of property rights, but out of our ability to imagine others' needs and expectations. Likewise, the notion of inheritance made more sense, Smith argued, if we allowed for the transference of our emotions with the dead and their wishes. Again, Smith based property and notions of justice in feelings – in an act of the sympathetic imagination – not reason.[139]

Smith's overall contribution to the development of a liberal economic order was also based on the Scottish system of natural liberty and, like his moral system, the power of accumulated human decisions and feelings to construct a spontaneously beneficent social order. Smith's central economic arguments are, of course, well known and more or less accepted by economists and social critics of all stripes.[140] In the *Wealth of Nations* (1776), Smith depicted a world driven by self-interested individuals competing in an economy marked and developed by the division of labour. Millions of consumers and producers free to choose from among the millions of products to consume and produce acted as an 'invisible hand' guiding the aggregate economy to the highest possible level of income. This system, though not wholly without pernicious side effects, allowed for the greatest levels of wealth and an increased quality of life for all. It was not the most equitable system – it was in fact driven by inequality – yet the poorest labourer enjoyed a quality of life unimagined in less developed societies. Overall the system was driven by the most pervasive of eighteenth-century ideals – freedom. Underlying his ideas was the belief that a 'socially beneficent ordered arrangement is likely to emerge out of the free actions of countless individuals, each aiming at the satisfaction of his own private ends'.[141] Freedom was the logic of Smith's political economy and its most radical message. This did not represent, however, simply a freedom of the body – the freedom to choose, to work, to buy, to sell, to alienate one's labour or to enter or exit markets, for example. It also meant the freedom of sentiments – of emotions – to think and want. Indeed, Smith's greatest contribution to political economy, *The Wealth of Nations*, is in effect, 'a description of the sentiments and agitation of mind of individuals in the ordinary events of life'.[142]

Using his system of natural liberty as a starting point, Smith's ideas on money, banking, wealth and consumption echoed Hume and directly contradicted Locke. Adam Smith more than any of the Scots saw free banking as central to the *summum bonum*.[143] He was by and large against the meddling of governments in banking and argued for both free note issue and the free chartering of banks. According to Smith, the more banks the better – the errors of the few would thus be spread out and the social consequences of speculation and failure diminished.[144] Banks increased the money supply, raised consumption, and thus unambiguously improved the quality of life. Specie drains associated with paper money posed no problem since money was not opulence. 'The opulence of a nation', he argued, 'does not consist in the quantity of coin, but in the abundance of commodities which are necessary for life, and whatever tends to increase these tends so far to increase the riches of a country'. 'Paper money', in his estimate, played a central role in increasing the abundance of goods. In this regard, he cited the 'flourishing ... American colonies, where most of the commerce is carried out by paper circulation'. Smith was very critical of John Law's idea that value was completely arbitrary. Nevertheless, he clearly outlined a 'utility' or circulation value of money, he legitimated consumption and goods – and not specie – as the measure of opulence, and he argued for an abundance of banks, and bank note issues regulated only by the community's acceptance of them.[145] Thus, according to Smith, trust and confidence in a bank, expressed by public opinion, was sufficient regulation of the extension of its credit; trust and confidence sufficed to maintain an economy's circulating medium.

Scottish Banking

The Scottish philosophers derived many of these ideas from their experience with eighteenth-century Scottish banking practices – though Scottish bankers often sorely tested the logic of their formulations.[146] Scottish banks were, of course, exempt from the Bubble Act of 1710 by virtue of the Act of Union of 1707; the Scottish banking system was, in effect, grand-fathered into the British financial system. Thus there developed in Scotland a formidable banking industry that innovated through the eighteenth century, successfully replacing specie with paper-credit instruments – bank notes. As Charles Munn notes, the specie reserves of Scottish banks dropped in the eighteenth century and were fractional by the early nineteenth century.[147] Furthermore, prior to the Act of 1765, the issue of small notes – often fractions of pounds – also meant that bank notes acted as the *de facto* currency of the nation for almost all transactions.[148] Scottish banks thus banked and prospered largely on note issues and deposits based on trust and confidence. More importantly, the key to both the Scottish social order and their paper-credit economy was this reciprocating notion of interdependence and trust. Scottish money, like Scottish morality, derived from the self-legitimating actions the people took: from human agency. It was a system designed by and for men and was not dependent on theocratic interventions.

Overall, both Hume and Smith derived their ideas on political economy in the context of their ideas about free moral will. The Scots in both their banking theory and practice measured the value of money first in utilitarian terms – as the facilitator of commerce (as opposed to the mercantile notion of wealth in money); and second in terms of trust and confidence, rather than intrinsic worth. Furthermore, they overwhelmingly saw no conflict between individual wealth and the wellbeing of the state. Individuals seeking their own prosperity assured social wealth; human agency best maximized economic potential. This development signified the end for mercantile ideas and marked the increased acceptance of *laissez-faire* ideas on commerce and consumption. This development, however, spoke to more than economic development and political economy. It also represented a fundamental epistemological shift from received theocratic value structures to anthropocentric, sociological constructions. The Scots internalized the sources of economic value and purpose.

There were, of course, many more Scottish Moral and Common Sense philosophers but, with few exceptions, the heart of their message was very similar.[149] Moral and aesthetic judgments derived from a heartfelt moral sense or intuition – from sentiment. Sentiment was, as Charles Taylor has noted, the measure of men – 'the touchstone of the morally good'.[150] This was a profoundly anthropocentric and sociological vision of the social order based on innate or instinctive, and ultimately *a priori*, ideas. It directly contradicted the theological voluntarism that Locke affirmed and supported with his sensational psychology. It was marked by human 'free will' and moral agency – ideas most often associated with liberal religion and anathema to orthodox Calvinism. This represented an internalization or subjectivization of external moral structures – and a legitimization of human agency and desires. As noted these ideas were both shaped and expressed by fundamental changes in financial theory and practice.

Thus far then, I have concluded that the external intrinsic value of silver was part of Locke's theocratic social order and hinged on the theological voluntarism of Calvinism. Furthermore, Locke's epistemology – his sensational psychology – buttressed theological voluntarism and its external value structure, including silver. Conversely, paper credit was the monetary equivalent of the Scottish reaction to Locke's external value structures. It represented the sociological construction and subjectivization of economic value, and directly contradicted both theological voluntarism and Locke's epistemology. More than half a century later, Americans struggling to come to terms with the financial and social dislocation of a revolution set out to reconstruct society and economy. In doing so they once again encountered many of the same ideas and problems which eighteenth-century philosophers and political economists had engaged. Struggling to stabilize their economy, they pondered the nature and origins of money, and the purpose of economic activity. Not surprisingly given the colonial history of these debates and their shared heritage, they carried out these debates using the language and ideas of Locke, Shaftesbury, Hutcheson, Hume and Smith.

3 AMERICAN MONEY AND POLITICAL ECONOMY, 1780–1828

> The Nation's Ruin'd, We Are Told
> If Paper Longer Pass for Gold
> And City Aldermen Grow Thinner,
> By Paying Thus for Abstract Dinner.
>
> William Pitt, *The Bullion Debate: A Serio-Comic*
> *Satiric Poem* (London, 1811).

Questions about the site and nature of money's value dominated eighteenth- and early nineteenth-century Anglo-American economic thought. Though colonial Americans flirted with liberal monetary ideas and institutions through the first half of the eighteenth century, Imperial decree based on mercantilist principles banished fundamental change.[151] The Revolution, however, liberated and recharged American financial and intellectual speculation.[152] Into the nineteenth century, Americans followed the Scottish political economists and increasingly adopted liberal ideas on money, banking and the nature of the economy.[153]

Americans' adoption of liberal economic ideas and practices touched on more than just the economy. This shift refocused ideas about the *summum bonum* – the good life – in everyday experience and undermined mercantilist notions of the organic social order.[154] Recent scholarship argues that trade policies during the Early Republic constituted a neo-mercantile strategy.[155] This literature, however, ignores the demands of mercantilism outside of trade relationships. Mercantilism's zero-sum economy denigrated individual consumption, equated specie with wealth, promoted its accumulation, and privileged the state-centred whole over its individual members. In other words, it distrusted and sacrificed individual freedom and desire for the benefit of the organic whole. It derived from and reinforced an empiricist world of fixed and limited 'real' values based on hierarchical – theocratic – authority. By legitimizing paper-credit instruments, liberal economic ideas located monetary value in trust and confidence – in the self and society – rather than in external theocratic or political value structures. In defining wealth as the individual consumption of goods rather than the accumulation of specie, contemporary liberal political economists stipulated that the social order served the people, and provided for their happiness, not vice versa.[156] Finally, the idea that human beings in their individual capacities spontaneously constructed a harmonious social and economic order undermined external authority and hierarchies. Once again, American bankers and political economists followed the Scots in imagining an economic order based on human subjectivity, not external or received values.

Revolutionary Experience

Revolutionary financial needs and practices opened anew the mid-eighteenth-century debate on the site and nature of economic value. The Continental Congress and the individual states financed the Revolutionary War with fiat money. Congress alone issued more than 200 million 'continentals' by 1780. The value of these instruments rode holders' waves of confidence and pessimism, rising and falling with American military success or failure. In 1781 Congress officially depreciated the currency to one-fortieth of its face value. In this manner Congress collected $119 million in 'continentals' for $3 million in specie. At the same time it issued new 'tenor' bills – interest-bearing promissory notes to be redeemed in specie five years from the date of issue – though they never kept the terms of the contract. These too depreciated on the open market and soon traded at 15 per cent of their face value. The states likewise emitted more than $200 million in currency – ultimately depreciated to $6 million in specie. Though the practical effect of the consistent depreciation of fiat currency was a tax on the note holder that effectively financed two-thirds of the war, the immediate effect was hyperinflation, contempt for fiat currencies, monetary confusion and debate.[157] Financial thinkers puzzled by the incessant inflation and monetary collapses in the midst of the Revolution attempted to formulate an understanding of how the economy worked. The 'quantity theory' of money popular in the late seventeenth and early eighteenth centuries argued that prices expressed the balance of goods and silver in the economy. Extreme versions of this idea imagined an absolute quantity of goods in the world in balance with an absolute quantity of silver. Price fluctuations thus reflected short-term imbalances and specie flows. Put another way, demand and/or production factors little affected prices. Enlightenment versions of the quantity theory espoused by the Scots David Hume and Robert Wallace dropped the specie dogma and promoted a currency adapted to the needs of commerce – in balance with trade.[158]

The hyperinflation of the Revolution revived attempts to understand the economy through the quantity theory. Too much money, paper or specie, financial theorists argued, generated the hyperinflation, and retiring the money might restore the balance. James Madison, Alexander Hamilton, Robert Morris and others disagreed. The hyperinflation of the Revolutionary period bore little proportion to the actual volume of emissions. Simply cutting the volume in half, for example, would not restore the value of the remaining currency by a proportionate amount. These thinkers thus revisited Locke's intrinsic-value-in-silver theory instead. Revolutionary emissions or 'continentals', Madison argued, lost their value because all paper credit depended on silver redemption. The value of money did not depend on the quantity of money or goods in the economy, but rather in the confidence people had that precious metals supported the note issue. Thus Revolutionary disillusion with paper money revived Locke's intrinsic-value ideas albeit in the form of specie-backed credit instruments.[159]

Robert Morris's Bank of North America quickly confirmed the value of specie-backed paper-credit instruments. Chartered in 1781, the Bank of North America assisted the Continental Congress through financial difficulties in the latter stages of the war. Its success, however, had a longer impact. It reaffirmed for many the need to back paper credit with specie and demonstrated banks' ability to increase and maintain credit markets. Imitators soon followed and in 1784 capitalists in New York and Boston established the Bank of New York and the Massachusetts Bank. Their success spawned numerous competitors, including the first Bank of the United States in 1791. By the 'Age of Jackson' more than 300 banks capitalized at over $160 million created hundreds of millions of dollars in liabilities and dominated American economic life.[160]

Specie-backed paper-credit instruments unleashed the tremendous economic potential of the young nation.[161] The American advent of specie-backed instruments did not, however, signify a complete return to a Lockean political economy based on intrinsic value. Specie-backed paper instruments, as Adam Smith and others argued, depended on the confidence note-holders expressed in the issuer. This was, in Pocock's phrase, an 'imaginary' value in the mind of the holder.[162] Furthermore, an economy based on these types of exchange instruments had no limits placed on its 'money' issue. As long as people expressed confidence in the circulating medium it maintained its value and, as Smith pointed out, there could never be too much money. Money in this system lost its 'fixed' value as a commodity and for commodities. 'Since money no longer had to balance the quantity of goods at market', Janet Riesman concludes, 'it no longer seemed to have the intrinsic value vis-à-vis goods at market which it was assumed that it once had. Money now must be seen as having a value that was essentially "fictitious" because only the "common consent" of all men gave money its value ... Indeed it was only the measure of value, only a medium; it facilitated trade, but did not regulate it.'[163]

Disquietude over the nature of money did not diminish with the widespread adoption of specie-backed bank notes. Bank notes were a halfway measure between specie and fiat money, but Americans universally saw them – in support and opposition – as part of the 'Paper System'.[164] In part this was a function of the nature of contemporary banking. The practice of fractional reserve banking meant that banks greatly exceeded their specie reserves and thus bank notes increasingly relied solely on confidence. Also, bankers and legislators, and, we can assume, ordinary Americans, confused 'capital' with specie reserves – voiding the effectiveness of legislation designed to curb credit market expansion. Increasingly, legislators also ignored book money – credit created through discounts deposited in the issuing bank – altogether. Book money, however, never physically 'real', often exceeded bank note emissions and thus silently multiplied credit without increasing specie reserves.[165] Widespread speculation and malfeasance also served to bring the new economic system into question. Frequent failures and a plethora of paper-credit instruments, banks and joint-stock companies of all sorts further diluted the connection between bank notes and specie – between *natural* economic value in silver and gold and a shifting and ever-changing value riding the psychology of the new paper-credit markets. Thus, although Riesman correctly maps the sea change in economic theory and practice in the 1780s, debates on the nature of money, and questions of economic value, dominated American political economy into the 1830s and beyond.

The language of these debates on money echoed the Lockean recoinage crisis. With every attempt to charter a large bank, and every periodic downturn, financial bubble or fraud, newspaper polemicists and pamphleteers argued the source of money's value. Was it intrinsic – a function of silver? Or was value extrinsic – constructed and legitimized by authority, trust and confidence?[166] Related to this issue was money's utility. If money was a sign and not a thing, its value derived largely from its exchange value or utility rather that its value as 'treasure'. Finally, associated with both of these issues were fundamental questions about the nature of the economy. These can best be expressed in terms of the definitions of wealth and economic purpose. Was wealth the sum total of resources at the disposal of the nation-state? Or was wealth an aggregate of individuals' ability to consume goods and achieve a higher standard of living? Finally, could the decisions of consumers and producers in and of themselves guide the economy – or were individual desires insufficient to maximize economic potential?

Money as a Thing

Debates on the nature of money filled the popular presses of post-Revolutionary America. In 1786, for example, in the midst of the Bank of North America's efforts to retain its Philadelphia monopoly, the *American Museum* devoted an entire issue to 'paper money'. Jonathan Witherspoon, the Princeton President and member of the Continental Congress, featured prominently in these debates as an advocate of specie, and a long pamphlet he published on the subject was reprinted in the *American Museum* 'paper money' issue. Witherspoon was, of course, best known as the Scottish Popular Party Presbyterian minister (Calvinist) who, ironically, did so much to introduce the Moderate Party's moral-sense philosophy to Princeton.[167] As a member of the Continental Congress, he served on the Finance Committee alongside Robert Morris and others. The pamphlet and article were part of a debate on money that included Benjamin Franklin, William Barton and numerous other theorists. Witherspoon strongly expressed a tremendous anxiety towards paper money and backed a commodity theory of money – based implicitly on Locke's ideas but ultimately also derived from his own orthodox Calvinism. For Witherspoon, money needed to be a commodity and silver was the obvious and 'natural' choice. He followed Locke and other metallists and presented a 'paper' system as unnatural and irrational; the 'sign', in Witherspoon's world-view, could not be traded for the 'signified'. Only 'real' property could satisfy an exchange for 'real' property.

Witherspoon's disquisition on money began with a rhetorical question: 'what gave rise to money and what is its nature and its use?'. An imagined solitary individual on the earth had no need for money, Witherspoon continued. It was only the exchange of surplus resulting from the division of labour as men best utilized their talents that gave rise to exchange instruments. Commerce necessitated instruments that might 'represent the absent commodities'. Indeed, the great 'conveniancy' of signs promoted their utilization. But very soon thereafter, Witherspoon continued, there grew confusion between the sign and the signified; between the goods being traded and the representatives of those goods. 'It must have appeared', he continued, 'and did speedily appear, that all mere signs labour under an essential defect. They depend ultimately on the faith or credit of the persons using or answerable for them. Now, whether these be individuals or the multitude by general custom and implied consent, or even the ruling part of the society, there is very great uncertainty'. Hence, he argued, the need for a more positive or reliable sign. 'An absent commodity well known, or even an idea well understood, may be a standard of computation and common measure; any thing almost whatever may be a sign, though, since the art of writing has been known, paper, is the best, but both are essentially defective; there is wanting a value in the sign, that shall give not only a promise or obligation, but actual possession of property for property'. This was, for Witherspoon, a great evolution. First, men dealt in 'gross barter; and after that invented signs, and were content with them for another period; and at last [they] perfected the plan, by getting signs possessed of real value'.[168] The precious metals, in Witherspoon's estimate, were a perfect circulating medium – they were signs possessed of value that allowed the exchange of 'property for property'.

Witherspoon developed a monetary history that reflected natural law ideas about social change current in his lifetime.[169] Ultimately, however, his notion of intrinsic value rested on the 'natural' and thus – from his Calvinist perspective – God-ordained value of silver. He readily discounted Franklin's and others' notions of utility-value in objects. As discussed below, theorists from Nicholas Barbon to Benjamin Franklin had argued that value was a function of utility. Following that logic, they concluded that iron and wheat both had greater utility and thus greater value than the precious metals. For Witherspoon, this was simply nonsensical. The utility value of iron versus gold did not factor into their relative prices. The *de facto* difference in their prices, Witherspoon declared, proved his point. Furthermore, a starving man might indeed hold a bushel of wheat in greater esteem than a pound of gold – but, Witherspoon asked plaintively, 'is this any argument against the intrinsic commercial value of gold, as it has taken place since the beginning of the world?'. Those authors who denied the value of precious metals as money, he continued, had simply 'abstracted the idea' and taken money 'in the single light of a sign, without considering it as a standard'. A nail had no value outside of its function as a nail. Melt it down, however, and it will serve as lock and key. 'So a guinea', he declared, 'while it continues as a guinea, is of no use whatsoever, but as an instrument of commerce; but the gold of which a guinea consists, can easily be converted into a ring, or any thing which its quantity will reach. This is what is called, with perfect propriety, its *intrinsic* value'. The value of silver and gold, Witherspoon insisted, had nothing to do with so-called accidental opinion; these qualities arose 'from the nature of things'.[170]

Witherspoon focused mostly on fiat money but also argued to limit the specie-backed notes of banks. Fearing the note circulating strategies of Scottish banks, he pushed for limited emissions of high-value bank notes and an economy dominated by specie. Others, such as James Sullivan, engaged the bank note question more directly. James Sullivan was a Massachusetts Democratic-Republican politician who occupied various elected and political patronage posts over his career. He was elected Governor of Massachusetts in 1811. In 1792, then Attorney General of Massachusetts, he published a lengthy and satirical essay on the nature of money and the economy. At the time of his writing, like many politicians of the period, he was deeply invested in a number of joint-stock companies.[171] His investments in stock did not prevent him, however, from lashing out at the banking system as it developed in Massachusetts. Writing in the midst of the great stock and securities speculations that followed Hamilton's assumption program and the creation of the First Bank of the United States, Sullivan condemned contemporary banking practices – even at this nascent stage.[172] Sullivan was a disgruntled former shareholder in the Massachusetts Bank (est. 1784), thus his condemnation of banks (and the Massachusetts Bank in particular) was, in part, initiated by his inability to continue to partake of the bank's riches.

Beyond the self-interested feud he had with the Massachusetts Bank directors, Sullivan clearly understood and opposed the fractional reserve banking system then current, which was ultimately based on confidence. Printing notes beyond the actual amount of specie in the bank, he argued, created 'fictional' money. Money, Sullivan argued, was strictly speaking specie – gold and silver coin. The very 'practice of coining money', however, 'introduced what is called imaginary money, or money of account'. Current coins did not, in Sullivan's opinion, correspond to actual weights. 'Coins were established in the commercial world as the representative sign of the articles of commerce ....' Paper credit instruments, the 'secondary representative of the articles in commerce', were created to reduce the risk and cost of transporting specie. Paper did not, however, maintain its value relative to specie. Paper, Sullivan quoted Dr Price, 'owes its currency to the credit of the emitter, or to an opinion that he is able to make good on his engagement, and that the sum specified may be received upon being demanded ... Paper, owing its currency to opinion, has only a local and imaginary value ... [N]othing can be more delicate or hazardous; it is an immense fabric with its head in the clouds, that is continually trembling with every adverse blast and fluctuation of trade; and which like the baseless fabric of a vision, may, in a moment, vanish and not leave a wreck behind.'[173] 'Paper' included bank notes and stocks emitted by private joint-stock companies, as well as the 'funded credit of the government', an appellation in this regard, according to Sullivan, 'entirely arbitrary ... for in this kind of business there is no existing stock unless the plighted public faith may have that appellation'.[174]

Sullivan found all paper pernicious but condemned contemporary banking stocks in particular. He resented the special privilege politically-driven bank charters allocated to groups of men, especially the Massachusetts Bank, which, he argued, had greatly exceeded its original capitalization, issuing double their money on the security of borrowers. 'Upon this idea', Sullivan observed, 'their notes are so far from being the representative of real money, that they are nothing more than the representatives of the credit of men, with whom the possessor has not acquaintance, and of whose circumstances he is totally ignorant'.[175] Furthermore, this special privilege created splendours corrosive to the social order. The riches of the few 'intoxicated ... a great part of the community'. In this climate, Sullivan argued, *too many are ready to lay aside their ordinary business, to pursue* chance *as the only goddess worthy of human adoration*.[176] The subscription meeting for the First Bank of the United States, Sullivan recalled, occasioned such a 'wicked' crowd that 'a golden mountain ... emitting from its crater a lava of purest gold', could hardly have attracted the number, or surpassed the 'intense eagerness', of those assembled.

Sullivan did not, however, disparage banking altogether. The last section of his pamphlet outlined a plan for a massive bank with a widespread subscription. It would not, however, be a bank of emission in the ordinary sense of the word. Sullivan eschewed fractional reserve practices – and thus banking on confidence. His bank would be limited in its liabilities to actual 'money' paid in to it.[177]

The idea of replacing silver with paper on a one-to-one basis also appealed to the pseudonymous and republican minded Nestor, who saw all bank notes issued beyond actual specie deposits as producing 'debt and dependence'.[178] Others were, however, less appreciative of the banks and their 'unnatural' note emissions at any ratio.[179] These critics of banks and their note emissions insisted that money needed 'real' commodity value to function as a means of exchange. Bank notes printed on fractional reserves served only to drive 'real' money out. Often they imagined social dissolution and misery as a result of the devaluation of the 'real' standard of specie and thus the erosion of objectively knowable standards – the immutable laws of nature.

These ideas, though often popular, did not, however dominate economic thinking during the Early Republic. Indeed, a competing idea of money 'backed' the tremendous explosion of banks and paper-credit instruments of all kinds during this period. Central to this bundle of theories was the notion that money was a sign. Furthermore, bank notes signified more than absent specie. Indeed, as Riesman argues, 'Americans believed that bank credit was in fact based on the productive potential of manufacturing, turnpike and canal companies, all of which were engaged in tapping the true wealth of the land'.[180] Banks and bank credit were backed by an imagined potential wealth brought into being by the very instruments based on it. They represented and banked on the future of the nation.

Money as a Sign

The first article in the *American Museum* issue dedicated to the paper money debate was a 1764 piece by Benjamin Franklin often used by paper credit promoters or engaged by supporters of specie. In this article Franklin spoke directly to the British Board of Trade Report that banned paper money emissions in the colonies, and challenged their reasoning point by point, especially their theory of money.[181]

According to Franklin, the Board of Trade report stipulated that paper could never be the equivalent of the precious metals – it was not property, it had no intrinsic value. Franklin countered with a utility view of money that also engaged the quantity theory.[182] Were there enough specie, he suggested, its standard as money would not be disputed – but as a result of the very scarcity of specie 'it becomes necessary to use something else, the fittest that can be got in lieu of it'. Bank notes, according to Franklin, clearly filled this role, and 'yet they have no intrinsic value, but rest on the credit of those that issue them, as paper bills in the colonies rest on those of the respective governments that issue them'. Furthermore, even specie current in Britain, Franklin continued, no longer represented the actual weight value of precious metals it contained. Many coins were lighter by half of their nominal value. As such they had less foundation than paper money: 'For this difference between the real and the nominal, you have no intrinsic value; you have not so much as paper; you have nothing'. Finally, Franklin echoed Nicholas Barbon's objections to the very idea of intrinsic value in precious metals placing it in opinion and not divine authority.[183] 'Gold and silver', he concluded, 'are not intrinsically of equal value with iron, a metal in itself capable of many more beneficial uses to mankind. Their value rests chiefly in the estimation they happen to be in among the generality of nations, and the credit given to the opinion that that estimation will continue: otherwise a pound of gold would not be a real equivalent for even a bushel of wheat'.[184]

Franklin's arguments were, of course, posthumous and did not engage the specific post-Revolutionary context. Matthew Carey did, however, include more recent paper-credit polemicists, like William Barton, who spoke directly to the financial dilemmas facing the new nation. The well-born and English-educated Barton had earned his peers' respect for his Revolutionary service but was more widely acclaimed for his intellectual prowess.[185]

Barton first expressed his theories on money amidst the creation of the Bank of North America in 1781. Writing in support of the bank, Barton differentiated between the intrinsic commodity value of specie and its extrinsic value as money.[186] Barton began his tract in the style of the day, with a history of money and civilization. Primitive men, he noted, had little use for money. 'But when mankind became more polished, the *conveniencies* of life, and at length its luxuries, were fought for; and these artificial wants necessarily opened an intercourse between the inhabitants of various climes'.[187] This intercourse demanded a medium of exchange. Gold and silver, Barton noted, derived their value from scarcity, and 'certain inherent qualities of purity' that gave them intrinsic value – and as such were the 'universal medium of commerce'. However, their intrinsic value was, for Barton, their value as commodities; their extrinsic value as coin was usually equal to their intrinsic value yet, on occasion, the 'supreme power' might raise extrinsic beyond intrinsic value.[188]

In a second defence of the bank, published in 1786 and reprinted alongside Witherspoon's essay (among others) in the paper money issue of the *American Museum*, Barton distanced himself further from the intrinsic theory of money and re-emphasized the dual nature of precious metals. Barton again conceded that gold and silver contained intrinsic value as commodities, though he quoted passages from Franklin basing that value on opinion. Nevertheless, 'gold and silver', he pointed out, 'derives not its intrinsic value from performing the office of money; but possesses it as a commodity'. 'Money, considered in itself', Barton quoted the Scottish political economist James Anderson, 'is of no value. – But among civilized nations, who have found out how convenient it is for facilitating the barter or exchange of one commodity for another, it has received an artificial value. – So that although useless in itself, it has come to be accepted among all civilized nations, *as a token proving that the person who is possessed of it had given something of real value in exchange for it*; and is in that account, accepted of by another in exchange for something that is of real utility and intrinsic worth.'[189]

Finally, Barton quoted the Scottish political economist Sir James Steuart and defined money as 'any commodity which purely in itself is of no material use to man, but which acquires such an estimation from his opinion of it, as to become the universal measure of what is called value, and an adequate equivalent for any thing alienable'.[190] Specie was thus both a 'merchantable commodity' and a 'medium of alienation'. Its value as a medium of alienation, however, did not derive from any intrinsic properties, but from its utility. Furthermore, Barton concluded, as a medium of alienation it could not add to the wealth of the nation any more than 'paper or leather money, or any other *sign* of property'.[191]

Numerous supporters followed Barton and promoted a liberal system of banking as socially beneficent. On the eve of the First Bank of the United States re-charter struggle, Erick Bollmann enthusiastically defended bank credit. Long-standing detractors of the bank included ambitious speculators anxious to increase the power of state-chartered banks, and southern planting interests suspicious of its power.[192] Bollmann, a charismatic cosmopolitan financier familiar with economic theory, undertook the defence of the bank in aid of Federalist and conservative republican interests.[193] Following a long tradition, Bollmann began with a long exegesis of bank credit and banking that patiently explained the origins of bank notes. He placed this genesis in the unused specie stocks of goldsmiths. The goldsmiths, taking note of the vast unused resources in their storage vaults, initiated the credit process. They maintained a fractional reserve of gold that satisfied the everyday demands of their depositors while their unused deposits circulated widely. Modern banks took this one step further and circulated only standard and widely recognizable representations of gold – bank notes. Furthermore, he continued, although bank notes ostensibly represented the '*actual circulating medium, the gold and silver* in the bank, yet the checks represent it no *longer*. On the contrary, they *take the place of it* and become *the circulating medium themselves*.'[194] These credit instruments had, in Bollmann's estimate, ably performed as money. In fact, Bollmann proclaimed, the first Bank of the United States had only ever collected $675,000 in specie, and yet that sufficed to carry more than $6 million worth of credit.[195]

Bank credit, Bollmann argued, was more than just a financial instrument; it formed the very basis for civilization. Thus the threat to the Bank of the United States, according to Bollmann, undermined the basis for society. Winding down the bank's operations, if undertaken at all, must be done very slowly, he argued. Furthermore, the credit 'must be replaced with something. Without being replaced, stagnation, confusion, dissolution of the social bond, barbarism, and ruin [would ensue]. [Replacement] can be effected *slowly by time, suddenly* only by *a deus ex Machina, by magic*.'[196] Winding up the Bank of the United States would be disastrous not only for the bank itself, but also for all other banks. 'The Banks appear to me', Bollmann concluded, 'like a fleet, buoyed up by confidence and credit gliding down the spacious stream of trade and prosperity, each *just comfortably ballasted with specie*, and all of them *linked together* by a mighty chain of debtors and creditors, fastened to that ballast'. To slow down one ship was to slow them all down or 'upset' them, 'or else swing [them] round and dash [them] to atoms against each other'.[197]

Six years later, after a tour in Vienna and London where he wrote a number of essays promoting banks based on inconvertible note issues, Bollmann directed a second pamphlet at American banking practices.[198] He still pursued a quantity theory of money explanation for the appreciation and depreciation of currency. The value of currency fluctuated, according to Bollmann, only when there was too much or too little of it. Double the money supply and you simply doubled the price level. Change the medium into specie, and the effect is the same. The investor/consumer then has 'something *heavier* in his possession, but nothing more *productive*'.[199] Bank notes, he argued taking a page from Adam Smith, worked best as currency because they bore a direct relationship to commerce. They, by and large, owed their existence to commerce, and if thus properly secured, could never exceed the demand for money. Bollmann concluded his discussion with yet another proposal for a National Bank that would emit a national inconvertible currency. This was to be a *bank of banks* – a massive institution to regulate the issue of bank notes, yet maintain a steady supply of money. Indeed, advocates for a 'National Bank' never seemed to tire. Writing on the eve of the 1819 crisis, James Swan, the Scottish-American Boston-based adventurer, constructed yet another proposal for a national Land Bank that promised to replace discredited specie as the basis for a national currency.[200]

Bank notes to these proponents of paper credit ably functioned as a medium of alienation – a sign that facilitated the exchange of goods – and were thus a suitable form of money. 'Land and other solid property', wrote an anonymous Virginian in the *American Museum*, 'are the real objects of the industrious, and whether they be represented by gold or by paper – that representative will be considered by industry, as its most estimable reward'.[201] The circulating 'medium of trade', wrote another anonymous author, was the 'legal creation' of the legislature of the state, necessarily made from material of 'very small intrinsic value, to facilitate the exchange of one necessary article for another'. 'Money to the state', continued the author, 'is like the mechanics tools, the very last things he should dispose of; it is the medium which facilitates agriculture, trade and business of all kinds – deprive a people of money and you reduce industry to the lowest ebb'.[202] Banking, claimed one polemicist in the *Pennsylvania Gazette*, was the 'great engine' of domestic circulation, unique in its ability to 'melt solid property down'. The capacity to 'liquefy' property was, according to this anonymous writer, essential to credit – and credit, he concluded, was confidence.[203] Numerous writers in newspapers, pamphlets and books expressed these ideas time and again.[204] In the short-run, banking, and the banking practices most often associated with Scottish bankers and political economists, provided a solution to the specie shortage and confusion over the site of value. In the long run Americans accepted banks as economically and socially beneficent. Banks (and all other joint-stock moneyed corporations) were, following Samuel Blodget, the 'golden chains' that held society together.[205]

The debate on the nature of money as expressed by Witherspoon, Barton and others also pointed to different ideas on money's role in the economy. For Witherspoon there was no possible shortage of the 'natural' circulating medium. 'Whether any particular person, city, or nation, is rich or poor, has more or less comparatively of it, is nothing to the purpose. Everyone will receive of the circulating medium', he argued, 'that quantity which he is entitled to by his property or industry'. Price levels adjusted to specie flows and if a man one day buys a bushel of wheat for a quarter of a dollar, he is no richer nor poorer if seventy-five years later, the same bushel now demands a dollar. He was, Witherspoon argued, simply more burdened by the greater weight. Thus there was no reason to increase the money supply or create alternative forms of currency.[206]

Barton, on the other hand, promoted a new vision of the economy. Money simply facilitated commerce. The 'real' wealth money stood in for was, for Barton, in no way to be confused with money; it was based on goods. Thus money need not remain stable or fixed in supply: 'if that stock of commodities be increased by the *industry* of its inhabitants, a larger quantity of money will be requisite to represent that increased value of this real wealth ... [The] sign of wealth ought to bear a certain proportion to it.'[207] Furthermore, given North America's continuous increase of wealth, the very scarcity of the precious metals worked against their utility as a medium for commerce. Hence, Barton argued, the need for a system of paper credit. Credit, Barton quoted the Scottish political economist James Anderson, was '*absolutely necessary* to an extensive commerce'. Private credit was one early answer; private bank credit was a more sophisticated solution; yet, for Barton, public credit was the most attractive option: 'A public debt is a benefit to a nation, provided it be confined within proper limits, as it increases the cash of the country, by the introduction of a new kind of currency.'[208] A public debt was also a new kind of wealth – a wealth that existed 'only in name, in paper, in public faith, in parliamentary security: and that is undoubtedly sufficient for the creditors of the public to rely on.'[209]

Paper-credit instruments redefined monetary value. They circulated not on intrinsic value but on utility, trust and confidence. The value of money was thus a function of human institutions, agency and desire. Furthermore, under a paper system wealth resided not in precious metals but in the consumption of goods – the satisfaction, following Barton, of the wants of the mind. Unregulated consumption did not, in the eyes of Adam Smith and others, undermine the social order. It was, in fact, the point of the social order. The 'consumptibility of goods', as he put it, 'is the great cause of human industry ...'.[210] In this new order, society best served the needs of its members when it attended to their wants. Furthermore, the ordinary everyday activities and desires of men now controlled society and indeed defined its purpose.[211] Confidence in this 'newly discovered capacity of human beings' signified the end for mercantile ideas and marked the increased acceptance of Adam Smith's *laissez-faire* ideas on commerce and consumption.[212] These changes can also be discerned in the growing literature that fashioned an American political economy, particularly as expressed in Early Republic Boston.

Adam Smith and Boston's Political Economy

Political economy, as Janet Riesman notes, was the science of happiness during the eighteenth century, especially for the Anglo-American world. In Britain, the efforts of political economists continued through the century to provide axioms for felicity. A new ideal took root – one that emphasized the power of everyday activities to regulate the economy and provide for the people's welfare. Commerce, paper-credit instruments, demand-fuelled economic growth, individual acquisitiveness, or the 'pursuit of happiness', and a society based on the division of labour and exchange, the prophets of modernity argued, civilized humanity and engendered sympathetic social bonds and happiness.[213]

In the American colonies a movement towards a political economy based on exchange, credit and the internal development of markets also developed through the colonial period.[214] The disastrous New England experience with paper money and the Massachusetts Land Bank disruptions of 1741, however, thwarted these developments. 'No one writing in the colonial period', Riesman concludes, 'ever again [after the Land Bank fiasco] made the case that value was set in the market and that, if the market could be expanded, the value of paper money would not only remain stable but even grow'.[215] Colonists nevertheless carried into the Revolution a legacy of innovative economic ideas.[216]

In the post-Revolutionary period, the freedom to innovate combined with Revolutionary economic experience to fuel a dramatic burst of economic and intellectual growth. In the 1790s in particular, Joyce Appleby argues, 'Adam Smith's invisible hand was warmly clasped by Republicans'.[217] Liberal market economic theory dominated Jeffersonian ideas, and promised political and economic equality. Jefferson widely promoted the works of political economists like Destutt de Tracy and Thomas Cooper – both devotees of Adam Smith. By the second decade of the nineteenth century, most literate Americans agreed with J. Gallison's warm praise of the 'beneficial' science in Boston's *North American Review*:

> In truth it would hardly be too much to say of this philosophy [political economy], that it has disclosed a new power in society to promote the happiness and moral

elevation of its members. The end to which it steadily aims, is the general diffusion of a spirit of order, decency and honest industry, to place within the reach of all the means of comfortable subsistence, and to make men happy and virtuous by the natural and easy development of their faculties and desires.[218]

In Massachusetts, theories of economic development seemed to change with perceived sectional interests. The Revolution's immediate and deleterious impact on commerce pushed Massachusetts shipping interests to demand protection. Indeed, they made protection key to their acceptance of the constitution.[219] Through most of the Napoleonic Wars and the period of 'neutral shipping' Massachusetts enjoyed unfettered free trade and prospered. Embargo, non-intercourse, and the War of 1812, of course, did the most to set back the shipping interests of Massachusetts and in the long run set the stage for the transformation of its economic base to manufacturing.[220] Up until 1828, however, the senators and shipping interests of Massachusetts, often one and the same, pushed for a free-trade economic policy. Boston critics strongly associated political economy with Adam Smith, and his 'disciple' J. Say, and hotly denounced any efforts to repudiate their ideas. Writing in the midst of a burgeoning American and academic theory of political economy and the continued efforts by Matthew Carey and numerous others to promote 'protection', the Boston intellectuals associated with the *North American Review* missed no opportunity to engage protectionist tracts.

Though Americans often wrote brief pamphlets and other polemics under the title 'Political Economy', it was not until the 1820s that a full academic treatise on the subject appeared. Daniel Raymond's 1820 *Thoughts on Political Economy*, touted by Joseph Dorfman as the first full treatise by an American 'economist', made a cogent argument for tariffs and thus the protection of manufactures.[221] In the process he set himself against Smith's revered free-trade doctrines and drew the fire of Smith's supporters. Raymond, a New England lawyer settled in Baltimore, was already famous for a substantial pamphlet on the Missouri Crisis when he undertook his book on political economy. As a northerner living in a border state, he straddled a number of worlds, and his ideas on the tariff, slavery and other controversial issues were nothing if not sincere. Writing in the wake of the 1819 financial collapse, Raymond pushed hard for tariff legislation and the so-called American System.

Raymond followed the Earl of Lauderdale and argued against the mighty and respected words of Adam Smith.[222] Smith, as discussed above, argued that a self-regulating economy based on desire and consumption best served society's needs. The satisfaction of human beings' wants, and thus the quality of their lives, was in fact the goal of social organization and economic activity. Money was in no way riches, but merely represented goods that were riches. National wealth consisted of the aggregate wealth of individual assets. In this sense, society was also an aggregate of individual decision-makers, rather than a single organic entity. This aggregate or myriad of decisions, Smith argued, created the best of all possible worlds.[223]

Raymond, on the other hand, following Lauderdale, espoused radically different ideas about society, wealth and value. Raymond differentiated between national wealth and individual wealth. Individual wealth, he argued, was universally understood as property: '*The possession of property, for the use of which, the owner can obtain a quantity of the necessaries and comforts of life*.'[224] Property included land, goods and money – but not stock, which was 'more properly denominated the representative of property'. National wealth meant something altogether different from individual wealth. For Raymond, a nation was a 'unity' – it was an organism, or 'corporation'. As an artificial being, it could never possess wealth in the same manner as an individual. National wealth he defined as the *capacity to acquire the necessaries and comforts of life*.[225] More importantly, however, national wealth did not always equal individual wealth. Individuals and the state might in fact have opposite goals and conflict. 'The interests of a nation and the interests of individuals composing that nation may be, it is true, and often are, in unison', he argued. 'They may be identical, but they are not necessarily so; so far is this from being the case, that they are often directly opposed.'[226] Thus for Raymond, the aggregate of individual self-interested decisions central to Smith's political economy did not produce the best possible society. Order was not 'spontaneous' but the product of legislation or direction.

Underlying Raymond's hodgepodge of ideas was the 'bullionist' argument on money.[227] Money was a thing, not a sign. Men valued money by weight. Paper representatives of money issued by banks 'should be the actual representative of gold and silver money'.[228] Raymond even included a table that professed to indicate the number of 'grains' of silver in – and thus the true value of – current British coins. Also attached was the new protectionist/mercantilist credo. According to Raymond, tariffs stimulated 'idle labour' and increased national capacity and wealth; public works likewise added to the nation's real productive capacity; monopolies regulated consumption to the nation's benefit; likewise, colonies increased the empire's capacity at the expense of third nations (and thus unambiguously benefited the empire). The common thread in each of these positions was the denigration of individual interests toward a larger goal. Tariffs injured individual consumers, but in Raymond's zero-sum world-view, allowed some to work, thereby, in his logic, diminishing the burden on the whole. Public works and monopolies exhibited the same logic. He even legitimized colonization on the same basis – the sum of the benefits, he argued, go to the whole. The colony is the lesser, but the imperial organic unity is increased – in large part because third parties are denied access to the relationship. Also implicit in his argument was a complete repudiation of any 'spontaneous' organization by independent agents.

Raymond's ideas evoked a critical response from Boston's F. C. Gray in the *North American Review*.[229] Gray denounced Raymond's ideas on wealth, value and the nature of society. No one, Gray argued, used the term wealth as Raymond insisted. For Gray, Adam Smith's disciple Say best defined national wealth, and included the aggregate wealth of all individuals and their property as a corporate body. As Gray understood it, the increase of national wealth as defined by Raymond was not properly speaking even the domain of political economy. 'To increase the property of the nation thus understood is the object not of political economy in general', Gray concluded, 'but of the single department of finance'. Political economy pertained to the happiness of the people – in Gray's opinion inseparable from the national wealth but distinct from any state-centred definitions of prosperity.[230] Furthermore, Gray condemned Raymond's ideas on tariffs and/or protection. Tariffs directed consumption and production to unprofitable industries. Public works perniciously put good money to waste, and diminished capital investment in profitable projects that expanded overall production. Likewise monopolies simply allowed one part of the population to tax the other. Most importantly, however, these measures stunted the natural and spontaneous order that economic and personal freedom guaranteed.

The New York Review and Atheneum Magazine likewise saw Raymond's ideas as pernicious, and tied them into discredited mercantilist notions of wealth. 'In the *mercantile* system', the *Review* authors argued, 'the metals were esteemed the only riches of a country, and all the regulations of commerce had in view a favourable balance of trade, by which it was conceived, that the import of bullion would be made to exceed the export'. Associated with this system, the authors argued, was the idea that the merchant and the nation might have conflicting interests. The authors pointed to Raymond's *Political Economy* overall and his specific idea that 'individual wealth is often national poverty' as a recent source of these fallacious notions. So pernicious were these ideas, that the *Review* even called upon the University of Virginia to dispel the unfounded rumour that it was using Raymond's treatise as a textbook, 'lest it affect its reputation with the lovers of true science'.[231]

The reviewers' harsh criticisms of Raymond's ideas and tone did not discourage all potential followers – even in then free-trade Boston. In a series of articles first published anonymously in the Boston-based *United States Literary Gazette*, and later in book form, Bostonian Caleb Cushing made similar arguments.[232] Cushing was concerned that theories of political economy developed in Europe promoted European interests. Americans were altogether too 'prone to regard the writings of certain English politicians and economists as little short of oracular'. His goal then was to 'give a plain exposition of economical principles adapted to our interest, not the interest of France, or of Britain, or of the British country Gentlemen, or of British stockholders'.[233]

Cushing followed Raymond's ideas on wealth. National wealth and individual wealth were not synonymous, and indeed might conflict. 'Although a portion of individual wealth enters to make up the aggregate of national wealth, namely, that portion which consists in material objects of intrinsic value and of debts due from abroad; yet it does not follow that every accession to individual wealth is an augmentation of national wealth, or that what promotes the interest of the individual must necessarily promote that of the public'. Thus, pace Smith, Cushing did not see the individual and his choices at the centre of a self-regulating system that ultimately best met the needs of the individual and society simultaneously. In the immediate context of Cushing's efforts to buttress protectionism, this was a nod to the regulation and/or protection of industry. In the larger context of the debate on society and political economy, Cushing (and Raymond) pointed backwards to a more corporate, less self-driven social order.

Cushing also seemed to follow mercantilist, or neo-mercantilist ideas on value. Money was both a medium of exchange and 'one of the constituents of wealth'. At the same time, however, he argued that value, or price, was determined by market-based demand – 'the want which others may have for [a product], and what they are willing to give for it'.[234] Furthermore, banks and bank notes, judiciously checked, benefited the community by releasing specie for foreign commerce.

The anonymous *North American Review* author disagreed strongly with Cushing's overall message. Though many of his propositions were 'sound and pithy', the author erred through 'precipitancy, imperfect examination, and a proneness to decide on first impressions'. More importantly, however, Cushing had slighted Smith and Say. 'Adam Smith was one of the master spirits of his age', the author argued, 'possessing a mind of extraordinary power and resources, and throwing a new and brilliant light upon every subject he touched ... Smith and Say have passed the ordeal of the world ... as writers of very great merit on political economy, who stand indeed at the very head of the list'.[235]

A more systematic defence of Smith's principles came from long-time free-trade advocate, Thomas Cooper. Cooper, Dorfman notes, 'was probably the first American academic economist whose positions were of concern to the national political leaders, especially on the protective tariffs and related questions in the 1820s'.[236] At the turn of the century, Cooper's strident defence of free trade led Jefferson to distribute his *Political Arithmetic* as campaign literature in the election of 1800.[237] Two decades later, after various political tribulations that included time in jail under the Federalist sedition laws, and after repeated efforts by Jefferson to secure him a position at the University of Virginia, South Carolina College hired him first as an instructor and then appointed him college president.[238] In 1826 Cooper wrote his first full textbook for American college students. Cooper's text in large part embraced Smith and the latest advocate of that 'new political economy', Ricardo.[239]

Overall, Cooper advocated positions consistent with Smith's ideas on trade, money, value and the ability of human beings to spontaneously generate order through their purposeful and self-interested activities. Government legislation and all other 'forced' steps and/or encouragements were despotic and inefficient, Cooper noted. 'Every step on the road which is made naturally, on the impulse of preceding circumstances, subject to the general laws of human nature, is surely made, and permanently gained.' 'The restrictive system', he warned, 'tells us in fact that we shall greatly profit by being confined as prisoners within our own houses, without intercourse out of doors'. These ideas derived from ignorance and were a 'national disgrace'.[240] According to Cooper, the fixation on tariffs derived from balance-of-trade theories, which confused gold and silver with wealth and had long ago been discredited by serious scholars. Gold and silver, Cooper concluded, did not constitute wealth in any sense of the word – nor were they essential to incite trade. The different endowments between nations incited and maintained trade. Cooper, though hardly consistent, followed similar 'liberal' positions with respect to other subjects. In the area of banks and money he deferred almost entirely to his long-time friend and one-time business partner, Erick Bollmann, whose ideas, discussed above, strongly favoured Smith's notions of money and value.[241]

North American Review author J. Porter championed Cooper's *Lectures*, save for one point. In his text Cooper engaged Bostonian and *North American Review* contributor Edward C. Everett, whose recently-published text on population refuted Malthus's 'gloomy and extremely injurious ideas'. Cooper, Porter argued, inexplicably opposed Everett and followed Malthus's ideas on population. Indeed, Porter read him correctly. On population, Cooper followed Malthus and argued that 'the tendency of population unchecked, will always and every where enable it to overrun the supply of food'.[242] This doctrine, Porter noted, contradicted Cooper's great lifetime achievement, his principle of '*vis medicatrix natura*'. According to Porter, in the corpus of Cooper's work, and in the rest of his analysis, he argued that 'the natural feelings and dispositions of man, undirected and uncontrolled but by the rules of justice, obviously tend to the most rapid advancement of his own condition, and to the most rapid advancement also in opulence and improvement, of the whole community to which he belongs'.[243] Under this self-organizing and spontaneous principle, Porter approvingly concluded, population could never outstrip production. The economy lacked fixed boundaries:

> Business, we say, continually increases; capital is always accumulating; employments are multiplying as constantly and as rapidly as human beings; greater calls for industry arise, and new broader avenues to wealth are opened for the spirit of activity and enterprise.[244]

Porter's lusty confirmation of these ideas culminated a fundamental transformation in American economic and social thinking. Human beings dominated economic life and the social order – and spontaneously generated the prosperity that Americans shared through the myriad of their activities. The 'enlightened selfishness' of acquisitive individuals adds 'immediately to the accumulation of their wealth, and leads, in the plainest manner and with unerring steps, to the rapid increase of national wealth, and to the general improvements of all the enjoyments of social life'.[245]

Of course, as material conditions changed, Boston's political economists shifted some of their thinking. Porter's celebration of 'spontaneous order and progress' proved to be the *Review*'s last. By 1828, after years of fundamental shifts in the economic base of New England, many critics and legislators shifted from a free-trade position favouring merchant activity to tariff promotion favouring manufactures. In 1828, the *North American Review* praised Willard Phillips's *Manual of Political Economy*, the first cogent explication of New England protectionism, for its defence of property, as protectionism was then euphemistically promoted.

The post-mercantilism protectionists of the late 1820s, however, included an important difference in their message. Certainly, markets benefited from protection. But the emphasis on national wealth was gone. Markets were protected so that infant industries might take hold, develop the internal trade and manufacturing of the nation, and eventually increase the level of consumption, and the quality of everyday life for individuals. Tariff promoters encouraged protectionism to increase individual power and choices, not to enhance the fiscal or political power of the state. The *summum bonum* was still defined by the people, and fuelled the economy. The protectionists expressed less confidence in the myriad of everyday human decisions behind Smith's theory; at the same time, however, they continued to emphasize human will and agency. 'Most men', argued Willard Phillips in his protectionist tract, 'from necessity or choice, devote the greatest part of their lives to procuring the means of supplying their real or fancied wants; industry – the earning of wages and the making of profits, – is the great business of the world'. Furthermore, all value was created by desire.[246] 'The desire to obtain any particular thing', concluded Phillips, 'gives it its value, and the motives of such desire are as various and numerous as the appetites, tastes, passions, wants and caprices of mankind'.[247] These appetites did not, however, always lead to the most favourable outcome. 'Though capital once accumulated has a tendency to find a channel', he concluded, 'it may find none, or one in which it will be lost. Almost every change of fashion, habit, opinion, institution or laws, may have some influence ... in checking or augmenting production and accumulation.'[248] Put another way, water may find its own level, but sometimes human agency is needed to dig the ditch. The individual will replaced the spontaneous order as the architect of the economy but the bounty remained the same – an endlessly expanding economy based on the 'appetites, tastes, passions, wants and caprices of mankind'.

Finally, even as they praised protectionism, the *North American Review* authors stressed important intellectual continuities with Smith. Put simply, the protectionists had a hard time legitimizing their ideas based on the intellectual heritage. In fact free-trade theorists dominated political economy debates even in areas linked to protectionism. As Joseph Dorfman notes, 'the protectionists could not supply a textbook that was simple, lucid and in good English. And there were too many conflicting interests in the protectionist cause to make it anything more than a jumble of interests'. Furthermore, the protectionists found in the infant-industry arguments of the free traders enough room to manoeuvre their message.[249] Indeed, as the age of Jackson approached, the important tariff and banking issues often complicated the established economic ideas of Smith and Say, but they did not seem to damage their prominence. The best schools continued to teach the two masters and the best gentlemen continued to read them. As late as 1829 Brown University adopted Say's textbook.[250] More importantly, certain principles remained despite political and economic changes. Money was a sign, not a thing; goods, not money were wealth; individual wants and the satisfaction of those wants composed the interests of the social order. These changes marked the end for the zero-sum mercantilism and bullionism of John Locke and his host of eighteenth- and nineteenth-century followers. They also signalled fundamental changes in the social order. Abstract exchange value ushered in the atomism of modernity and an epistemology based on feelings. Subjective value based on self and desire undermined the objective value structures that buttressed empiricism – in economic practice and theory, aesthetics and morality.

These ideas were not, however, vague intellectual notions. Indeed while the political economists debated the issue, bankers in major seaboard cities like Boston both expressed and shaped new ideas about monetary value – and thus *de facto* undermined age-old notions of intrinsic and/or objective value structures. As discussed in the next chapter, Boston banks multiplied exponentially during this period. In 1802 Boston maintained two banks capitalized at $1.6 million, with liabilities of $1.9 million and more than $0.5 million in specie reserves. Massachusetts-chartered banks outside of Boston, or 'country' banks, numbered five, with just over $0.6 million in capital, $1.2 million in liabilities, and more than $0.5 million in specie. By 1825 Boston boasted fourteen banks capitalized at $10.3 million, with $6.2 million in liabilities and $527,000 in specie. At the same time there were twenty-seven country banks capitalized at $4.2 million, with more than $3.4 million in liabilities on $511,196 in specie. Furthermore, the greatest period of growth was yet to come, and by 1837 Boston had thirty-four banks and country banks numbered ninety-five.

This tremendous explosion of credit combined with frauds, bubbles and busts to make economic value during this period highly volatile. Nevertheless, American and Boston thirst for credit continued unabated. Bostonians, and Americans overall, judged that more money was better than less. They immersed themselves in a world of paper-credit instruments of their own devising and undermined intrinsic notions of value in specie – and subsequently, intrinsic value overall. Increasingly, Americans accepted new notions of value founded on a Scottish emotive epistemology; value resided exclusively as a function of trust, emotions and the imagination.

4 BANKING AND MONEY IN BOSTON

'I entered into the service of a "Change Buck", one of the many Jews and Gentiles, *Loungers* about the *Rainbow* and *Batsons*, from eleven 'till four daily, (Sunday not excepted) manufacturing and throwing upon the public the nauseous foam of the day, commonly called news', began a story of 8 July 1815 in the *Intellectual Regale; or Ladies' TEA Tray*.[251] The story, an 'extract from a satirical work, [and] supposed to be the adventures of a bank note, or piece of money ...', was a first-person narrative by a bank note about its life and its master, 'Change Buck'. Change Buck's chief quality was 'blowing' – 'this swell of the cheeks and distortion of the countenance is undoubtedly very graceful, there is sublimity in it, suitable to the union of riches and ignorance, and it is as necessary to an overgrown trader, or stock jobber, as a chaise and country house are to him who has been in business six months: they equally give him consequence, they are equally as respectable ...'. Change Buck's chief occupation was news, or 'fabrications' so 'plausible, that they have been known even to effect more than once, that criterion of national wealth, the Stocks ...'. Upon this foam rode the stocks, the nation's prosperity, and Change Buck's fortune too.

This and other similar fantasies scattered throughout Early Republic popular culture emphasize the volatility of paper-credit instruments, their easy imitation and their tendency to ride, or be puffed and swollen by, the wind of opinion.[252] The notes' subjective posturing and volatility in these popular narratives speak to tensions about the nature of money, knowledge and value in late eighteenth- and early nineteenth-century Anglo-American society.

Ideas about the nature and purpose of money and the economy were hotly debated in newspapers, books and magazines like the *North American Review* and the *American Museum*. Encyclopaedias were filled with long articles detailing the debate between specie and paper. Pamphlets cited authorities from Smith to Ricardo to Locke in defence of their various positions. Popular magazines like the *Ladies Port Folio* or the *Intellectual Regale; or Ladies' TEA Tray* explored these issues in more fanciful ways. Even at the theatre, Early Republic Americans watching the romantic comedy *The Bank Note* could not leave these issues behind.[253] These narratives expressed continuing uncertainty about the nature of money and the location of economic value but did not, however, slow the expansion of credit markets. Doubters may have insisted that specie was the only true money or castigated the stock jobbers and money men who sprouted like mushrooms in the dewy exchange alleys that every American city now seemingly possessed, but capitalists kept on increasing the number, capital and liabilities of banks. Furthermore, for all the disquietude with regard to money, banking institutions and the financial instruments they created and/or traded thrived and drove the American economy throughout this period.[254] Americans thirsty for money and economic growth grew comfortable with a variable and often volatile medium of exchange. For Americans of this period, 'too much money', Bray Hammond notes, 'was better than not enough'.[255]

Massachusetts and Boston in particular early on became important banking centres and led the way in innovations even as they seemed to weather the worst excesses and crises that Early Republic bankers faced in the first three decades of the nineteenth century. From the 1780s into the 1830s, Boston's elite merchants as well as rising middling men hungry for economic power pushed for and got access to bank charters. Boston capitalists' consistent and successful pressure for access to new credit institutions confirms Bostonians' *de facto* immersion in and acceptance of this new political economy and the widespread acceptance of the new financial instruments associated with banks.

This proliferation of bank notes and paper-credit instruments revolutionized the economy, and fuelled a seemingly endless number of bridges, canals and other internal improvements in Boston and across the country. More to the point, in terms of this discussion, paper-credit instruments demanded a new way of looking at society and the economy; economic transactions based on paper-credit instruments demanded trust and confidence – not just in individuals, corporations or the state, but in a whole new and innovative economic system. Men and women accepting bank notes for their pay; retailers and landlords accepting them for their produce and rent; businessmen for their goods; investors accepting bank stock for their portfolios – they all had to believe that the abstract signs they traded for real goods and labour had economic value. Along with the proliferation of joint-stock corporations and the credit instruments they issued, banks and bank notes created an economy of interdependent investors, producers and consumers – fuelled by self-created and self-legitimized exchange instruments. These instruments both shaped and expressed a new confidence in the power of men to create value; they both shaped and expressed a new emotive anthropocentric epistemology first delineated by the Scottish Moral Sense philosophers.

Banking Practices

Both state-chartered banks and the first and second Bank of the United States were private companies that issued notes and created deposits that acted as currency. Typically banks were capitalized *vis-à-vis* stock subscriptions. In theory the investors paid for their stock in specie and this became the operating capital for the bank. In practice, as we shall see, bank stock purchasers often paid for their stock in the bank notes of other institutions and/or other financial instruments. Not infrequently, investors paid for the first instalment of their stock in specie – or another financial instrument – then took out a loan from the institution collateralized by the stock (often for the full face value), and used the institution's own notes or the 'book money' created by the discount to complete the purchase.

In their structure and practices banks followed British banking systems. In particular, they utilized the fractional reserve ratio system to regulate bank note emissions. Banks did not store or maintain the total specie promised by their notes – but only a fraction that allowed them to meet the everyday demands generated by their note emissions and deposits. Typically, bank note issues far exceeded the banks' specie reserves. Deposits too created 'money'. Discounts (loans) appeared on one side of the ledger as an asset (money due to the bank), and most often on the other side as a deposit, or a liability (money due to the depositor). Seldom did a discount or loan applicant walk away with the bank notes. Rather, the bank credited the discount to his account as a deposit. This form of 'book money' often exceeded note issues and was an important form of currency creation and credit market expansion.[256]

Banks made two kinds of loans or discounts during this period: real bills discounts and accommodation loans. Banks made 'real bills' discounts collateralized by actual goods for short-term periods of time to facilitate commercial transactions. They made accommodation loans for longer periods of time, often backed by bank stock or other property, for numerous types of investments, from manufacturing and commercial investments to speculation in securities. The evidence available indicates that over the period examined, 'country' banks in Massachusetts made more accommodation loans. Boston preferences fluctuated, though individual bank records suggest a division of labour between the banks. Overall, however, banks began as merchant entities dealing strictly in 'real bills' loans and moved to accommodation loans.[257] Furthermore, accommodation loans, based as they were on the liquidity of the debtor's property and the feasibility of 'projects', were more 'imaginary' than 'real bills' discounts. As noted above, many institutions made loans collateralized by the actual purchase, stocks – often those of the lending institution itself.[258]

Liabilities determined a bank's risk exposure. A bank note was in effect a 'promise to pay' or cheque – a credit instrument – that circulated as currency. Likewise 'book money' simply extended bankers' credit to third parties. Deposits (book money generated by discounts or actual deposits) plus note emissions (bills in circulation) constituted a bank's liabilities. Depositors and note holders could at any time demand their specie. Thus the liabilities to specie reserves ratio represented the risk exposure the bank willingly consumed as part of its operations. A higher liabilities to specie ratio meant more profits – more notes and discounts maintained on lower levels of specie – but more risk. A lower liabilities to specie ratio, of course, meant the opposite – less profit, less risk. Bank directors in Massachusetts were typically personally liable for 'obligations' that exceeded two times the bank's capital. This restriction was clearly part of the General Court's efforts to curb speculation. Confusion surrounding the nature of capital and deposits, however, prevented this from being an effective brake on credit market expansion. The legislation assumed that a bank's capital was specie paid into the bank and maintained in the vaults. Bankers and legislators seemingly ignored the fact that no bank ever received or maintained anywhere near its capital in actual specie.[259] Furthermore, a great deal of bank capital in this period was paid in through 'stock notes' – discounts to stockholders collateralized by the bank stock.[260] Put simply, much of the capital was 'fictitious' and bore little relationship to the bank's daily operations. In 1803, for example, the Boston banks reported $3,400,000 in 'Capital stock paid in' but held only $225,690 in specie to satisfy $1,546,893 in liabilities. This confused state of affairs was further muddled when legislators began to ignore deposits as liabilities to focus more on note issues.[261] Typically, the bulk of discounts were simply notations in the ledger – the money never left the bank. These deposits or discounts often equalled or excelled bank note issues yet did not 'count' as liabilities and thus had a wholly 'fictitious' existence.[262] Without exception, over the period under study, through 'book money' and note issues, banks increased their liabilities to specie ratio, consumed more risk and greatly expanded credit markets. By 1819, contemporaries agreed that the 'system of a paper currency has been carried to a greater extent in America than in any other part of the world'.[263]

Boston's Banking History

Efforts to alleviate the perennial money scarcity in Massachusetts through banks dated back to the seventeenth century. In 1686, 1714, 1721 and 1741 Boston merchants attempted to establish a Land Bank to issue paper credit or notes on land security.[264] All of these efforts failed, or were banned by imperial decree, and ended colonial hopes for an increased exchange medium.[265] The Revolution of course ended Parliament's control of American would-be bankers. In 1780 Robert Morris and a number of important Philadelphia merchants chartered the Pennsylvania Bank to finance the Revolution. In 1781 the Continental Congress incorporated Robert Morris and others as the Bank of North America, a carbon copy of the Bank of England.[266] In 1782 Massachusetts incorporated a short-lived branch of the Bank of North America in Boston, and accepted its notes as payment for taxes.

In 1783 William Phillips, Thomas Russell and John Lowell, all prominent Boston merchants, wrote to Thomas Willing, the President of the Bank of North America, for advice in establishing a bank. Willing described banking as a 'pathless wilderness, ground but little known to this side of the Atlantick'.[267] Their guide was, of course, British bank law. Yet, according to Willing, 'the world is apt to Suppose a greater Mystery in this sort of Business than there really is. Perhaps it is right they should do so.'[268] In 1784 these men created the Massachusetts Bank.

The Massachusetts Bank was the first bank created by Boston capitalists, and the first local bank in Massachusetts and in Boston. Generally a conservative institution, it nevertheless greatly added to Boston's credit structure. The group of projectors that created the Massachusetts Bank first capitalized it at $100,000 in 1784. They increased this to $400,000 in 1792, and $1 million by 1811. Over time the bank also increased its liabilities to specie ratio and thus created more credit with less specie. In 1792 the bank maintained a weekly average of $135,311 in specie, $40,099 in deposits and circulated $206,766 in notes. Thus the liabilities to specie ratio was 1.5:1 (the bank created or assumed $1.5 in liabilities for every $1 in specie). At the end of 1802 the bank reported $463,200 in deposits, $210,000 in notes in circulation and $253,100 in specie, or a 2.7:1 liabilities to specie ratio. The liabilities to specie ratio was 1.76:1 in 1812 and 4.69:1 in 1819 (see Chart 1: Select Boston Banks' Liabilities to Specie Ratio, 1803–19).[269] Evidence also suggests that around 1814 the bank, along with the other Boston banks, increased its accommodation loans, indicating more liberal and speculative practices. Between 1808 and 1814 bank reports in Massachusetts differentiated between debts due and debts due on interest. Debts due were short-term loans banks 'discounted' for the cost of the money or interest. Debts due on interest referred to debts paying interest and thus longer-term accommodation loans, or discounts 'rolled over' (see Chart 2: Debts Due to Town and Country Banks, On Interest, Not on Interest, 1803–22).[270] By 1815 bank reports no longer differentiated between 'debts due on interest' and 'debts due', referring simply to 'amount of all debts due', though the evidence suggests these were now 'debts due on interest'.

The Massachusetts Bank enjoyed a great deal of success. In the 1790s it traded in government securities and made substantial profits. Though dividends averaged only 5.7 per cent from 1784 to 1789, they jumped to 21.75 in 1790, 19 per cent in 1791, and 29.26 per cent in 1792. Dividends averaged 8.6 percent from 1793 to 1811. Massachusetts Bank shares sold well above par throughout most of this period; they dipped below par momentarily only in 1814, 1816 and 1817 (see Chart 3: Select Boston Bank Stock Prices, Percentage Increase, Par=$100, 1799–1822).[271]

The success of the Massachusetts Bank invited competition and in 1792 the General Court chartered the Union Bank. The Union Bank represented a substantially different type of institution from the Massachusetts Bank. Its genesis was a Tontine scheme that Boston capitalists organized but the General Court refused to charter.[272] Tontines were speculative subscription ventures popular in France and Britain.[273] In France they were basically an annuity, paying dividends for a lifetime. In Boston, however, the scheme included a lottery, or what today is often called a 'shotgun' or 'survivor' clause. Put simply, investors bought their ticket; the capital was invested and dividends paid, but at the end of a certain period of time (1850 in this case) the whole of the remaining investment was to be divided among the survivors. Higher premiums for younger investors equalized the costs and benefits of this scheme (under five years of age, the ticket was $16; eighty to eighty-five years of age the ticket was $2). Its scrip sold out in hours and immediately traded at a premium; $1.10 paid on the ticket traded at $6 to $8 within days of the original issue. A 26 October 1791 *Boston Gazette* story described the Tontine fever: 'Tontine – Now or Never. Many of those who so sorely regretted their inattention, to adventure in Bank Scrip, now eagerly embrace the opportunity to retrieve their *imaginary* losses, by purchasing shares in the Tontine ...'.[274]

When the General Court refused the Tontine charter, the applicants turned their efforts – and the scrip already sold – to chartering a bank. Union Bank incorporators honoured the original scrip deposits for the Tontine Association toward the purchase of Union Bank stock. Virtually all scrip holders accepted this arrangement. Thus the original 100,000 Tontine 'tickets' became 100,000 shares in the Union Bank. The shares, $8 each, originally provided the bank with $800,000 dollars in capital, and the low share price encouraged small investors. Also, the Union Bank's state charter reserved one fifth of the capital for loans outside of Boston, purportedly to farmers, on land security. Furthermore, the Commonwealth of Massachusetts under its charter rules could and did subscribe $400,000 to the bank's capital – thereby increasing the bank's final capital to $1.2 million.

The Union bank was also decidedly more enterprising or risk-taking than the Massachusetts Bank; it consistently maintained a higher liabilities to specie ratio. In 1803 the Union Bank's liability to specie ratio was 3.86:1; by 1811 it was 5.23:1; in 1819 the ratio was 6.4:1 (see Chart 1).[275] The Union Bank also had a good share of its debts due on interest by 1811 and 1812, and by 1813 had all its debts due on interest (see Chart 2). It paid yearly dividends of 7 to 10.5 per cent from 1793 to 1813. During the War of 1812 dividends decreased to between 4 and 5 per cent and hovered in the 5 to 7 per cent area for the rest of the period under study. Union Bank stock sold well above par through this period. In 1802, $100 in Union stock sold for $150. It fell below par ($100) for the first time in 1811 and fluctuated through the war. In 1821, $100 in Union Bank stock was worth $110 on the Boston market (see Chart 3).[276]

The banking profits of the Massachusetts and Union banks during these early years encouraged a banking mania of sorts. During the 1802 and 1803 sessions, the Massachusetts General Court chartered sixteen banks and fourteen insurance companies (all joint-stock companies) and greatly increased access to paper-credit instruments.[277] Many bank and insurance company incorporators were, if not the same people, connected by blood, marriage, politics or interests.[278] All of these banks save the Boston Bank derived from the 'country', towns across Massachusetts and what later became Maine.

The Boston Bank, chartered in 1803, was, like the Union Bank, a more speculative risk-driven institution. Harrison Gray Otis and others involved in the bank were primarily concerned with real state development, internal improvement stocks, and speculation in securities. In 1826, for example, an over-extended Otis, one of the bank's original directors, wrote to the bank asking them to endorse a personal line of credit – from $10 to $20,000. At the same time he rolled a previous discount for $6,000 and asked for another $1,700 – or whatever his stock could 'secure'. In the letter he noted that real state speculation was the cause of his current difficulties.[279] Other records indicate that the bank's directors consistently and almost perfunctorily renewed discounts for themselves and their clients.[280]

The Boston Bank consistently maintained a higher liabilities to specie ratio than did the Massachusetts and the Union Banks (see Chart 1).[281] It also had all of its loans out as accommodation loans by 1811 (see Chart 2). It maintained dividends between 7 and 8 per cent up to 1812, between 3.5 and 4 per cent through the war, and 5 to 8 per cent to 1822. Boston Bank stock reached a high of $120 on $100 worth of stock in 1810. It traded well above par ($100) from 1803 to 1811, fell below par in 1812, was lower through the war, but climbed back and traded at $113 in 1821 (see Chart 3).[282]

The Union and the Boston Banks greatly increased liabilities, or credit, in Boston. At times the Union Bank's liabilities to specie ratio fluctuated wildly. In January 1804, for example, it had $626,183 in deposits and circulated $604,965 in bank notes with only $160,127 in specie (7.7:1 liabilities to specie ratio). At the same time, the Boston Bank also had its highest number of notes in circulation, $338,210, and $193,796 in deposits, with $181,266 in specie (3:1 liabilities to specie ratio).[283] The newly-chartered country banks also increased liabilities over this period. In 1803, they started out with $1,193,504 in liabilities and $518,259 in specie. By 1807, they maintained $1,648,852 in liabilities with $489,903 in specie (2.3:1 liabilities to specie ratio in 1803; 3.4:1 liabilities to specie ratio in 1809).[284]

In the wake of the chartering frenzy that took over the General Court in the 1802–3 session, an avalanche of bank notes swamped Boston. The multiplicity of banks and bank notes in conjunction with the novelty of the system created a babble of institutions and paper-credit instruments. Newspapers like *Cohen's Lottery Gazette and Register* published weekly sheets detailing the exchange rates of notes from city to city and state to state (further establishing in the mind of the reader the relationship of money to chance).[285] In Boston, *Gilbert and Dean,*

Chart 1: Select Boston Banks' Liabilities to Specie Ratio, 1803–19.

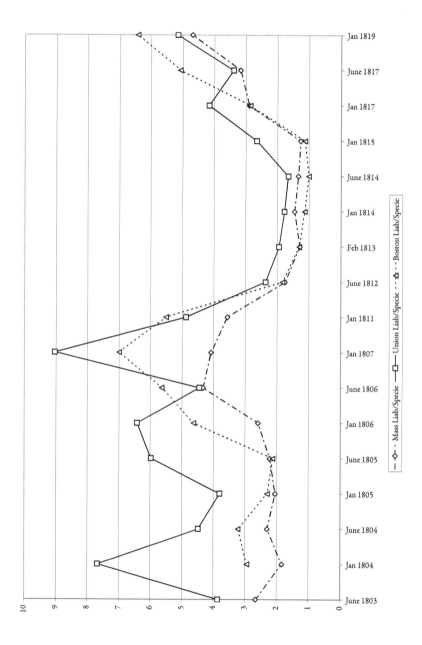

Chart 2: Debts Due to Town and Country Banks, On Interest, Not on Interest, 1803–22.

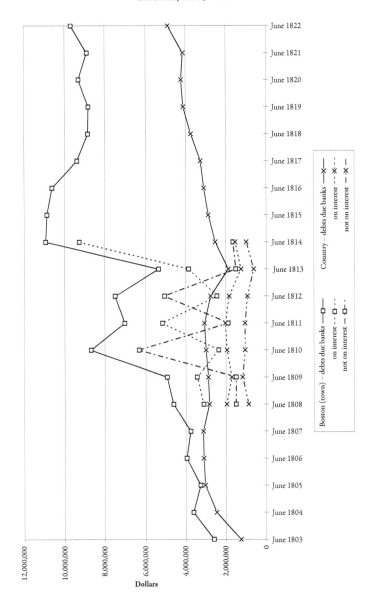

Chart 3: Select Boston Bank Stock Prices, Percentage Increase, Par=$100, 1799–1822.

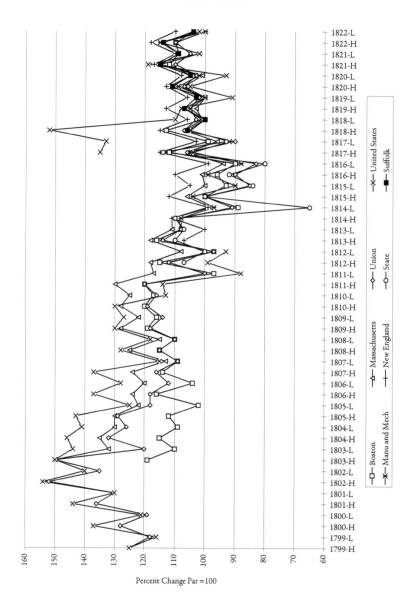

Percent Change Par = 100

Lottery and Commission Brokers, published their own pamphlet advertising the exchange rates of bank notes from Massachusetts, New Hampshire, Rhode Island and Connecticut.[286] This proliferation of currencies soon created problems for the Boston banks and residents. How, after all, could anyone be sure of the value of bank notes from Rhode Island? Boston dealers took individuals' bank notes at a discount (typically 2 to 3 per cent for 'good' country paper) – a perennial complaint of the country banks and note holders who saw this as a vast conspiracy directed at the countryside.[287] But what of the banks themselves – how would they deal with the thousands of dollars that accumulated in their vaults from distant and unknown institutions? As early as 1803 the Boston, Massachusetts and Union banks corresponded to find a solution to this dilemma. Initially their intent was to collaborate to collect specie from country banks. This process was, however, to say the least, complicated. Even when the specie was collected there were problems. On 26 September 1803, for example, the Boston Bank opened a box of specie delivered from the Lincoln and Kennebeck Bank, only to discover that it was $842 'short'.[288] This dilemma, and the bitter political infighting at the heart of bank charters, gave rise to one of the Early Republic's most prolific financial innovators, Andrew Dexter Jr, the proprietor of the Boston Exchange Office.

The Boston Exchange Office originated in the effort by Democratic Republicans and so-called 'Middling Interest' Federalists to charter the 'Town and Country Bank', an institution designed to specialize in the exchange of bank notes between the Boston banks and the banks chartered in the rest of Massachusetts, New England and even beyond.[289] Though the divisions were not complete or absolute, politics played an important role in many of Boston's bank charters. In 1803, Boston's four banks (including the Bank of the United States) represented a monopoly on credit by a group of elites associated by marriage, friendship and politics. A coalition of Democratic Republicans and dissatisfied Federalists calling themselves the 'Middling Interest' tied a bank charter to their political 'ticket', and attempted to win office and gain a bank in one swift move. The press referred to this group as the 'Middling Interest List'. This list included James Bowdoin, David Tilden, Russell Sturgis, Nathaniel Fellowes, Abiel Smith, Charles Paine and Jonathan Hunnewell. Hunnewell was on both the Federal and the 'Middling Interest' lists and won election. The rest of the list lost by about 300 out of a total of 2,000 votes.[290] Abiel Smith, Jonathan Hunnewell, Russell Sturgis and Charles Paine were not only candidates for election, they were also four of the nine petitioners for a new bank to be established on a 'more general and diffuse plan than has hitherto been adopted'. The petitioners claimed that they planned to include 1,100 subscribers in 53 towns in their 'Town and Country Bank'.[291]

The *Independent Chronicle* directly associated the bank and the election. Under the headline the 'Middling Interest List' they claimed that the 'proposed New Bank, emphatically styled the Middling Interest, embraces the general interest of the community more extensively than any other moneyed institution ever before the General Court'. The *Chronicle* urged voters to support the 'Middling Interest List' 'in order to bring the [bank] subject immediately before the public'. The paper claimed that the candidates had 'no interest detached from [the New Bank] by their connections with other institutions & will not use an insidious policy of pretended friendship while counteracting [illegible] object by out and out stratagem'. Further, the *Chronicle* promised that all 'their exertions will be unequivocally in favour of [the bank's] incorporation'.[292] '[I]t is time that the Middling Interest consisting of mechanics, shopkeepers, manufacturers and tradesmen', the paper proclaimed, 'should place themselves in such an attitude as to counteract the overbearing influence operating within the banks and other pecuniary establishments'.[293] Popular support for a new bank based on an extended subscription even found its way into the pages of the Federalist *Columbian Centinel*. 'Are the rich because they are rich and powerful to receive the exclusive benefits of being incorporated into banking companies?' 'Justice' asked. 'There can be no monopoly more invidious than to give exclusive privileges by the acts of government to a very few rich men for improving their money in banks and to refuse the same privilege to the [illegible] merchants and to the widow and the orphan', 'Steady' proclaimed.[294]

Bipartisan support did little for the Town and Country Bank. After the Middling Interest list lost the election, the Federalist-dominated General Court denied the petitioners their charter. The *Chronicle* linked the electoral loss directly to the bank charter petition. The citizens of the 'Middling Interest', claimed the paper, voted for the 'Middling Interest List ... with a view to carry a ticket that would support the application of that class for a new bank. Thus the middling interest have lost their election by the overwhelming preponderancy of the moneyed interest'.[295] Political and economic power continued to reside in the same persons, and in the same party. For example, in 1805, ten of Boston's twenty-six Representatives to the General Court, three of five Senators, and the one representative to Congress, were bank directors. All were Federalists.[296] The only Democratic-Republican candidate listed as an officer of a financial institution was Samuel Clap, who was the President of the newly-established Exchange Office.

After the 1803 'Middling Interest' loss, Democratic Republicans continued to attempt to secure access to financial institutions and credit markets. The Democratic-Republican *Independent Chronicle*, in a four-part series of long articles, explained and promoted the idea of an 'exchange' bank. In 1804, after much debate, a number of Bostonians, some associated with Democratic-Republican and Middling Interest politics, many associated by marriage and blood, and others associated by membership of Boston's First Church, obtained a charter for the Boston Exchange Office.[297] While it is impossible to guage the extent to which the Exchange Office represented the interests of widows and orphans, the men presenting these petitions clearly represented a new 'moneyed' (or would-be-moneyed) interest. Tax records from 1802 indicate that the 'Exchange Office' directors consistently represented a different economic strata than that of Boston's dominant banking elites (see Table A: Select Boston Bank Directors' Assessed Property, 1802).[298]

The Exchange Office issued no notes and therefore was not a bank (though it took in deposits). It was a clearing house for bank notes and discounted them according to the market's confidence in the issuing institutions. It exchanged the notes of 'country' banks for 'town' banks and vice versa. This 'exchange function' had originally served as the rationale for the 'Town and Country Bank' charter attempt. According to its charter the Office opened with $150,000 in other banks' notes and $50,000 in specie to back up deposits.[299] In its 'Prospectus', published in the Democratic-Republican *Independent Chronicle*, the directors promised to provide safety for notes, to accumulate dormant dollars, and to facilitate the exchange of notes.[300] Democratic-Republican/Middling Interest candidate Russell Sturgis was an original petitioner. As noted, Samuel Clap was the first President. Future Democratic-Republican candidates David W. Child and Eliphalet Williams were directors.

For all of its avowed altruism, the Exchange Office was simply a way to bank without a Massachusetts bank charter.[301] Many of the original petitioners were affiliated with the Detroit Bank, an institution chartered in the Michigan Territory at the same time the Exchange Office was chartered in Massachusetts. The short-lived Detroit Bank was one of the first 'wild-cat' banks and in its brief and eventful life issued a surplus of notes on little specie. Russell Sturgis and other Boston capitalists were among those involved in both the Exchange Office and the Detroit Bank. Jefferson's appointed Governor to the Michigan Territory, General Hull, was also a partner and the source of the Detroit charter.[302] Control of the Detroit Bank was an important part of the Exchange Office 'scheme'. The Exchange Office could not print notes under its charter, but it could circulate and exchange the notes of the Detroit Bank for Boston notes. These men contributed $19,000 in specie to the Detroit bank and issued $400,000 in notes. Subsequent note issues topped $1,000,000 and flooded the Boston market. Sturgis distanced himself from the fiasco early on though a number of Democratic Republicans tried to save the institution.[303]

The excessive note issues of this and a number of other banks associated with the Exchange Office can be traced to one man, Andrew Dexter Jr. Early on in the life of the Exchange Office, Dexter seized control of the enterprise. He was the son of Andrew Dexter, a prominent Boston businessman, whose brother, Samuel Dexter, was a United States Senator, Secretary of War and Secretary of the Treasury under Adams and Jefferson. In a brief and glorious banking career, Dexter bought the Exchange Office, the Detroit Bank, the Berkshire bank of Pittsfield, the Bangor Bank of Bangor and the Farmers' Exchange Bank of

Table A: Select Boston Bank Directors' Assessed Property, 1802.

United States	Real	Personal	Boston	Real	Personal
J. Coolidge	11000	0	Thomas C. Amory	7500	35000
P. R. Dalton	3500	5000	John T. Apthorp	10350	5000
S. P. Gardner	4250	20000	Peter C. Brooks	7250	60000
Gard. Greene	5000	75000	Joseph Chapman	1000	250
Joseph Hurd	3000	7500	Isaac P. Davis	9750	7500
John Joy	8400	5000	Ste. Higginson Jr	6000	17500
H. G. Otis	20500	25000	Jonathan Jackson	3250	6250
S. Parkman	21750	115000	Nathaniel C. Lee	2250	7500
T. H. Perkins	6500	0	Eben. Prebele	12750	50000
Thomas Perkins	2250	10000	William Sullivan	3250	2500
David Sears	10500	75000			
Timothy Williams	1750	15000	*Total*	63350	191500
			Average	6335	19150
Total	98400	352500			
Average	8200	29375	**Boston Ex.**	**Real**	**Personal**
			David W. Child	1500	4000
Massachusetts	**Real**	**Personal**	Samuel Clap	3700	5000
Rufus Amory	4250	12500	John Fox	3000	3000
Thomas Dawes	2450	4000	Joseph Loring Jr	3500	3500
Aaron Dexter	3000	15000	Joseph Nye	3250	7500
Benj. Greene	5000	125000	Geoge Odiorne	750	5000
W. Parsons	7850	17500	Thomas Odiorne	1000	0
J. Phillips	2450	3250	Nathaniel Parker	750	250
W. Phillips	14250	200000	William Ritchie	5000	2500
S. Salisbury	1750	5000	Daniel Scott	2050	1000
James Thwing	1750	1500	Samuel Spear	1750	4000
			Samuel Sumner	5500	2750
Total	42750	383750	Thomas K. Thomas	3750	2500
Average	4750	42639	Beza Tucker	5900	3000
			John West	3500	3000
Union	**Real**	**Personal**	Eli. Williams	900	0
Samuel Brown	6750	25000			
Bejamin Bussey	7500	30000	*Total*	45800	47000
Samuel Cobb	9700	25000	*Average*	2863	2938
Stephen Codman	6850	7500			
Joseph Head	2000	0			
Benjamin Joy	11750	10000			
Josiah Quincy	7000	20000			
John Welles	6150	10000			
Oliver Wendell	4250	12500			
Total	61950	140000			
Average	6883	15556			

Glocester, Rhode Island, and printed a fantastic number of bank notes.[304] In all of these endeavours, Dexter profited from his position in the Exchange Office, and the inability of Boston residents to physically redeem notes issued by distant banks.[305] In other words, he used the Exchange Office to flood the Boston market with out-of-state notes. In this and other efforts Dexter seems to have consistently chaffed against the boundaries established by the General Court's charter and contemporary banking practices. As early as 1804, the Exchange Office attempted to establish a line of credit with the Boston Bank. The Boston Bank first of all demanded substantial collateral against any line of credit; second it was unsure if the Boston Exchange Office's charter gave it the authority to borrow money.[306] More egregiously, on 22 May 1807, the *Columbian Centinel* announced in its 'Bank Thermometer' that the '*Worcester* and *Keene* Banks have issued a species of *irredeemable* bills, *receivable* not *payable*, at the Banks from whence they issue'. The *Centinel* queried how these notes, 'no better for the public than blank paper', circulated in Boston. 'A certain Office in *Boston*', whose deposits had apparently collapsed, had taken to 'palming' them off on the 'ignorant and unwary'.[307] Dexter's efforts also included a brief and ill-fated effort to get control of a stillborn institution, the Massachusetts Annuity Fund. After a number of prominent Bostonians attempted and failed to establish an Annuity Fund, Dexter seemingly picked up the reins, trying to convince the would-be investors that he could devise a plan to run the Annuity Fund without benefit of incorporation, 'and to greater advantage'. Interestingly the original 'Annuity Fund' plans included substantial investment in Boston real state and an elaborate 'Coffee House' and 'Exchange' much along the same lines as the Boston Exchange Coffee House eventually built by Dexter as the centre of his banking 'empire'.[308]

During its brief existence the Exchange Office held a great deal of power and political factions coveted its favour.[309] Furthermore, Dexter exerted considerable economic influence in Boston and used the notes of his country banks to construct the first luxury hotel in Boston and possibly the United States, the Exchange Coffee House. Embargo and non-importation worked against him, however, and explain, at least in part, his desperate efforts to print bank notes. By 1809 Dexter's financial innovations had worn Boston's financial community thin. In 1809 a number of influential bankers led by Nathan Appleton moved against the Exchange Office and demanded specie for Dexter's banks' note issues. Unable to put them off any longer, Dexter's pyramid collapsed. His downfall brought a wave of bank failures and recriminations against the lethal combination of banks, speculation and politics. An investigation by the Rhode Island legislature of his Farmers' Exchange Bank reveals the full extent of Dexter's financial manipulation and highlights the ambivalent nature of economic value in this period.[310]

The Farmers' Exchange Bank enjoyed a turbulent if brief life. Incorporated in 1804, the bank was capitalized at $100,000 – 2,000 shares at $50 each – to be paid, as was the norm, in instalments. From the beginning, however, only a fraction of the capital was ever paid in. The directors for their part never paid in any specie whatsoever but simply paid in their personal notes. Thus, out of 2,000 shares, investors paid for only 661 shares with any specie – and the total specie capital of the bank was $19,141.86. In the normal course of its operation, note issues varied from $20,000 to $70,000 and specie deposits often dwindled to hundreds of dollars.[311] The bank directors used a number of ingenious methods to circulate their notes. Taking a page from the Scottish banks, for example, they sent agents out to different states to purchase grain and other commodities with the bank's notes, reselling the produce for specie or competing bank paper.[312]

It was this unstable institution, 'conducted, as the perplexed and confused state of the books sufficiently evinces, negligently and unskillfully ... [whose Directors] had at no time a proper knowledge of the Affairs of the Bank', that Andrew Dexter Jr purchased using the bank's own assets. He could do this without difficulty, paying for the bank with its own debtor's notes and assuming the liabilities associated with existing bank notes. Bank notes were, after all, not an asset in the normal sense of money, but a liability – a promise to pay. The bank directors in many cases simply exchanged their stock for the promissory notes they had originally used to purchase the stock – in effect, their capital.[313]

Dexter from the very first exercised complete control of the bank and used it largely as a producer of bank notes to funnel through the Boston Exchange Office. Even before he gained full control of the bank he undertook this effort. In December 1807 he wrote to the bank with a proposal to accept their paper through the Boston Exchange Office, paying 2 per cent interest on it and yet maintaining complete liability for the money. Dexter promised to '[keep] the bills from circulation entirely, or pay them out [in such a manner] as will be most likely to prevent their return to the bank, and that in any case any of them should return, the [Exchange] Office will be at the expense of redeeming them'. Dexter agreed to accept any and all drafts from the bank.

At the height of his desperation Dexter plaintively appealed to his cashier and bank president to sign more notes: 'I am sorry you have signed no more bills and beg you to sign at least twice as many more during the next week. I wish you would work day and night so as to sign if possible $20,000 a day. Have the goodness to mention it to the president that he may do the same.'[314] When other directors, including his brother Samuel Dexter, became concerned, he had the cashiers sign the notes at night.[315] The bank's neighbours noted the odd hours kept by the cashier, who apparently often arrived at two in the morning to sign bills late into the dawn.[316] As his house of credit tumbled Dexter pleaded with his cashier to take all the material out of the bank and return to Boston: 'Pray come immediately and bring with you all the papers respecting my business ...'. The postscript was especially plaintive: 'I SHALL think you wholly unpardonable if you do not come instantly, and never shall forgive you if you don't'.[317] Unfortunately for Dexter, the game was up long before the Rhode Island legislature intervened.

During Dexter's tenure his debts to the bank (he generated them as personal loans to himself) exceeded $800,000. He printed well in excess of $600,000 in paper that he funnelled through the Exchange Office into the Boston market.[318] The Rhode Island Committee that examined his books in December 1809 found only $86 in specie, and as best as they could ascertain, more than $500,000 in outstanding bank notes trading at a large discount. The crash of Dexter's branch-bank empire also brought down its anchor, the Boston Exchange Office. In June 1805 it held $52,380 worth of specie and $255,944 of liabilities (4.9:1 liabilities to specie ratio). By January 1807, it had only $2,467 in specie and $278,643 in liabilities (113:1 liabilities to specie ratio).[319] Party organs blamed each other for the bank fiasco. Many blamed 'the speculation of one individual', doubtless the unnamed Andrew Dexter Jr. Expressions of distrust filled the newspapers. On 16 August the *Boston Patriot*'s 'Bank Thermometer' denounced the notes of the Detroit Bank: 'Those [notes] of the Detroit Bank were originally intended as the currency between rogues and fools; and they have answered the end of their destiny to admiration'. In the 11 September *Boston Patriot* a retailer advertised boots and shoes for Detroit bills at fifteen cents on the dollar. The *Columbia Centinel* blamed the whole crisis on 'democratic' banks. In 1809, the Exchange Coffee House, which cost $800,000 to build, was on sale for $250,000.[320] Two years later, the *Boston Patriot* still used the Farmers' Exchange and the Detroit Bank as synonyms for fraudulent banking.[321]

Bostonians even found occasion to poke fun at their feverish fantasies. The 9 September 1809 *Boston Patriot* ran a poem from a reader lamenting the 'state of the banks':

> *Mr. Editor* – Poetry is not always fiction.
>
> ON THE STATE OF THE BANKS
>
> Bank *Notes* like riches take their wings
> And fly from all their *owners*,
> And hide themselves in *Broker's vaults*,
> From *borrowers* or *donors;*
> So '*Shon ap Morgan*' told his Lord,
> His sheep were changed to *goats;*
> And all who lose their Notes and Bills
> Will want their winter *coats*.
> The Boston *Brokers* play their game
> With *Banks* in every town,

> The Country *Bankers* rise in turn,
> And knock the *Brokers* down.
> Had they secur'd them under *bond,*
> Some hopes they might have found,
> Let such as wish to pass the *bridge,*
> Be sure the bottom's sound.
>   '*GORE AND NO BANKS*'

The November 1809 Boston *Omnium Gatherum* joined in the fun and announced a '*A Grand Chance for Speculation! – or, another New Bank!*'. The paper proposed a new '*Potatoe Bank* – to consist of 15,000 shares, each share to be 100 bushels of good merchantable potatoes, of the red kind ... As the buildings necessary for the deposits, together with the salaries of officers, clerks, &c. will be attended with considerable expense', the author continued, 'I think it would be advisable to petition for a lottery, for promoting my plan, as it will have a vast tendency to encourage the landed interest of the state, and create an emulation to establish almost the only article of produce that has escaped the notice of the monopolist and the speculator'.[322] The joke was so good and the thirst for banks still so great that the *New England Galaxy* reprinted the entire 'proposal' verbatim in 1822.[323]

The circumstances surrounding Dexter's collapse, though 'irregular', were by no means singular. In 1811, for example, the Massachusetts General Court investigated the Penobscot Bank and found tremendous irregularities. The Bank was first chartered in 1806 with a capitalization of $150,000. This amount was due from the stockholders in two instalments of $75,000. Within four days, however, 'seven-eighths of the amount was loaned to the stockholders on pledging their stock, and giving their notes renewable once every six months'. When the second instalment became due, it was paid. 'But it was a mere nominal thing', concluded the Committee, 'for on the same day the greater part was borrowed by the stockholders, as before; and within six months, from that time, *the whole capital, excepting 600 dols. was loaned to the owners of the stock and so continued till August 1809. It might therefore be truly called a Bank without capital; created not by those who had money to lend, but who wanted to borrow*'.[324]

The bank came to the notice of the General Court when it failed to redeem large numbers of notes in circulation. The Committee estimated that at any one point perhaps as many as $170,000 circulated on virtually no specie. The author of the report, Peter C. Brooks, an old hand in the insurance, banking and stockjobbing business, lamented the situation. The stockholders, many from Boston, were the principal creditors of the bank. The success or failure of the bank depended, however, according to Brooks, on the directors' willingness to collect debts outstanding – an unenviable task, since the directors were the principal debtors.

The collapse of the Hallowell and Augusta Banks in 1818 led to yet another Massachusetts General Court investigation. The *Report of the Committee of Both Houses, on the Hallowell and Augusta Banks* revealed that 'it was permitted and practiced in both corporations, to loan to any stockholder, the whole amount of his stock, on his private note, and a transfer of his stock to the corporation'. Furthermore, this made up the overwhelming amount of discounts extended by the banks. Of the $150,648 in discounts credited to the Hallowell and Augusta banks (debts due to the banks), $131,215 was 'By Cash Discounted on Stock Notes'.[325] The Second Bank of the United States also largely operated on these principles. The Committee investigating the Second Bank of the United States after the 1819 financial downturn was surprised to find how little commercial paper the bank actually handled. The greater part of the discounts extended by the bank were collateralized by stock alone. While commercial paper was commonly rejected, 'not an instance has occurred of a note secured by a pledge of stock being rejected'. Furthermore, the original purchases often involved imaginative transactions. Discounts were often made to cover the second specie instalments of the stock purchase (which made up the capital of the bank). In these cases, the bank was supposed to discount only the amount due for that instalment. 'It appears', however, the Committee concluded, 'that in many instances the directors did not confine themselves to the amount prescribed in the last resolution, that is to the coin part of the second instalment, but discounted to the full value of the stock, which was paid for by the proceeds of the same discounts, and the discounts, the payment of the second instalment, the payment of the price to the owners, the transfer, and the pledge of the stock were, as it is termed, simultaneous acts'.[326]

These acts appear at first, bizarre and possibly corrupt – not unlike Dexter purchasing a bank with its own assets. Given the nature of banking, however, it is not difficult to see why many thought that their promise sufficed. Bank notes were liabilities – promises to pay. As Nicholas Biddle realized, however, they were not ordinary debts. A farmer who accepted notes for his produce *de facto* accepted them for their purchasing value and not their convertibility. 'Why should he rush to the bank and exchange them for coin?' – Biddle queried rhetorically. 'The debts of a bank', he concluded, '[were] an exceptional and peculiar category because they [had] a monetary use which the obligations of other debtors [did not have]'.[327] The increased liabilities issued by a bank during this period depended on the perception of the bank's legitimacy – at best a subjective evaluation of other people's economic worth and honesty – at worst, a function of bank note iconography. Nevertheless, given the unprecedented extension of the banking system, most Americans concurred that more money was better than less money, and accepted financial innovation with periodic disturbances.

Despite these disturbances banks continued to multiply, paper credit flourished, and the connection between paper and its specie anchor deteriorated. In 1811 Democratic-Republicans flush with political victory and in control of the state chartered the largest bank in Boston and the state. Democratic Republican office holders had originally proposed a plan for a 'State' bank designed to dominate and eventually overtake all Massachusetts banks in 1808.[328] This proposal was the product of a special committee established in the midst of the various crises that Dexter imposed on Massachusetts's banks from 1807 to 1809 – but also, tellingly, when the Democratic-Republicans held the governor's chair. The plan proposed a very large bank with capital of 12 million dollars. It was truly to be a 'State' bank – with branches established in the towns of Massachusetts. The plan also included a proposal to refuse any possible new banks or extensions of existing charters in Massachusetts: 'Be it further enacted, That no new charter for any banking institution within this commonwealth nor any extension of the existing charters or new privileges shall be granted to any person or persons, bank, exchange office, or other body politic or corporate within this commonwealth for banking purposes for the term and during the continuance of this act creating a State Bank.'[329] The Boston Gazette reported on 11 February 1808 that the lower house of the General Court had passed the act by a 'large majority' but that it was unlikely to pass in the Senate. In March the Senate referred the bill to the next session. Over the next couple of years (1809 and 1810) the Senate established two committees to look into the State Bank Bill. In 1811, when the Democratic Republicans were once again in power, they finally got a bank, though it did not represent the monopoly on banking that they had originally explored.[330]

Capitalized at $3 million, the State Bank, by its sheer size, soon became an important institution in Boston. Though the capital was not yet fully paid in, in 1813 the State Bank generated an additional $2,183,549 in liabilities, and in 1814 it had a respectable specie to liabilities ratio. The association of the State Bank with Madison's wartime administration also raises some interesting questions with regard to its genesis and financial affairs. In 1815, asked to make a loan to the Commonwealth of Massachusetts under its charter obligations, it failed to comply. As its stock plummeted (see Chart 3), a General Court Committee inquired as to its finances. Subsequent investigation revealed that the bank accepted Federal Treasury notes as specie. Furthermore, it had loaned out all of its capital ($2.7 million, or nine-tenths of its capital stock) to Madison's administration during the War of 1812.[331]

Despite the economic setbacks New England suffered during this period, the War of 1812 did not impede the progress of banks of Massachusetts. In the middle of the war the General Court chartered two new banks in Boston: the New England Bank in 1813 and the Manufacturers and Mechanics Bank in 1814. The New England Bank undertook the exchange business anew. It promised to charge depositors a nominal fee to receive 'country' and out-of-state notes at par. The New England Bank's efforts to recover specie from the New York banks led to a famous episode in which a Federal Customs Officer in New York State refused to allow three wagonloads of silver coin to leave the jurisdiction on the flimsy charge that Boston bankers planned to export the specie to the British in Canada. Boston bankers eventually retrieved the silver and the New England Bank continued in its exchange role until the establishment of the Suffolk System in 1824. In 1822 it carried $122,474 in 'Bills of Instate Banks', and $297,343 in 'Bills of Outstate Banks'.[332] In 1824 the Suffolk Bank took over this function and the New England Bank expanded its interests in other directions.[333]

Another financial innovation Boston bankers developed in this period was the 'savings' institute. The Massachusetts General Court chartered America's first savings 'bank', the Provident Institution for Savings, in 1817. Chartered only to receive deposits and not to make discounts or issue notes, the Institute was part philanthropy, part capital accumulation. The Directors accepted interest-bearing deposits with only a few limitations and promptly – as a function of their by-laws – invested the funds in 'the stocks of the United States or of this State, or in the capital of some of the Banks within the town of Boston, or in that of National banks, or employed in the purchase of certificates of stock issued by this Institution, and for their benefit'.[334] Bankers had previously debated the issue of interest-bearing demand deposits and no Boston bank in 1816 paid interest on deposits. The prominent bank directors who created the Institute created a committee to restudy the idea and as a result modified it to suit their goals. Depositors could not withdraw their money on demand but were instead issued certificates for their interest-bearing deposits ($5 minimum) that could then be sold or redeemed yearly. Also, 'at the end of the year, the whole capital stock is appraised at the market price and every depositor is enabled to take his proportion of the joint stock in money'.[335] By 1823, the yearly distribution of 'all the extra income' was modified to a distribution every five years made on top of the 4 per cent interest per annum paid on deposits of $5 or more. The Institute styled itself a philanthropic agency and appealed to the poor and workers to deposit their money for personal improvement; the directors took no salary for their efforts. It advertised its services in a popular sentimental didactic pamphlet that showed how the 'good brother' who saved his money thrived, while the 'reckless brother' with a 'fashion'-addicted wife fell prey to vice and died. A detailed explanation of the Institute's services, the rates of interest (and indeed, how interest worked), and a list of the Board of Directors, followed the sentimental tale.[336]

In 1817 the General Court chartered the Suffolk Bank to some of Boston's largest capitalists and Bostonians continued to expand credit markets in more conventional ways. Within a few years of its establishment the Suffolk became the 'central' bank of Massachusetts. It began by offering country banks their exchange services if they kept a minimum deposit in the Suffolk Bank. Of course, non-compliance meant that the notes of those banks would not be accepted and would suffer severe discounts elsewhere. In 1824 all the Boston banks gathered together and further modified this system, creating a $300,000 fund for the purpose of exchanging and thus regulating the emissions of the country banks – to be managed exclusively by the Suffolk Bank. By 1826 the Suffolk bank held $221, 238 in country notes and $172,722 in out-of-state notes. At the same time (1826), the State Bank held only $43,578 in country notes and only $910 in out-of-state notes. Boston's banks greatly reduced their exposure to these notes through the so-called Suffolk System.[337] The Suffolk Bank played this role into the 1850s when a group of country banks chartered the Bank of Mutual Redemption for the purpose of undermining the dominance of the Suffolk in their affairs. For almost three decades, however, the Suffolk System, as Hammond notes, 'showed *laissez faire* at its best'. It greatly stabilized banking in Boston, and oversaw a period of tremendous growth.[338]

Overall, between 1784 and 1822 capitalists incorporated 10 banks in Boston, 23 in Massachusetts and 87 in New England. Nationally the number of banks increased from 53 to 338 between 1803 and 1818. In New England, bank capitalization increased from $100,000 in 1785 to more than $30 million in 1822; liabilities (notes in circulation plus deposits) jumped from $84,373 to almost $13 million (up 15,308 per cent); loans and discounts from $15,864 to $28.6 million (up 180,182 per cent); yet specie reserves climbed only from $160,587 to $2.4 million (up 1,395 per cent). The aggregate liabilities to specie ratio for New England climbed from 1.9:1 to 5.4:1 (See Chart 4: Town and Country Bank Data, 1803–22).[339]

Bank charters and liabilities increased at an even greater rate between 1822 and 1825. In 1821, Boston had seven banks capitalized at $6.5 millions, just over $6 million in liabilities and $2.2 million in specie. By 1825 there were fourteen banks in Boston capitalized at $10.3 million, with $6.2 million in liabilities and $527,000 in specie.[340] Country banks, the chartered banks of Massachusetts excluding Boston banks, experienced even greater growth. In 1821 there were twenty-one country banks capitalized at $3.25 million, with $787,000 in deposits, $1.7 million in bank notes, and $770,000 in specie. By 1825, there were twenty-seven banks chartered in Massachusetts outside of Boston. They were capitalized at $4.2 million, had more than $1.3 million in deposits, and issued more than $2.1 million in bank notes on $511,196 in specie. Consistently, the country banks issued more bank notes and created fewer deposits than the Boston banks. These notes, however, circulated in Boston. In 1824, for example, the twelve Boston banks held $380,000 of 'Bills of other banks in the State', and $127,000 in bills from banks incorporated 'elsewhere'.[341]

In keeping with national trends, between 1830 and 1837 Boston experienced yet another round of explosive bank growth, with the number of banks doubling from seventeen to thirty-four. Capital stock increased from $12.35 million to $21.35 million. In 1830 the Boston banks carried almost $7 million in liabilities with $910,000 in specie (7.7:1 liabilities to specie ratio); by 1837 Boston banks carried almost $15 million in liabilities with $1.1 million in specie (13.3:1 liabilities to specie ratio). Massachusetts had forty-six country banks in 1830.

Chart 4: Town and Country Bank Data, 1803–22.

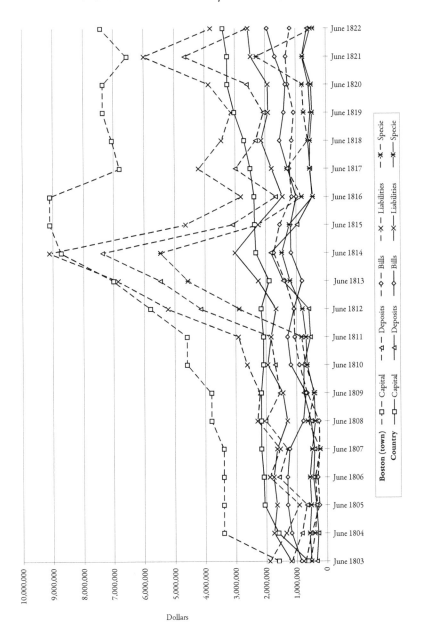

This more than doubled to ninety-five by 1837. Capitalization of state-chartered banks outside of Boston increased from $6.9 million to $16.9 million from 1830 to 1837. In 1830 the country banks carried $4.6 million in liabilities with $348,000 in specie (13.2:1 liabilities to specie ratio). In 1837 this increased to $9.3 million in liabilities with only $388,000 in specie (24:1 liabilities to specie ratio).[342] Banks were also part of a much larger development – a 'Paper System' that included bridge companies, land development corporations and numerous other joint-stock companies that issued paper-credit instruments; these instruments were widely held by Early Republic Bostonians.

Property-Holding in Boston 1795–1821

The popularity of paper-credit instruments increased through the period under study.[343] Looking at 219 Suffolk County probate records in 1790 and 1791, only one probate record indicated stock ownership and 23 listed state financial paper – loan certificates and other state notes – as assets. By 1821, of 214 Suffolk County probates examined, 41 listed bank and other joint-stock company paper, often in conjunction with government securities.[344]

Many of these probates reveal very sophisticated and diversified patterns of investment. Prominent Boston businessman Andrew Sigourney's probate records, for example, record more than $33,000 in a variety of securities, over $13,000 in personal notes – more than $9,000 designated as 'bad' – and real state that included two houses and stock in the Boston Theater, totalling $9,000. His securities investments included stock in five insurance companies, two canals, one bridge, one turnpike, two banks, one academy and two mills.[345] Other inventories reveal much simpler investment patterns. Catherine Hay's probate included one pianoforte ($50.00), one chest of drawers ($15.00), wearing apparel ($50.00) and twenty shares in the Boston Bank, originally worth $1,500 – but at the time of the inventory, worth $1,600.[346] In her will, Miss Hay left everything to her aunt and adoptive mother. Still others reveal some poor decisions. Eli Brown's inventory of 29 January 1821 indicates he owned four books – '1 practical navigator, 1 Dictionary, 1 French Dictionary, 1 Other Old Book', and the 'Scrip' for 324 shares in the Hillsborough Bank at Amherst, apparently having no value at the time of inventory. His only other worldly possession was a 'Paper purporting to be a claim on the Government of the United States for about six hundred dollars'.[347]

Town of Boston tax records also reveal the same pattern of increased investment in financial instruments. Under tax legislation for Massachusetts, 'Real Property' was by and large land and other 'real' or fixed assets. Personal property included a person's furniture, clothing and other 'personal' items – it also included financial instruments. Overwhelmingly, Personal Property values fluctuated strongly (and positively) with the rise and fall of security and bank stock prices in Boston. The correlation is especially evident during peak speculative periods such as 1802 when the legislature of Massachusetts incorporated sixteen banks and fourteen insurance companies. This was true overall for the town but particularly true in wealthy wards such as 9, 10 and 12 (see Charts 5–9).[348]

Finally, joint-stock corporations were in and of themselves large consumers of the paper credit they emitted during this period. For example, the Boston Marine Insurance Company established in 1799 was capitalized at $500,000 – 5,000 shares of $100 each (payable in instalments). There were approximately 136 shareholders in Boston, Salem and Newburyport. The corporation held its assets in the stock of other companies and government securities. In December of 1799, for example, it held $102,000 in 8 per cent securities, $151,420 in 6 per cent securities, $10,000 in 5.5 per cent, $5,963 in 3 per cent, $5,200 in United States Bank Stock and $14,188 in Union Bank stock. Correspondence from Thomas Davis, then President of the Boston Marine Insurance Company indicates that the company employed an agent, Allen Crocker, to travel to Philadelphia and New York for the purpose of securing the best deal on government securities. Crocker made purchases of $20,000 in 6 per cent securities and $10,000 in 5 per cent securities in the space of one week in Philadelphia (6–13 May 1799).[349] Furthermore, there is evidence of a continuous pattern of diversification and increased investment in private joint-stock paper by some corporations. In 1801 the Massachusetts Mutual Fire Insurance Company, with 154 subscribers, invested just over $90,000 in 8 per cent and 6 per cent government securities. By 1822 they invested close to $150,000 in eight different kinds of government securities (1812, 6 per cent; 1813, 6 per cent, etc.) as well as stock in the Union, Manufacturers and Mechanics, Boston, Worcester, and Massachusetts banks.[350]

Increasingly Bostonians and Americans everywhere lived in a paper economy and circulated promises based on a value they imagined. Some Americans judged this pernicious and poetically compared the new market in paper ('Scripomania') to John Law's infamous South Sea Bubble and other financial disasters:[351]

NOW Sixty years have roll'd about,
    Since grandame Britain saw,
The famous South-Sea-bubble-rout,
    Rais'd by that schemer *Law*.

Of golden mountains – in the moon,
    What pictures did they draw!
And diamonds dimming sol at noon,
    Form'd by that conj'rer *Law*.

But soon they found the bubble burst-
    The baloon had a flaw;
And thousands found themselves accurst,
    That built their hopes on *Law*.

This fatal fact one would have tho't
    Should fill mankind with awe!
But *we* by ruin still untaught,
    In scrip have distanc'd *Law*

Still other Americans, and especially Boston's Samuel Blodget, praised the new economy for its benevolent features. Writing in 1806, Blodget sang the praises

Chart 5: Aggregate Assessed Personal Property Taxes Ward-by-Ward, 1795–1821.

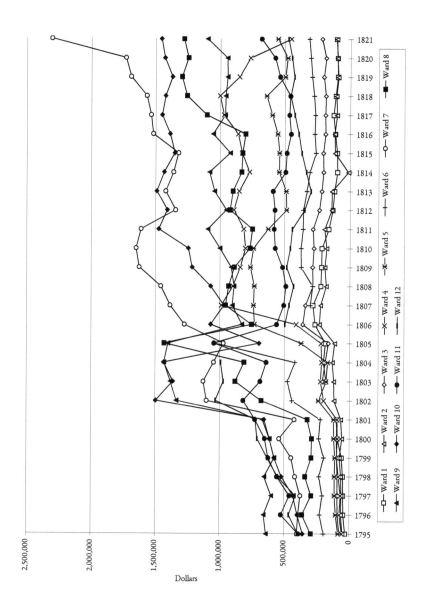

Chart 6: Aggregate Assessed Personal and Real Property, 1795–1821.

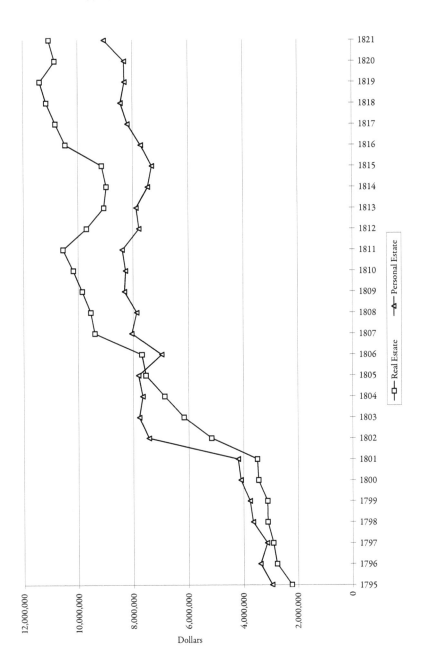

Chart 7: Ward 9 Assessed Personal and Real Property, 1795–1821.

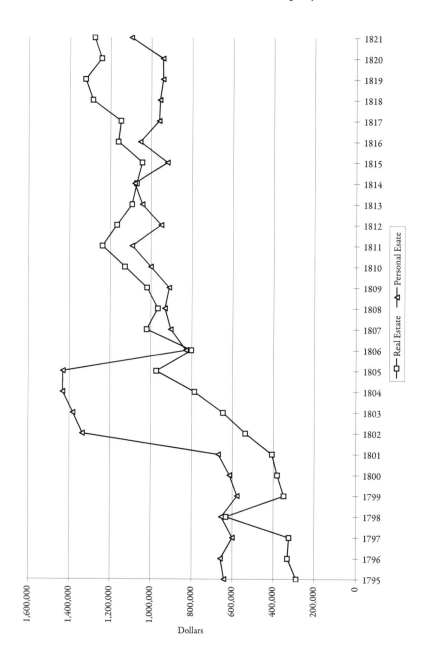

Chart 8: Ward 10 Assessed Personal and Real Property, 1795–1821.

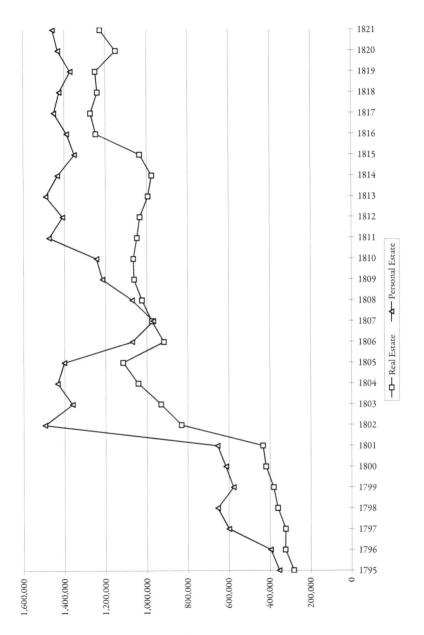

Dollars

Chart 9: Ward 12 Assessed Personal and Real Property, 1795–1821.

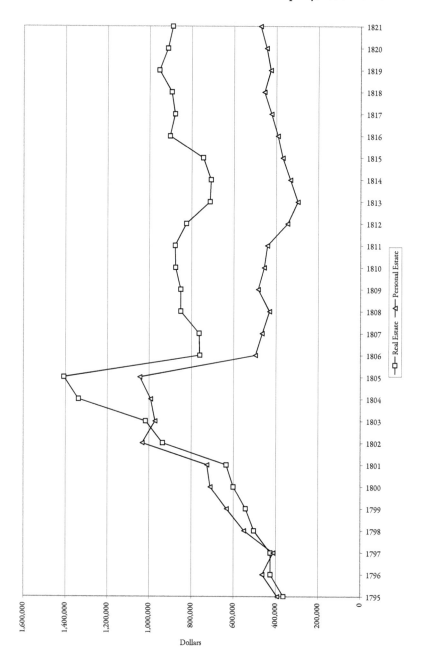

of paper-credit instruments. Blodget delineated four kinds of social ties: kinship (*'silk bands'*), legal (*'iron bands'*), culture (*'flowery bands'*) and 'the fourth, and perhaps the most to be depended on of all, are those of incorporated moneyed commonwealth associations, they are therefore stiled *golden chains*'.[352] He continued:

> In England these [golden] chains are the most numerous; they are there distinguished by the names of funded debt, national and state banks, insurance companies, canal and turnpike; and toll bridge and mining and commercial and tontines, and orphan and widows funds, which, with the India and other mercantile companies, by innumerable divisions of the whole into small shares, the people of all classes and descriptions, the rich and the poor are so linked and riveted together, by their interest, in these constitutions, that they are by many conceived to be the strongest tie against a revolution that the British government possess.

Paper credit's golden chains held mankind together.

The men who created this world did not, however, cease to play an innovative role outside of their functions as bankers. Indeed, the bankers who made Boston the financial centre of New England also created and influenced numerous other institutions and spheres of life. In Boston, religion was still of tremendous social and spiritual importance. Here too a faith in human causation, action and institutions dominated. Here too a new epistemology – a new way of thinking – prevailed. Boston's elite, deeply immersed in the paper-credit world they created, dominated liberal religion and partook of and promoted a spirituality that confirmed the worth of the subject self they engendered.

5 LIKENESS TO GOD

Take, for example, the delight that we find in the vast scenes of nature, in prospects which spread around us without limits, in the immensity of the heavens and the ocean, and especially in the rush and roar of the mighty winds, waves and torrents when, amidst our deep awe, a power within seems to respond to the omnipotence around us. The same principle is seen in the delight ministered to us by works of fiction or of imaginative art, in which our own nature is set before us in more than human beauty and power. In truth, the soul is always bursting its limits. It thirsts continually for wider knowledge. It rushes forward to untried happiness. It has deep wants, which nothing limited can appease. Its true element and end is an unbounded good. Thus God's infinity has its image in the soul; and through the soul, much more than through the universe, we arrive at this conception of the Deity.

William Ellery Channing, 'Likeness to God', *Discourse at the Oration of the Rev. F. A. Farley, Providence, Rhode Island* (1828).

Changes in political economy and the nature of economic value encouraged and reflected an increased subjectivity or interiority. Economic value, once resident in silver, increasingly derived from the imagination, trust and confidence; it was an abstract and subjective evaluation. Furthermore, human actions, feelings and desires unselfconsciously and spontaneously constructed a self-regulating and beneficent economic order.

Moral value also reflected this increased subjectivity and confidence in human agency. In particular, the conflict in Boston between orthodox Calvinism's received and external moral structures and heart-based Unitarian humanism replicated the conflict between empiricism and the imagination; between specie and paper credit; between subjective and objective systems of value. Though Boston's heartfelt Arminian spirituality developed over the eighteenth century, not until the early nineteenth century did it conflict directly with orthodox Congregationalism. Complex social and material attitudes and circumstances exacerbated this struggle – but underneath the material elements lay completely distinct and opposing visions of humanity, the deity and the cosmos. At stake was the nature and location of moral value – did value exist as an external and received ideal delivered to man from the hand of God? Or did moral value derive from the heart and soul of man – ultimately known to him through his feelings and emotions? Orthodox Congregationalism ultimately placed moral value outside of man – it was an external and objective reality that God ordained through the scriptures. Unitarian Arminianism imagined a divine humanity – innately good and ultimately connected to the 'providential' order through the emotions of the heart. For Unitarians, moral value derived from an inner and thus subjective voice within – the Unitarian conscience. Furthermore, in Boston the rise of liberal religion was fundamentally associated with Scottish Moral Sense philosophy, and indicated an increased subjectivity in religious and/or moral beliefs and practices.[353] Over this period, Unitarians increasingly defined morality as a function of conscience, emphasized the innate benevolence and sociability of humanity, and trusted their inner feelings as sources of virtue. Thus a moral system based on an internal and anthropocentric epistemology replaced received empiricist theocratic rule.

The roots of the changes in moral value (as in aesthetic and economic value) were not particular to the United States. In all of the Protestant world liberal religious notions undid years of Calvinist orthodoxy.[354] In the Anglo-American world scholars have traced these changes to the rise of the so-called 'latitude' men or British Latitudinarians.[355] In British North America, Jonathan Edwards reinforced yet complicated orthodox Calvinism in the mid-eighteenth century. Though he never abandoned most of the principles central to Calvinism, he embraced the heart and reconfigured the idea of free agency as important parts of his theology.[356] Likewise Ebenezer Gay, 'Liberal patriarch' of numerous Unitarian ministers, practiced a liberal form of Calvinism in the same period.[357] Nevertheless, although liberal religious notions circulated at this time, on the eve of the Revolution only three of twelve Boston ministers were liberal theologians. In the immediate post-Revolutionary period, liberal or 'Unitarian' ministers headed seven of the nine surviving Congregational churches. By 1809 only one orthodox church, Old South, remained.[358]

Boston's Religious Institutional Structure

Boston's unique institutional framework differed substantially from the rest of Massachusetts. It allocated greater power to parishioners as opposed to full communicants and made it particularly prone to changes in the nature of religious practice. From 1692 to 1833 the state financially supported the 'established' congregational ministers of Massachusetts. Each town resident (except in Boston) had to pay a tax to support the church and the minister. In many ways this fundamentally changed the relationship of the minister to the town. He became a 'civil servant' dependent on the state for his income and was, at the least, day-to-day financially independent of his parishioners. 'Establishment', however, also empowered the town residents and gave them a voice in the election of ministers. Previously only communicants retained the power to choose the minister. After the establishment of the church, the town members 'approved' the selection of a minister by the church elders. Still, given the religious homogeneity of Massachusetts into the eighteenth century, there was little cause for alarm and/or dissent on these issues.[359] Scholars have referred to the overall religious institutional structure of Massachusetts as the 'Standing Order'.[360]

The Revolution reinforced this agreement. By and large strong supporters of the Revolution, the Massachusetts Constitution of 1780 did not diminish the Congregational ministers' financial support. In fact Article 3 of the Constitution strengthened the state's relationship to the congregational churches. Previously, under pressure from parliament, the state exempted dissenting church members from church taxes. Thus Baptists for the most part had been able to avoid taxes and supported their own church on a voluntarist basis. Article 3 of the 1780 Constitution made church taxes mandatory for all residents. Dissenting church members might apply to have their money diverted to their church, but this called for the confirmation of the church and minister's status by the General Court. It also undid the voluntarist ethic central to a number of denominations.

In Boston, however, the state never 'established' the churches. No doubt a function of the numerous churches in Boston in 1692 (eight of them), the town of Boston remained voluntarist through the eighteenth and into the nineteenth century. This created a much closer relationship between the worldly merchants who dominated Boston's social and cultural life and the ministers who depended upon them for their salaries. The ministers' salaries had always been a point of power for the parishioners. In Boston, the extended influence of the parishioners may account for the increasingly latitudinarian nature of the Boston church. 'Convinced they were masters of their own fate', Peter C. Field concludes, 'Boston's elite sought pastors ... who served a rational and benevolent deity'.[361] A more likely explanation, however, turns not solely on the financial support and power of the so-called Boston Brahmins, but on the overall nature of Boston culture during this period.[362]

In the late eighteenth and early nineteenth century Boston's culture increasingly reflected cosmopolitan interests. In the colonial period urban merchants throughout British North America partook of eighteenth-century polite culture. Addison's *Spectator* as well as the *Tatler* and other polite English journals characterized this polite commercial world.[363] Post-Revolutionary America saw a dramatic increase in the number of home-grown expressions of this culture with little relative change in content from their English counterparts.[364] Numerous magazines and social libraries testified to the increased interest in *belles-lettres*.

Nevertheless, though the relationship between merchant financial power and church culture was hardly instrumental, Field is correct to suggest a large role in the church for elites. In Boston the same men who transformed the economic order dominated the church pews. The aristocratic Anglican King's Chapel proprietors – an ultra-liberal institution whose radical minister led the Arminian challenge – included Joseph Coolidge, Dr Aaron Dexter, James Swan, Joseph Barrell and other prominent bankers and merchants. King's Chapel became a truly Congregational church in 1785 when the American bishops refused to ordain their young minister, recent Harvard graduate James Freeman, precisely because of his very un-Episcopalian views. A member of the church, Dr Thomas Bulfinch, ordained him as their minister with the full support of most of the members. Its historian referred to King's Chapel as the first Unitarian Church.[365]

Members of William Ellery Channing's Federal Street Church included bank directors Nathan Appleton (Suffolk Bank), T. H. Perkins (United States Bank), Russell Sturgis (Exchange Office, Detroit Bank), his nephew William Sturgis (New England Bank), Josiah Quincy (Union Bank), John Phillips (Massachusetts Bank) and other capitalists.[366] Many of the candidates for office in the effort to charter the Town and Country Bank in 1803, as well as a number of the original incorporators of the Boston Exchange Office, owned pews at the First Church of Boston, the senior Emerson's parish and, for a time, the epicentre of Boston's liberal, cosmopolitan religion. The First Church was not a one-bank institution, however. Exchange Office directors Eliphalet Williams, John Fox, Beza Tucker and John West worshipped alongside bank directors James Thwing (Massachusetts Bank), John Joy (United States Bank), Peter C. Brooks (Boston Bank) and Benjamin Austin (State Bank).[367] Harrison Gray Otis (United States and Boston Bank) married into the more conservative Episcopalian Christ's Church – as did Samuel G. Perkins, of the Perkins clan, which had two bank directors in the family. He married the daughter of Stephen Higginson (Boston Bank).[368] Even the orthodox had their bank. The Massachusetts Bank, operated largely by William Phillips and family, was associated with the orthodox (Calvinist) Old South Church. Many of its directors, including William Phillips, the founder and long-time head of the bank, worshipped at Old South. Many directors were deacons. Phillips also avidly supported orthodox causes including the Andover Seminary. The Massachusetts Bank was a conservative, high specie to liabilities, real-bills bank – only in 1819 did they begin to circulate small bills of one, two and three dollars.[369] In this sense there is a connection to Jonathan Witherspoon, the orthodox President of Princeton College, who maintained a bullionist position and advocated only high-denomination bank bills.

Clearly Boston's elite religious structure mirrored its elite financial structure. Indeed, if we multiply the family ties across religious and financial institutions we uncover a veritable web of faith and money. In this web, the Massachusetts Bank and Old South stood out as exceptions. By and large the cultural, religious and financial leadership of Boston fell into the hands of men comfortable with self-created and legitimated exchange instruments and a moral law writ upon the heart.[370]

Boston's Liberal Religion

The founding of Brattle Street Church in 1698 set the trend for Boston's religious structure. The Brattle Street Church was the first ministry to decide 'a public relation of one's conversion experience was no longer a prerequisite to full church membership'.[371] Implicitly, liberal religion was at its roots a personal affair. Wealthy and worldly merchants dominated the Brattle Street Church from the beginning. They raised the funds for the building and the minister and they were also among the first to institute pew purchases. This practice became the standard in the nineteenth century and aligned church and economic power. Though this hardly represented a revolution – the wealthy had always enjoyed their townsmen's visible deference within the church's seating arrangements – it institutionalized their power.[372] Thus in Boston a mercantile, cosmopolitan elite dominated the congregational (later Unitarian) churches that largely reflected their interests.[373] Brattle Street Church was also the first congregation to follow the teachings of Arminius. Throughout the eighteenth century numerous Boston churches followed.

Arminian ideas on the nature of man emphasized man's ability to overcome sin through 'works'. This increased confidence in human nature reflected and shaped an increased interest in human achievement and the arts. An increasingly urbane and sophisticated laity partook of a succession of ministers more attuned to oratory and 'high' culture than theological orthodoxy.[374] Furthermore, these ministers increasingly played an active role in secular high culture. They founded the *Monthly Anthology* magazine and the *Athenaeum* social library. Boston's liberal ministers played important roles in organizing these institutions, sponsored and patronized by Boston's elite merchants. They partook of and supported the liberal, cosmopolitan Atlantic culture of letters that thrived in Boston during this period.

This new alliance of religious authority and secular high culture could hardly coexist alongside an orthodox Congregationalist structure devoted to a strict Calvinism, marginalized within Boston but still popular in the countryside. This power struggle led to conflict for the first time in 1803 around the Hollis Professorship of Harvard University. Following their defeat in this conflict, orthodox ministers created alternative cultural and institutional structures in the Andover Seminary, the *Panoplist* Magazine and the Park Street Church, only the second orthodox church in Early Republic Unitarian Boston. The larger conflict continued with the Dorchester controversy in 1811, was further exacerbated by increased tensions between communicants and parishioners within the different ministries, and finally reached a climax in the Dedham decision of 1821.[375]

The religious elements of the conflict centred on the different and opposing definitions of spiritual knowledge and moral value. Calvinists believed in 'the doctrines of the trinity, of the divine decrees, of particular and unconditional election and reprobation, of total depravity, of the special influences of the spirit, of justification by faith alone, and of the special perseverance of the saints'.[376] In other words they believed in the received knowledge and spiritual power of God. An omniscient God had clearly stipulated his doctrines. These doctrines were indisputable facts. The Unitarians believed in reason, and feelings as the arbiters of moral value. They opposed doctrinal rigidity and external authority. Each minister and each person went to God's light in his or her own way. Indeed, as Channing eventually argued, the light and the way existed within humanity and the spiritual journey of man was a subjective experience. Again the conflict was between internal and subjective systems of value and external and received authority; between a damned and depraved humanity that must follow God's rule, and a benevolent humanity ruled over by an internalized deity that expressed Bostonians' warm humanism.

Social and Religious Conflict

The religious ideas held by these two groups came into conflict over a series of issues. The Hollis professorship became the front line in these increasingly contentious debates in 1803 when a number of deaths opened up an opportunity for the liberals to dominate Harvard. David Tappan, Hollis Professor of Divinity, Joseph Willard, Harvard President and Harvard Corporation member, and Simeon Howard, Harvard Corporation member, all died in succession in 1803. This left the Hollis Professorship, the Presidency and control of the Harvard Board of Overseers in a state of limbo and the site of a struggle for the heart of the institution. The struggle centred on the nature of Hollis's instructions and religious beliefs.[377] The orthodox Jedediah Morse insisted that Hollis, as an orthodox parishioner, would have been outraged that the money he left behind to create a professorship supported liberal religion. The liberals disagreed and after a long struggle mustered more votes than the orthodox and won their professor.[378] The victory by the increasingly more powerful Brahmins signalled the orthodox retreat from Harvard – made complete by the creation of two alternative institutions – the *Panoplist Magazine* (1806) and the Andover Seminary (1808).

The *Panoplist* was the orthodox answer to the Brahmin *Monthly Magazine*. As noted above, Boston ministers in alliance with their wealthy parishioners established the *Monthly Magazine* prior to the controversies. Overall, the *Monthly Magazine* devoted itself not to scripture but to literature. It reflected the changed expectations Bostonians had of their religious clergy as well as their ministers' own predilections. Good taste, as expressed in poetry and other forms of literature, was extremely important to and/or for successful Boston ministers during this period. The *Panoplist* countered this voice with a singly orthodox message, expounding doctrinal rigidity and stressing the basic ideas of orthodox Calvinism at every opportunity. During the controversies it acted as the mouthpiece of Jedediah Morse, Moses Stuart and other orthodox polemicists.[379]

Orthodox ministers and parishioners established the Seminary at Andover as an institutional balance against ideas of the liberal Harvard clergy; they imagined a ministry prepared to preach in the style of their 'fathers'. In large part, Yale graduates and followers of Jonathan Edwards and Yale President Timothy Dwight staffed and supported Andover, which was structured to counter the difficulties incurred during the Hollis controversy. Specifically, professors at Andover had to take an elaborate oath that confirmed their orthodoxy.[380]

Boston's Brahmins did not ignore the creation of the new seminary or its controversial oath. 'We consider the establishment of the Institution in Andover', they pompously declared, 'as the most important event, which has occurred in the ecclesiastical history of our country'.[381] It was important because for too long Americans had ignored theology's '*critical* and *exegetical*' elements. Having only recently discovered this weakness in American religion and letters, the Brahmins claimed to 'delight' at the creation of an institution that might alleviate this shortcoming. The Brahmins questioned, however, 'whether the principles, on which it is established, are such, as, in any degree to impair or destroy the good, which such an institution is calculated to effect?'.[382]

The *Monthly Anthology* attacked the Constitution and Associate Statutes of the Andover Seminary on two fronts: first, as revealed in the decree, the union of the groups that created the Seminary represented a cynical marriage of opportunity between Hopkinsinians and Calvinists; second, the idea of swearing an oath to a creed undid, in their opinion, the very tenets of Protestantism. The first was an effort by the Brahmins to undo the alliance created against them by two groups of orthodox Calvinists – or in their language, by two 'funds under the convenient denominations of the Calvinistick and Hopkinsinian'. The Hopkinsinians were a group that followed the ideas of Dr Samuel Hopkins. Briefly, Samuel Hopkins, a devoted follower of Jonathan Edwards, created a 'New Divinity' brand of Calvinism to deter the rise of Arminianism in New England. The Hopkinsinians differed from the Calvinists in their theories of 'moral agency', 'atonement', 'imputation' and 'preparationism'.[383] Through these modifications of Edwards's ideas Hopkinsinians attempted to 'strengthen Calvinism' against Arminian assaults on innate depravity, predestination and the perseverance of the saints – as well as against the radical antinomian tendencies of Calvinism. Within a Hopkinsinian system, the free agency and moral responsibility of man were reconciled with

God's absolute power, the innate depravity of man and the perseverance of the saints.[384]

According to the *Monthly Anthology*, the new Andover Seminary, though nominally a victory for the Calvinists, was in fact a Hopkinsinian institution. Both the Calvinistick and Hopkinsinian systems, the *Monthly Anthology* argued, believed in the basic structure of Calvinism. Both believed in 'the doctrines of the trinity, of the divine decrees, of particular and unconditional election and reprobation, of total depravity, of the special influences of the spirit, of justification by faith alone, and of the special perseverance of the saints'. However, the creed maintained important concessions to the Hopkinsinian ideas of imputation, atonement, preparationism and moral agency.[385] Most importantly, however, according to the *Monthly Anthology*, the creed pointed to the idea 'upon which the Hopkinsinian founds his doctrine, that God is the author of all evil'. This essential idea was contained in one of the creed's final passages:

> That it is the prerogative of God to bring good out of evil, and that he will cause the wrath and rage of wicked men and devils to praise him; and that all the evil which has existed, and which will *forever exist* in the moral system, will *eventually* be made to promote a most important purpose under the wise and perfect administration of the Almighty being, who will cause all things to work for his own glory and thus fulfil his pleasure.[386]

Overall, the *Monthly Anthology* found the new institution's creed and its malevolent deity offensive to its enlightened and optimistic notions of humanity and God. The Brahmin deity benevolently loved his creations and diffused earthly pleasures among them. Man needed no 'wise and perfect administrator'; he had one within. The *Monthly Anthology* also objected to the very idea of creeds because creeds demanded conformity in religious thought; creeds stipulated that religion and spirituality were facts received by men from God – that they were objectively knowable realities beyond interpretation. For the Brahmins doctrinal rigidity was impossible – men knew all knowledge through their subjectivity. 'You may make men use the same words', the author concluded, 'but it is beyond your power to give them the same ideas'.[387] Indeed, the Brahmins concluded that, with a creed, Andover could in no way contribute to the study of theologies' '*critical* and exegetical *elements*'. The orthodox, in the Brahmin view, created the new institution to counter those tendencies. After welcoming the Andover Seminary in its first few sentences, the *Monthly Anthology* closed with a lustful dismissal of the institution and its creed as barbaric and unenlightened. The creed, the *Anthology* proclaimed, 'is a yoke too galling to be endured by any man, who had felt the difficulty of investigating truth, a yoke, which neither we nor our fathers were able to bear'. Furthermore, the institution that demanded such a creed 'would have disgraced the bigotry of the dark ages'.[388]

Of course, the *Panoplist* responded in kind in an emotional and long two-part article picking apart the *Monthly Anthology* article.[389] In both these articles they reiterated the basic Calvinist belief-structure: a profound belief in the Trinity, in the holiness of Christ, in innate depravity, in predestination and the perseverance of saints. They downplayed the differences between 'Calvinists' and 'Hopkinsinians', pointing to the *Monthly Anthology*'s recognition of their fundamental similarities. They emphasized their own continuity to the religion of their 'fathers', and concluded their polemic with an emotional denouncement of the *Monthly Anthology* and its Unitarian constituency: 'Degenerate offspring of such ancestors! – Un-happy apostates from the faith of god's elect, thus to spurn the evidence, which the events of providence afford of the existence and government of God!'.[390] Put another way, how could you denounce the obvious and objectively knowable ('evidence') existence of God and thus his authority?

The orthodox response thus stressed the received authority and physical reality of a God who governed men. The orthodox also established a more concrete manifestation of their ideas through the creation of the Park Street Church, which they established to counter liberal Boston religion. In the post-Revolutionary period, Old South was the last remaining orthodox institution in Boston's centre. By creating the Park Street Church the orthodox ministers took the truths of orthodox Calvinism into the homes of the Brahmins.[391] Of course, much ado was made about the real need for such an institution and the minister Edward Griffin, in his dedication sermon, downplayed politics for demographics. Nevertheless, the emphasis at Park Street Church was on the direct challenge to Calvinism that liberal Boston religion represented to orthodox Congregationalists.[392]

The Unitarian response to these events was typical of their attitude throughout the controversies. They espoused a critical and catholic reading and interpretation of the scriptures; they critiqued their earnest opponents' efforts to keep old wine in new bottles.[393] Continued orthodox efforts to uphold the received knowledge of the scriptures as the very word of God brought on the ridicule of their worldly opponents. The Trinity is exemplary of this dilemma. 'Nothing so much exposes the religion of Jesus Christ to the contempt of mankind', the *Monthly Anthology* concluded, 'as such pitiful attempts to dogmatise on this unsearchable subject'.[394] At the same time, however, they did not often readily espouse their beliefs. Throughout these debates the orthodox Congregationalists seldom missed an opportunity to emphasize their continuity with the true faith of the Puritan Fathers. They also never missed an opportunity to recite their beliefs, point by point. The liberal or Unitarian faction, firmly in control of Harvard and Boston, felt less urgency and seldom expressed clearly their doctrinal ideas. The best such explications of Unitarian ideas are William Ellery Channing's 'Unitarian Christianity', 'The Moral Argument Against Calvinism' and 'Likeness to God'.

Unitarian Christianity

Written in the heat of the continued confrontations between the orthodox and Unitarian factions in Boston, Channing intended 'Unitarian Christianity' to clearly describe the principles of Unitarian religion. He structured the address in two sections, outlining '1ˢᵗ, the principles which we adopt in interpreting the Scriptures; and 2dly, some of the doctrines which the Scriptures, so interpreted, seem to us clearly to express'.[395] Implicit in this structure was the idea that moral knowledge flowed from interpretation and/or speculation upon texts that did not clearly outline moral truth beyond dispute; or, put another way, that moral knowledge was subjective.

The doctrines expounded by Channing in the second section expressed then current latitudinarian and Arminian ideas. First, Unitarians denigrated the idea of a 'trinity' as incomprehensible and thus unbelievable. Second, they emphasized the unity of Christ, in effect constructing a human Jesus. Third, they constructed a morally perfect God. 'God', Channing declared, 'is infinitely good, kind benevolent, in the proper sense of these words – good in disposition as well as in act; good not to a few but to all; good to every individual as well as to the general system'.[396] Taking for granted a benevolent deity, Unitarians found it excessively difficult to understand the doctrine of innate depravity and predetermination. Thus they imagined a benevolent humanity that could through works approach divinity. Fourth, as developed by Channing, Unitarians believed that Christ's mission on earth was that of a teacher, 'to rescue men from sin and its consequences, and to bring them to a state of everlasting purity and happiness'. He did not, however, come into this world to die for man's sins. It was completely illogical that Christ should have died for man's sins. In this context, Channing concluded, God never forgives – since their punishment is 'borne by a substitute'. 'A scheme more fitted to obscure the brightness of Christianity and the mercy of God', Channing concluded, '... could not, we think, be easily framed'.[397]

These liberal religious doctrines clearly opposed orthodox teachings. More galling to the orthodox, however, was the doctrinal speculation through which the Unitarians derived these ideas. Channing defended 'reason' as an interpretive tool of scripture. 'Our leading principle in interpreting scripture', he proclaimed, 'is this, that the bible is a book written for men, in the language of men, and that its meaning is to be sought in the same manner as that of other books'.[398] The Bible, as the word of God, was for Channing even more demanding of the faculties of reason than other books. Its language was figurative and demanded 'more continual exercise of judgment'. Also, the Bible was not confined to 'general truths' but demanded historical analysis – lest we 'extend to all times and places what was of temporary and local application'.[399] Finally, the Bible's authors possessed particular points of view and 'feelings'. It behoved the reader to understand these feelings and 'influences' in order to decipher their work. Overall, according to Channing, Unitarians felt duty bound 'to exercise our reason upon it perpetually, to compare, to infer, to look beyond the letter of the spirit, to seek in the nature of the subject and the aim of the writer his true meaning; and in general, to make use of what is known for explaining what is difficult and for discovering new truths'.[400] Thus for Unitarians, 'the great question of truth is left by God to be decided at the bar of reason'. Revelation could not be at odds with reason but must complement it. God created the reasoning faculty and must expect us to use it, Channing argued. Through their subjective faculties men thus established the doctrines of God.

Unitarians arrived at God's truths through the exercise of their human faculties in reading the Bible. 'Christian virtue, or true holiness', however, did not derive from any 'new' or old truths therein discovered or expounded. 'We believe', Channing declared, 'that all virtue has its foundation in the moral nature of man, that is in conscience or his sense of duty, and in the power of forming his temper and life according to conscience'. The 'moral faculty' of man was the highest expression of his humanity – it replaced 'God's irresistible agency on the heart' and created a system of 'self-government'. This did not deny the role that God played in human life – 'conscience without the sanction of God's authority and retributive justice, would be a weak director ... benevolence unless nourished by communion with his goodness, and encouraged by his smile could not thrive amidst the selfishness and thanklessness of the world ... self-government without a sense of the divine inspection, would hardly extend beyond and outward and partial purity'.[401] Nevertheless, self-government replaced God as the springs to moral judgment and action.

Channing's famous sermon quickly drew the fire of Moses Stuart. He responded to the twenty or so page sermon with a 180-page tirade against the logic of Unitarian ideas and once again reiterated the orthodox position. Most offensive to Stuart was Channing's idea that 'reason' precluded revelation.[402] 'Do you mean', Stuart exclaimed, 'that common sense may determine first, independently of Revelation that the doctrine cannot be true; and then maintain the impossibility that Revelation should exhibit it?'. According to this system, Stuart argued, men decided *a priori* what was true and what was not regardless of revelation. To admit to this logic Stuart concluded was to throw out all revelation – all received authority. Common sense, as he understood it, played a role in 'judging of the evidences that the Bible is of divine origin and authority'. It played an important role in establishing the rules of 'exegesis'. It was a tool to investigate the writings of inspired writers. If, however, common sense was used to *a priori* 'cast off the divine authority of the Bible' then it was no part of 'any sincere lover of truth and sober investigation'.[403] Furthermore, concluded Stuart, you could not accept the Bible as a source of inspiration and truth and reject the doctrines therein found.[404]

The consequences of these ideas were, for Stuart, fraught with peril. The application of *a priori* logic to scripture led to complete chaos and relativism. In this scenario, conceivably, one man could interpret the Bible differently from his neighbour on the basis of superior knowledge. 'The same text in the Bible therefore, may be received by one, as a consistent part of revelation, and rejected by the other. The measure of a man's knowledge, consequently, cannot be a proper rule, by which we may test the meaning of Scripture.' Individual knowledge could not determine if scripture was true or false – scriptural knowledge was a fact. Furthermore, scriptural knowledge could not be measured by a 'rule' that varied from person to person – it was measured by a fixed and immutable standard. If these standards collapsed, Stuart implied, chaos followed.[405]

Stuart feared where this was headed. Unitarians need only to look at Germany and the path of religion in that country. In Germany too the conflict began with the question of the 'divine authenticity of the bible'. Now, Stuart continued, miracles, the resurrection and other revelations had been dismissed. Schelling, a German divine, preached that God and nature were the same. The English Unitarians, raptly absorbed by German idealism, had also proceeded on this slippery slope and now they too espoused doctrines, in Stuart's opinion, '*fundamentally subversive of Christianity*'.[406] 'Not long ago', Stuart recalled, 'almost all the Unitarians of New England were simple Arians'. Before long, however, Stuart predicted, they would become 'simple *Humanitarians*'. This was, in his estimate, precisely the pattern that subjective speculation led to. Before long, he concluded, the issue will be whether 'natural or revealed religion is our guide and our hope'.[407]

Stuart was prescient in his analysis. Unitarians of course resisted his observations and Andrews Norton undertook a long defence of Channing's position.[408] Channing too followed up his explication of Unitarian principles with a further pointed assault on orthodox religion.[409] A close reading of Channing's 'Likeness to God' sermon preached at the 1828 ordination of Rev. F. A. Farley, however, reveals fully the powerful differences between Unitarian religion and Calvinism in this period, and points to the Scottish Moral Sense philosophers and their mentor, Shaftesbury, as the source of these ideas. In 'Likeness to God' Channing undoes any notions that his thought pertained to an objective reality, or a 'common sense' philosophy. Channing's sermon betrays his Neo-Platonic, Scottish Moral Sense roots. Not surprisingly, it both resembled and inspired the work of the Transcendentalists, and points squarely to romanticism's complete subjectivity.

Likeness to God

To 'seek accordance or ... likeness to God', Channing began, is the purpose of true religion. Yet this likeness, according to Channing, 'has its foundation in the original and essential capacities of the mind'. Thus the spiritual journey of man is an inward and ultimately subjective experience. For Channing, God is real to the extent that his nature is unfolded within the individual. To seek 'likeness to God' is to transform the self and enter into 'intercourse' or friendship with the deity. Furthermore, to seek likeness to God – ultimately a principle of 'sympathy or accordance with his creation' – is 'the true and only preparation for the enjoyment of the universe. In proportion as we approach and resemble the mind of God', Channing concluded, 'we are brought into harmony with the creation; for in that proportion we possess the principles from which the universe sprang; we carry within ourselves the perfections of which its beauty, magnificence, order, benevolent adaptations, and boundless purposes are the results and manifestations'. The human soul, Channing argued, was the source of the knowledge of the 'attributes and perfections of the Supreme Being'. Put another way, 'the idea of God, sublime and awful as it is, is the idea of our own spiritual nature, purified and enlarged to infinity'. Indeed, God was 'another name for human intelligence raised above all error and imperfection and extended to all possible truth'.

In Channing's system, the idea of God was a function of mind, but so were God's attributes – goodness and moral perfection. These were all 'writ in the law of the heart', principles 'implanted' and 'unfolding' in 'our own breasts'. Did this undermine the 'new' Continental idea so dreaded by Stuart that God and nature were one? Channing readily acknowledged the place of God in the beauty of the universe. 'The Universe, I know, is full of God', he concluded. But how did man come to know this? These truths were not 'apparent to the outward eye; not to the acutest organs of sense, but to a kindred mind which interprets the universe by itself'. It was the mind and thought which revealed God and his works to humanity. 'In truth', Channing concluded, 'the beauty and glory of God's works are revealed to the mind by a light beaming from itself. We discern the impress of God's attributes in the universe by the accordance of nature, and enjoy them through sympathy.'[410]

This inwardness or interiority expressed by Channing was at the centre of the Unitarian idea of human 'divinity'. Man resembled the deity ('has a character of infinity') insofar as he partook of the 'higher actions, in original thought, in the creations of genius, in the soarings of the imagination, in its love of beauty and grandeur, in its aspirations after a pure and unknown joy, and especially in disinterestedness [and] in the spirit of self-sacrifice ...'.[411] These were not, however, hopeless dreams, aspirations or prescriptions. Indeed, for Channing, the 'human mind seems to me to be turning itself more and more inward, and to be growing more alive to its own worth and capacities of progress ... There is a spreading conviction that man was made for a higher purpose than to be a beast of burden or a creature of sense.'[412]

Channing's ideas and words in this and other sermons betray his debt to the Scottish Moral Sense philosophers. Daniel Walker Howe has argued that the key to understanding Unitarian ideas is Thomas Reid's Scottish Common Sense. The now familiar narrative of Scottish Common Sense stipulates that Reid, in reaction to Hume's scepticism, constructed a philosophy that reintroduced Lockean empiricism to moral philosophy. Hume had followed Berkeley and Descartes into a subjectivity so deep it threatened the existence of reality. If everything we know to be true or real derives from our mind and/or sense experience, Hume asked, then how do we know things really exist? Reid attempted to draw philosophy back from this ledge with the bold common sense assertion that they exist because they exist. Things were not objects in the mind but things in and of themselves.

Reid further differentiated himself from the Scottish Moral Sense philosophers, namely Francis Hutcheson, but also, by implication, Shaftesbury. According to Howe, Reid followed a 'rational-intuitionist' branch of Neo-Platonic thinkers and developed a different and opposing theory of the moral sense than that of Shaftesbury and Hutcheson. 'The "moral sense" for Reid', Howe concludes, 'was no involuntary emotion but an active, rational power. Reid considered that the sentimentalists had by reducing the moral faculty to an involuntary emotion, robbed ethics of ultimate validity and man of genuine moral responsibility'.[413]

In Howe's narrative, Boston Unitarians grasped Reid's ideas as a way to maintain religion, reason and Lockean epistemology. At Harvard especially, Howe argues, Common Sense reigned supreme. For Unitarians, 'Scottish realism was basically a device to justify empiricism, to restore confidence in natural science and natural theology'.[414] Locke himself continued to be read well into the nineteenth century in new American editions. Indeed, for Unitarians like Alexander H. Everett, Locke provided an important bulwark against the 'palpable absurdities' of Kant and other German idealists and the French philosophers Voltaire and Rousseau.[415] But most Americans came to Locke through the works of Thomas Reid, widely excerpted and read at Harvard, and refashioned in Levi Hedge's *Elements of Logick*. Furthermore, according to Howe, the 'natural religion' of someone like Channing was possible precisely because 'Common Sense rescued man by transforming sensation into a reliable key to nature'.[416] Reid's Common Sense, Howe concludes, was 'certainly a more influential concept in America than the moral sense of Shaftesbury and Hutcheson'.[417]

Certainly, Reid's philosophy was important at Harvard (and elsewhere). Furthermore, there is plenty of evidence that Harvard students read Locke diligently. But was it really the source and/or formative influence of the natural religious transcendentalism that Channing so ably precipitated? Was it the source of the emphasis on benevolence and sympathy that so distinguished the Unitarians from their fellow Congregationalists?

Howe's book is at least nominally about the Unitarian *Conscience*, which he describes not as a function of Common Sense realism but 'benevolent affections'. In Howe's words, 'Certain faculties were normally singled out [by Unitarians] for special praise as indispensable to human activity. Few were extolled more than the benevolent affections, those emotional impulses of fellow-feeling that Unitarians considered the basis for society.'[418] Furthermore, as Howe ultimately acknowledges, even Reid bent to the power of feelings and emotions. For Reid, Howe concludes, 'the most important power cementing society together was not the rational moral sense but the benevolent affections'. Sounding very much like an 'ethical sentimentalist' rather than a 'rational intuitionist', Howe quotes Reid, 'the security, happiness, and the strength of human society spring solely from the reciprocal benevolent affections of its members.'[419]

It is no surprise that Reid believed strongly in the benevolent affections. He was born into and educated in an environment saturated in Scottish Moral Sense.[420] Further, as Richard Teichgraeber has argued, the lines of demarcation between Moral and Common Sense have been drawn too tightly – Reid may have modified aspects of the Scottish Moral Sense philosophy, but as his own words reveal he was deeply influenced by the main ideas.[421] Reading the words of the Unitarian Harvard-educated ministers, it is clear that the most important influence for Harvard Unitarians was not Scottish Common Sense, but a Neo-Platonic tradition carried forward by the Scottish Moral Sense philosophers, especially Shaftesbury and Hutcheson.[422]

This difference between these two traditions is important because the emphasis on emotions and the heart so central to Scottish Moral Sense philosophy and political economy led, as Charles Taylor notes, to increased subjectivity and eventually to romanticism.[423] If we follow Locke's empiricism and/or Reid's 'rational intuitionism' down this path, we reach a dead end. We cannot explain the rich emotional life that was at the centre of the Unitarian experience using Locke or Reid. Indeed, Howe is at a loss to explain his ministers' embarrassing sentimentalism and seems to ascribe their sentimental poetry to a personal emotionalism rather than a widespread cultural phenomenon.[424] Furthermore, he is unable to explain their romantic obsession with the sublime and nature.[425] 'For supposedly "corpse-cold" rationalists', he plaintively concludes, 'the Liberal moralists were strangely infatuated with the mysterious, the mighty and the remote.'[426] This infatuation was no passing or singular phase. As noted in Chapter 6, the sublime and the picturesque were part of a growing aesthetic of the imagination and worldly Unitarian ministers, and Channing in particular, were at the centre of these ideas, as derived from Scottish Moral Sense philosophy.

The Scottish Moral Sense Roots of Unitarian Religion

The intellectual influence of Scottish Moral Sense philosophy on Channing is obvious from a brief examination of Scottish Moral Sense versions of his ideas.[427] As discussed above, sympathy and benevolence were central to Channing's ideas on man and God. 'That God can be known and enjoyed only through sympathy or kindred attributes is a doctrine which even Gentile philosophy discerned', Channing concluded. Furthermore, 'Likeness to God must be a principle of sympathy or accordance with his creation'. Howe argues that Unitarian aspirations to a 'God-like' character were uniquely American. 'In daring to avow such an aim', he concludes, 'the Unitarian moralists were manifesting the glorious optimism, the unlimited perfectionism of nineteenth century America ... In the New-England aspiration toward "likeness to God", Christian humanism reached what was probably the highest development it ever achieved anywhere.'[428] No doubt that may be so if the qualifier 'Christian' is rigorously applied – but the Unitarians' language and message was decidedly Neo-Platonic, especially as developed by the Scottish Moral Sense philosophers.

Adam Smith recognized the power of benevolent affections and the human 'likeness to God' at work in his *Theory of Moral Sentiments*. He traced these ideas back to the Cambridge Platonists and his old teacher Francis Hutcheson. The Cambridge Platonists, Cudworth, More and John Smith – along with Hutcheson – Smith argued, recognized in benevolence the highest attributes of man and the deity. Indeed, insofar as it was benevolent, mankind aspired to God. In this system, Smith noted, 'benevolence ... was still the supreme and governing attribute, to which the others were subservient, and from which the whole excellency or the whole morality ... of the divine operations was ultimately derived'. Insofar as man aspired to benevolence he aspired to the divine – or as Smith put it, 'the whole perfection and virtue of the human mind consisted in some resemblance or participation of the divine perfections, and consequently in being filled with the same principle of benevolence and love which influenced all the actions of the deity'. Only through this imitation could we 'express our humble and devout admiration of his infinite perfections, that by fostering in our minds the same divine principle, we could bring our own affections to a greater resemblance with his holy attributes, and thereby become more proper objects of his love and esteem; till at last we arrived at the immediate converse it was the great object of the deity to raise us'.[429] Or, put another way, 'Likeness to God must be a principle of sympathy or accordance with his creation'.

Channing was, of course, well aware of Hutcheson. According to his biographer, Channing's first religious experience came upon reading Hutcheson's ideas on disinterested benevolence. 'It was while reading [Hutcheson] one day', his nephew William Henry Channing recalls, 'some of the various passages in which he asserts man's capacity for disinterested affection, and considers virtue as the sacrifice of private interests and the bearing of private evils for the public good, or as self-devotion to absolute, universal good, that there suddenly burst upon his mind that view of the dignity of human nature which was ever after to "uphold and cherish" him, and thenceforth to be "the fountain light of all his day, the master light of all his seeing"'.[430] Channing's religious epiphany and thus his calling came through a reading of Hutcheson. Contemporaries familiar with Channing knew well his repudiation of Locke's ideas and his predilection for Hutcheson and Rousseau, and even the German philosophers.[431]

Hutcheson's disinterested benevolence was the linchpin to his system of moral sentiments. Without disinterested benevolence society necessarily operated on the principle of self-interest. Furthermore, a benevolent deity could not exist in a social order operated on the principle of self-love. 'But how is the DEITY concern'd in this *Whole*, if every Agent always acts from *Self-Love?*', Hutcheson queried. 'And what Ground have we from the idea of a *God* it self, to believe the DEITY is *good* in the Christian *Sense*, that is, *studious of the Good of his Creatures?*' Without benevolent affections there was no reason to think that the 'Deity will make the *Virtuous* happy.'[432] In part, Hutcheson assumed a benevolent deity. He recognized that 'we shall perhaps find no demonstrative Arguments *a priori*, from the Idea of an *Independent Being* to prove his *Goodness*. But there is abundant probability deduced from the *Frame* of *Nature*, which seems, as far as we know, plainly contriv'd for the *Good* of the *Whole*.' Furthermore, a benevolent God implied a benevolent humanity. 'For if the DEITY be really *benevolent*', Hutcheson reasoned, 'or *delights* in the Happiness of others, he could not *rationally* act otherwise, or give us a *moral Sense* upon another Foundation, without counteracting his own *benevolent Intentions*.'[433]

Ultimately, however, as Hutcheson readily acknowledged, for eighteenth-century thinkers these ideas originated from the pen of Shaftesbury.[434] Men believed in and followed God for one of two reasons, Shaftesbury reasoned. 'It must be either *in the way of his* Power, as presupposing some disadvantage or Benefit to Accrue from him: or *in the way of his* Excellency and Worth, as thinking it the Perfection of Nature to imitate and resemble him.' Under the system of self-interest ('*in the way of his* Power ...') man had no virtue or goodness. 'The Creature', Shaftesbury concluded in reference to self-interested man, 'notwithstanding his good conduct, is intrinsically of as little worth, as if he acted in his Natural way, when under no Dread or terror of any sort'. However, in the second case, when man aspired to '*imitate and resemble*' a benevolent God who had a 'Love towards the *Whole*; such an example must undoubtedly serve to raise and increase the Affection towards Virtue, and help to submit and subdue all other Affections to that alone.'[435] Furthermore, for Shaftesbury, the natural world was itself a sink of virtue. 'But if *the Order of the World it-self* appears just and beautiful'; he explained, 'the Admiration and Esteem of *Order* must run higher, and the Elegant Passion or Love of Beauty, which is so advantageous to Virtue, must be the more improv'd in its exercise in so ample and magnificent a subject. For 'tis impossible that such A *Divine Order* shou'd be contemplated without Extasy and Rapture.'[436]

Channing, although greatly inspired by natural religion, broke with many of these ideas. Nature and the universe were a function of God and ultimately, as he emphasized, a function of the human spirit. As he explained in 'Likeness to God', 'Should I deem a property in the outward universe as the highest good when I may become partaker of the very mind from which it springs, of the prompt-ing love, the disposing wisdom, the quickening power through which its order, beauty, and beneficent influences subsist?'.[437] He might have quoted the new edi-tion of Mark Akenside's famous poem, *The Pleasures of the Imagination*: 'Mind, Mind alone, bear Witness Earth and Heav'n, / The Living Fountains in it self contains / Of beauteous and sublime ...'.[438]

Channing's sermons and ideas represented Unitarian thought during this period and clearly demonstrate a Scottish Moral Sense pedigree. That these ideas had more currency than the pulpit is easily ascertained by a perusal of the magazines from this period. Bostonians obsessively discussed benevolence and sympathy on a number of intellectual levels. Was man driven by self-love or benevolence? This was the debate between a 'Philanthropist' and a 'Mandevillian' in the *Boston Spectator*, carried on using the words of Mandeville as derived from his book *Private Vices, Publick Benefits*.[439]

'What!' cried the 'Philanthropist' indignantly, 'will you ascribe every action to the mere principle of *self love*? Is there not sentiment of true patriotism? No such thing, in any case, as disinterested benevolence? Do our views wholly centre in self love when we console the afflicted; when we relieve the distressed; when we pity the unfortunate; when we spontaneously rush to save the unknown stranger from peril?' 'Mandevillian' replied coolly that 'every motion of that kind' is based on vanity. Everything humans do, he retorted, follows from their selfish nature and they never sacrifice material goods or leisure lest it accrue some sort of benefit that outweighs the cost.

'Mandevillian' and 'Philanthropist' thus debated numerous fantastic scenarios for several pages, column by column, each side insisting on the other's error. But 'Philanthropist' was laying a trap for his selfish friend: 'I am traveling in haste through a strange country', he implored 'Mandevillian' to imagine, 'having just passed a cottage to which I can never expect to return. I see an infant, uncon-scious of his danger, approaching a rattlesnake, ready to spring upon him. Should I pass on with indifference; suffer the infant to be destroyed; or should I not instantaneously, with a blow of my cane, kill the serpent?' 'Mandevillian' con-ceded that no human would delay to instantly and without consciousness save the child. But, he explained, 'I could not go on, and leave this child exposed to danger, for the thought would give me pain – and the act of saving him gives me pleasure. From a disposition to shun pain and enjoy pleasure both of which are wholly selfish, I secure the child.'

Now 'Philanthropist' had his catch. Even if the selfish principles you claim existed, he declared – '*Whence arise this pleasure and pain, but from violating or gratifying the benevolent principle?* ... There is undoubtedly a pleasure to be derived from good actions, and it originates in my conformity to the constitution of my mind – in obeying a "natural impulse."'

This natural impulse, often expressed as benevolence and/or sympathy, was at the centre of a new moral value structure. No longer did men act or refuse to act for fear of God. No longer did they seek the wise counsel of religious authority as expressed in the scripture or the teachings of Calvin. Instead, Unitarians and, in the long run, most American Christians, aspired to divinity and sought the counsel or knowledge innately part of their natural constitution: the heart. This idea dominated the sentimental culture of Atlantic cosmopolitans for almost a century. It derived from a different epistemology – an increased confidence in the self and feelings as simultaneously expressed in changes to economic and aesthetic value. It was not, however, an idea limited to the pulpit. Indeed, the greater part of the discussion on benevolence and sympathy came through the large and increasing public sphere of letters. The novels and magazines of the period consisted of the greatest 'school for sympathy'.

6 THE LUXURY OF PITY

And if a sigh would sometimes intervene,
And Down his cheek a tear of pity roll,
A sigh, a tear, so sweet, he wished not to control.

Remarker, No. 29, *Monthly Anthology and
Boston Review* (January 1808), p. 25.

Sentimental literature, and especially novels, both expressed and resolved the crises of knowledge inherent in the construction of modernity and the self: epistemological questions of 'truth' and sociological questions of 'virtue'.[440] Epistemological questions of truth spoke to the nature and site of value. Where was truth and/or value located – in objectively knowable and received empiricist systems of knowledge, or in the 'private system' and subjectivity of emotions, feelings and the imagination? Likewise, the fashioning of self in an age of economic volatility, advice books, sociability and manners undermined accepted notions of trust – who was true and who was false?[441] Self-fashioned subjective identities, like the new bank notes based on trust, circulated and/or were discounted, but might also bankrupt the holder. The story of the virtuous maiden seduced by the rake was thus first a sentimental tale designed to inflame the spectator's sympathy. Second, it was the story of counterfeit value.

Americans of the Early Republic – especially Boston's cosmopolitan Unitarians – perceived the sympathetic feelings engendered by sentimental representations as the production of society.[442] The culture of sympathy and benevolence, best expressed by the eighteenth-century Scottish Moral Sense philosophers, emphasized the role that romances, seduction novels and sentimental fragments played in the fabrication of sympathy for the consumers' edification and pleasure. These thinkers argued that these representations engaged the readers' imagination, stimulated pleasurable feelings and engendered sympathetic bonds critical to social cohesion. Though there was considerable debate on the issue, by the 1820s Anglo-American readers and critics by and large concurred. Novels, the theatre, poetry – indeed all art forms that expressed pathos – were 'schools of sympathy' 'teaching man to feel for man'.[443] Indeed, they were a central part of the new emotional and/or moral landscape – the site where culture manufactured moral value. Thus the social bonds engendered by subjective emotions and feelings replaced hierarchies and received value structures undermined everywhere in the Atlantic world by a new subjectivity, itself derived from the radical psychological changes engendered by paper credit.

Numerous scholars have looked at the phenomena of sentiment.[444] Fewer have recognized the relationship between sentiment and capitalism.[445] Others have focused on the role that novels and/or romances played in a sentimental culture. Many of these analyses have positioned sentiment in terms of the possible radical or reactionary content and message.[446] Few scholars have, however, looked at the issue of origins.[447] By positioning the work of America's sentimentalists as part of a larger change in the nature of value knowledge and personality, this chapter more fully develops the cultural, intellectual and social origins and implications of sentiment. Sentiment was part of a much larger epistemic shift that included moral and economic value. It was the cultural ethos of an interdependent commercial society saturated by paper-credit instruments based on trust and confidence. At the heart of the sentimental narrative was a truly radical message – feelings count. In fact, feelings and emotions were the most important factors in determining moral and economic value, as well as self-knowledge and societal cohesion.

Scottish Notions of Pain, Pleasure and Fiction

For Unitarians sympathy and sentiment dominated religious feeling. Channing and other Unitarian ministers followed the Scottish Moral Sense philosophers in equating disinterested benevolence with divinity.[448] Thus disinterested benevolence and/or sympathy were central to a moral life and constituted the social affections or bonds between human beings. Nevertheless, expressions of sympathy and benevolence often took the form of pathos. The whole culture of sentiment was, in effect, seated in this idea – and a veritable industry of tears testified to the complete identification of sentiment, sympathy and pleasure.[449] Contemporaries did not overlook these connections and often asked the very direct question – what is our pleasure in others' distress? The answer to this question begins once again with the Moral Sense philosophers.

For Shaftesbury, the mind decided wrong and right, beauty and deformity. 'THE MIND', he declared, 'which is Spectator or Auditor of *other Minds*, cannot be without its *Eye* and *Ear*; so as to discern Proportion, Distinguish Sound, and scan each Sentiment or Thought which comes before it'. Shaftesbury thought it ludicrous that the mind was in any way created void of judgment and/or a disposition to goodness. 'Sense of Right and Wrong' was as 'natural as *natural Affection* itself ... there is no speculative Opinion, Persuasion or Belief, which is capable *immediately* or *directly to* exclude or destroy it'. Only 'contrary custom' and frequent 'contrary affection' might thwart this 'first Principle in our Constitution and Make'.[450]

'Natural Affections (such as are founded in Love, Complacency, Good-Will and in a Sympathy with the Kind or Species)' constituted the very source of happiness. They were the 'CHIEF MEANS AND POWER TO SELF-ENJOYMENT'. Shaftesbury numbered these 'satisfactions' (natural affections) among the '*Pleasures of the Mind*' and thought them far superior to the *sensual* pleasures. Thus, concluded Shaftesbury, 'whatever can create in any intelligent Being a constant Series or Train of Mental Enjoyments, or Pleasures of the Mind, is more considerable to his Happiness, than that which can create to him a like constant Course or train of Sensual Enjoyments, or Pleasures of the Body'.[451]

The '*Pleasures of the Mind*', however, did not always derive from joy. Indeed, 'the very disturbances which belong to natural Affection, tho they may be thought wholly contrary to Pleasure, yield still a Contentment and Satisfaction greater than the Pleasures of indulg'd Sense'. Mankind preferred the illusion of misery, 'as in a *Tragedy*' – the exhibition of 'fears, sorrows, horrors, griefs' – anything that 'moved the Passions in this mournful way' on behalf of 'Merit and Worth' – to any other entertainment 'of equal duration'. Indeed the melancholy scenes that exerted 'social Affection and human Sympathy' brought about a greater enjoyment than any possible objects of '*Sense* and *common Appetite*'. 'How much', Shaftesbury concluded, '*the mental Enjoyments* [of pathos] *are actually the very natural Affections themselves*'.[452] Thus, for Shaftesbury, the creation of mental pleasure was intimately associated with the social affections – natural bonds that held society together – and connected directly to the scenes of distress evoked in tragedy and other imagined narratives.

Francis Hutcheson made a very similar argument. For Hutcheson, disinterested benevolence played a central role in a theory of moral sentiments that described the natural affections between men. '*Compassion*' proved that *Benevolence* was natural to humanity. Tragedy moved witnesses to compassion with the sufferer, Hutcheson noted. Furthermore, real tragedy moves us to assist the sufferers and thus 'indulge our compassion'. People were hurried 'by a *natural, kind instinct*, to see Objects of *Compassion*, and expose themselves to this Pain when they can give no reason for it; as in the instance of *publick Executions*'. Accordingly, 'this same principle' led men to '*Tragedys*'. The urge to compassion, combined with the '*moral Qualitys*' of the sufferers, drew men to tales of pathos.[453]

The emotion and the beauty of representations were based, in Hutcheson's estimate, on the Moral Sense. 'But as the Contemplation of *moral Objects*, either of *Vice* or *Virtue*, affects us more strongly, and moves our Passions in a quite different and more powerful manner, than *natural Beauty*, or (what we commonly call) *Deformity*; so the most moving Beautys bear a relation to our *moral Sense*.' '*Epic or dramatic*' poetry and other powerful narratives were much more effective in both providing pleasure and 'recommending virtue'. Poetry 'will make us admire the *Good* and detest the *Vitious,* the *Inhuman,* the *Treacherous* and *Cruel,* by means of our *moral Sense* ...'.[454]

Adam Smith clearly articulated the same kind of didactic message in his *Theory of Moral Sentiments.* For Smith the 'impartial spectator' held the key to the system. As discussed above, Smith argued that sympathy derived from the spectator's ability to enter into the physical sufferer's predicament *vis-à-vis* the imagination. It was not, as is often surmised, the ability of the spectator to imagine the sufferer's predicament his own – the impartial spectator imagined himself as the other. Indeed it required a powerful act of the imagination to evoke this theatrical transference between the spectator and the sufferer. The impetus for this effort arose from the sufferer, but the 'mutual "concord" of the emotions or sentiments, "mutual sympathy," [was] pleasurable to both actor and spectator'. It was 'natural' and pleasurable to seek sympathy with others.[455] Human beings reaped pleasure from others' pain and suffering through the 'pleasure of mutual sympathy'.[456]

Smith's spectatorial vision of morality, like Shaftesbury and Hutcheson's, also succumbed to the lure of the theatre and novels. Love stories, in Smith's estimate, stirred the most powerful human emotions – and disappointed love stirred them most. 'The happy passion, upon this account [the love story], interests us much less than the fearful and the melancholy. We tremble for whatever can disappoint such natural and agreeable hopes', Smith declared, 'and thus enter into all the anxiety, and concern, and distress of the lover'. This was especially true if the lover disappointed or deceived was a woman. 'The reserve which the laws of society impose upon the fair sex, with regard to this weakness, renders it more peculiarly distressful in them ... her fear, her shame, her remorse, her horror, her despair, become thereby more natural and interesting.'[457] Perhaps the clearest articulation of these ideas, however, came from Dugald Stewart. Stewart is often described as a Common Sense philosopher. He was, however, an eclectic thinker and synthesizer – he borrowed widely and was very catholic in his intellectual tastes.[458] Overall, he did point to his teacher Thomas Reid for important ideas. Still, his dismissal of *tabula rasa* and his embrace of emotions and the imagination suggest that he was closer to the Scottish Moral Sense thinkers and his biographical subject, Adam Smith, than many scholars have supposed.[459]

In the *Elements of the Philosophy of the Human Mind,* Stewart noted the superiority of fiction to reality in producing effect. In a section on '*the Influence of Imagination on Human Character and Happiness*', he noted that 'what we commonly call sensibility depends in great measure, on the power of the imagination'. A scene of common distress, he argued, will affect two people very differently. One stunted in imagination will feel only that which 'he perceives by his senses'. The other of more developed imagination follows the unfortunate soul to his 'dwelling and partakes with him and his family in their domestic distresses. He listens to their conversation, while they recall to remembrance the flattering prospects which once they indulged; the circle of friends they had been forced to leave; the liberal plans of education which were begun and interrupted; and pictures out to himself all the various resources which delicacy and pride suggest, to conceal poverty from the world.' Thus when he wept it was not from what he saw, but from what he painted in his mind's eye. It was the 'warmth of his imagination' that increased and prolonged his sensibility.

A fine example of this phenomenon, Stewart noted, came from Laurence Sterne's *Sentimental Journey* in which the main character, 'engaged in a train of reflections' on prisons in France, 'indulges his imagination, and looks through the twilight of the grated door to take the picture [of the suffering of the prisoner]'. Quoting at length from Sterne's book, Stewart presented the imagined scenario (of an imagined scenario) as an example of the superiority of novels or 'exhibitions of fictitious distress' in their effect on some people otherwise unaffected by real distress. The novel more completely filled in 'every circumstance upon which the distress turns ... [and] the sentiments and feelings of every character with respect to his situation'.[460]

In his *Outlines of Moral Philosophy*, a distinctly clear exposition of Stewart's Moral Sense origins, he stated more clearly his ideas on the impact and/or role of theatre and novels. Stewart, like Hutcheson, Smith and Shaftesbury, argued that the 'exercise of all our kind affections is accompanied with an agreeable feeling or emotion. So much indeed of our happiness is derived from this source', he concluded, 'that those authors, whose object is to furnish amusement to the mind, avail themselves of these affections as one of the chief vehicles of pleasure'. This was, Stewart argued, the appeal of tragedy and other forms of 'pathetic composition'. Indeed, the powerful emotional resonance of these compositions eclipsed reality. 'How far it is of use', Stewart concluded, 'to separate in this manner "the luxury of pity" from the opportunities of actual exertion, may perhaps be doubted'.[461]

Americans in the Early Republic understood and appreciated the 'luxury of pity' and the social and entertainment power of benevolence and sympathy. The Scottish Moral Sense thinkers were, of course, widely read in Boston and elsewhere. Their ideas and variations upon them were central to the 'new' 'public sphere' culture of magazines and novels familiar to Americans, especially in seaboard cities like Boston.[462] Circulating libraries and thinly capitalized journals promoted a popular culture of sentiment mixed with moral philosophy.[463]

The Pleasures of Melancholy

Harriet Otis, for example, the twenty-four-year-old daughter of Massachusetts Senator Harrison Gray Otis, specifically called up the ideas of Dugald Stewart to understand the tragic events of the Richmond Theatre fire. Sitting in her father's Washington parlour, she reflected on the day's events: 'Papa came home at noon with the sad intelligence of the devastation of the Richmond Theatre by fire, in which many noted and interesting people perished'. One of these 'noted and interesting people' was a recent acquaintance and Harriet 'felt a sensation of horror at hearing he was no more'. Meditating 'at sunset upon sweet Venus just sinking into the west', she put these thoughts behind her and read Millot ('a charming historian, admirably translated') into the evening. Later, with her 'dear father, mother and sister', she 'sat over the coals discussing the beauties of Dr. Young and lost, for the time, in ... tranquil domestic comforts the sad recollections of the anguish which was rending the hearts of the whole city'. Upon reflection, however, she felt guilty: 'Was this selfishness and insensibility? It was human nature most certainly – I dare not defend it, nor am I much disposed to condemn it as unfeeling. I must adopt Professor Stewart's opinion that what we denominate as feeling and unfeeling often depends upon the power of the imagination in representing scenes of distress in vivid colors to the mind – we on this occasion suffered our fancy to sleep while gratitude and cheerfulness woke to the numberless blessings around us.'[464] The imagination safely asleep, vivid thoughts of distress were out of mind, feelings of sympathy abandoned the heart, and the Otis family enjoyed other forms of domestic bliss.

The idea that the imagination was central to the sentiment of benevolence or sympathy was often a *de facto* assumption of many 'sentimental fragments' in American journals. These fragments and short stories deliberately invoked the spectatorial perspective that dominated Scottish Moral Sense to evoke scenes of pathos, as the 'spectator' imagined the suffering of others. 'To visit the abodes of wretchedness, to enter into the feelings of the unfortunate, to sympathize with their sorrows, and to relive their distresses, are actions truly elevated and ennobling', the pseudonymous 'Benevolus' declared. 'Benevolence, the source of these actions, is that godlike affection, which exalts its proprietors, above the rest of mankind both in dignity and happiness.' It was through the acts of benevolence that men might 'imitate the actions of the deity' who created humanity as a benevolent gesture. Furthermore, benevolence was the source of happiness. 'The exercise of benevolence', 'Benevolus' concluded, 'is a positive enjoyment which may justly be stiled happiness.'[465] It was also very clearly an imaginative act – the spectator did not merely observe and/or alleviate the sufferers' condition, following Smith and Stewart, he 'entered into their feelings and sympathized with their sorrows'.

Often tracts on benevolence, encouraging the practice and extolling its virtues, played a dual role – praising benevolence and providing warm examples for the reader's pleasure. Indeed, it was their 'work' to evoke pleasure through pathos. 'To drop a tear over the manes of virtue; to wait with trembling anxiety around the bed of sickness; is the lot of sympathetic benevolence, and divine humanity', declared the 'Investigator'. Benevolence and 'its sister, humanity' were indeed subjects approximate to religion – 'the noblest companions of the soul and the brightest ornaments of character; teaching man to feel for man, pointing out the duties necessary for society and fellowship and guiding the arm of strength to the support of weakness'. It brought succour to the needy, and pleasure to the 'proprietor' of feeling – as well as the third-party spectator (the reader). 'When life's lamp glimmers, and the rosy cheek turns to a ghastly pale', 'Investigator' concluded, 'to behold a companion with anxious trembling hand, watching each change of pulse, feeling almost alike with us the increasing malady, is a sight grateful to the soul, and sacred to sympathetic benevolence and divine humanity'.[466] The 'Investigator' then continued his or her fragment with the brief pastoral tale of Eliza, the shepherdess. The shepherdess theme was a sentimental pastoral trope often repeated in American and British journalism of the period.[467] So familiar were the tropes of sentiment that when the 'Investigator' related the story of the death of the 'shepherdess', he felt no need to develop any of the events. He introduced the characters, described her forlorn parents dead at the shock of her passing, hinted to the romantic circumstances of her demise, and declared the feat accomplished. 'But – I would that ye had not tears, then I would proceed: yet having tears, which mark you as the children of benevolence and humanity, I desist from relating the catastrophe.'[468] The work of this story, 'Investigator' surmised, was simply to evoke emotion.

The idea that benevolence and sympathy were both acts of the imagination and products of spectatorial consumption spoke directly to the power of the theatre, novels and fictional fragments in magazines. It was, however, a convoluted nest of spectators peering in on the unfortunate when the reader watched the watcher watch the benevolence of a fourth party (not to mention the modern historian peering in on them all). Such was the scenario anonymously described in the *Massachusetts Magazine* of April 1795. 'If I have any knowledge of you', said the friend as he beckoned his companion to the window, 'you will be as much delighted within these few minutes, as you ever were in your whole life'. What was this vision of delight? 'A young lady of an elegant figure' who several times a day punctually assisted her invalid brother into their carriage. 'This little melancholy scene of affection, said my friend [and in turn, the anonymous writer related to the reader] is acted here three or four times a day; and such a fine melancholy pleasure does it bestow upon my heart, that I sometimes postpone my ride for an hour, lest I should not enjoy it.' 'He was in the right – he knew me well!' the second spectator to the pathetic scene rejoiced. 'I never was more delighted in my life', claimed the connoisseur of pity. The next day as he passed by their lodgings he peered again through their open window. The invalid brother rested his head on her bosom while she held his handkerchief and supported his 'frame'. 'Oh! Thought I, what a fine discipline is this business, as I have seen it performed, to prepare the sister for the wife – This school of fond attention, where every amiable feeling of the mind is in continual exercise; where affection keeps her vigils, and with a vestal patience and piety watches over the flame of expiring life.'[469]

Given the rest of his story this connoisseur knew well his subject. In a mere few pages the writer plumbed the depths of his spectatorial imagination – dwelling on recent tragedies and other pathetic scenes. Indeed, first imagining his own death, and second his imagined lover's imagined passing, he savoured the moments of 'possible' emotional ecstasy: 'And when, with a pale face and streaming eyes, with an air of desolation and a look of inexpressive tenderness and anguish, she shall strive in vain – how shall I be able to wave my hand as a signal to bid her depart; and not arrest my thoughts in their passage to heaven! ... Or, if it is decreed by the great Arbiter of humane allotments that I should survive thee: how, Amanda, shall I support those fearful moments ....' And so on – delighting in the consumption of imagined and heightened emotional distress.[470] Here again, as in the excerpt from Sterne quoted by Stewart, the reader stands in as an impartial spectator, peering in on the feverish imagination of the subject – as constructed in the feverish imagination of the author.

In this and other tracts, the message was similar.[471] Benevolence was a 'virtue exceedingly beneficial and necessary to society'.[472] At the same time, it provided the benefactor and in turn the spectator 'moments of exquisite pleasure'.[473] Indeed, it was a connoisseur who knew best how pity stimulated the heart. 'What can afford more refined enjoyment, than to walk by the side of an unhappy friend, in the cooling shade, and hear him repeat the history of his misfortunes, count over the number of his troubles, and kindly drop a tear of pity and condolence when his heart bleeds?' The 'balm of pity, kindly emitted from a sympathizing heart' soothed the sufferer and provided refined pleasure to the benefactor and the 'spectator'.[474]

American critics speculated on the source of the 'pleasure that we derive from witnessing scenes of distress both in real life and in fiction'. H. Holley, in an essay for the *North American Review*, aptly titled '*On the Pleasure Derived from Witnessing Scenes of Distress*', synthesized numerous ideas into a multi-causal explanation. Pleasure from witnessing distress derived 'from sympathy, from curiosity, from the love of novelty, from our attachment to strong emotions and excitements, from the valuable and practical end which our interest in the distress of others promotes, from the development of our faculties and the formation of character, from mental exercise generally, from a sense of injustice and retribution, from the ideas of a probation in order to deserve future reward, from invention and skill in the productions of genius, and from the social and generous nature of our passions'. Of these sympathy and curiosity furnished a 'large part' of the pleasure derived from scenes of distress. Curiosity drove men to take an interest in others and vice versa. Ultimately, however, sympathy allowed humanity to be 'affected by the affection of another'. Furthermore, it was a general 'law of nature' that whatever excited sympathy generated pleasure.[475]

Writing in the *Monthly Anthology and Boston Review*, the 'Remarker' readily agreed. Men exercised a 'deliberate choice in the favour of pity'; they solicited 'objects and representations with a view to be moved, and demand that their hearts shall be filled with palpitations and their eyes with tears ...'. Clearly there was a 'real attractiveness in sympathetick grief'. But where did these feelings come from? Pity, sympathy and compassion, the Remarker explained, moved the 'emotions or passions', including the 'mildest of these affections' – love – and diffused a 'pleasurable tranquility over the mind'. The 'narrative of the historian, the tale of the novelist, a picture, a poem, a drama, or a theatrical representation' stirred these natural feelings of sympathy, or *'sympathetick curiosity'*. These 'works of art', created by the imagination, display 'our fellow human beings in situations of trial and distress, or accentuated by painful passions' that awaken and 'enchain our attention'.[476]

Certainly, there were critics of this sort of consumption. 'There is a sort of bounty which arrogates to itself the name of *feeling*, and rejects with disdain the influence of a higher principle', claimed an anonymous author. This was not, the author frankly declared, an indictment of the 'humane and exquisitely tender sentiment, which the benevolent author of our nature gave us as a stimulus to remove the distresses of others, in order to get rid of our own easiness'. Instead, it was a reminder that distress was 'no less real [when] it did not obtrude upon the sight and awaken the tenderness of immediate sympathy'.[477]

Contemporaries loudly acclaimed the work of sympathy. As noted above, this often did not signify actual acts of benevolence but also took in the consumption of such acts and, more often, the consumption of fictional representations of such acts (and even, as in the case of the invalid brother, the consumption of fictional representations of the consumption of benevolent acts). Contemporaries understood that sympathy and sentiment played a part in creating a community of feeling that might reorganize relationships between people on a basis different and opposed to the hierarchies of the early modern order. At the same time, however, many were genuinely concerned with these ideas, the medium in which this new sympathy was expressed and, concurrently, the nature of these expressions.[478] Were sentimental representations of virtue 'true'? Were the emotions shed by young men and women reading romantic novels 'real' or did the imagination dupe and seduce them into vice? Sentimental narratives and novels in particular expressed the crisis in epistemology discussed above in terms of economic and spiritual value. Sentimental narratives, and especially novels, critics claimed, were 'true' as they mirrored nature; they were 'fictitious' insofar as they reflected the private system of the imagination. Again, the conflict was between objectively knowable standards and the perceived or suspected chaos of subjectivity and the imagination.[479]

The Impression of Examples

'Perhaps no class of writings have more effect upon the morals of the age than novels', declared the anonymous reviewer of *Self-Control*, 'and it is unfit that these powerful agents should be arrogantly employed by any one, who has invention or imitative power to plan a story, and words enough to make sentences'. Some modern writers, the reviewer argued, created 'pleasing' characters 'in acts of extravagance, rashness or folly' – they pictured them in love, so obsessed with their emotions that they 'neglect all duty, destroy all common feeling and propel to what is criminal'. These authors 'confused our idea of virtue and destroyed the definiteness of the boundaries between right and wrong'.[480] Fortunately, *Self-Control*, as the title suggested, was not one these narratives. 'We cannot but approve the intention of the author to recommend habits of self-government', the reviewer concluded, 'for we wish that it should be believed that it is our duty to direct and not be guided by our feelings'.[481]

Levi Frisbie agreed heartily. In his Inaugural Lecture as Alford Professor of Natural Religion at Harvard he touched upon the practical influence of moral philosophy. Some of the 'means' of disseminating this practical influence were 'those compositions in poetry and prose, which constitute the literature of nation, the essay, the drama, the novel ...'. These, 'it cannot be doubted, [had] a more extensive and powerful operation upon the moral feelings and character of the age'. Fiction operated directly on the heart – especially the story of the hero driven by 'feelings and sentiments'; here the 'magick of fiction and poetry [was] complete'. And herein lay the danger for Frisbie. Authors inattentive of their power crafted deep associations in the mind of the reader. 'Thus the powers of fancy and of taste blend associations in the mind, which disguise the original nature of moral qualities.'[482]

For the pseudonymous 'Corneille', novels and novel reading were pernicious. They 'impaired the understanding and rendered the mind incapable of receiving the solid truths of nature'. The novel created fantasies and took the mind 'to an aerial world, there to frolick amid imaginary beings – "Giving to airy nothing, / A habitation and a name!"'. This 'bubble' of unreality, however, 'the being of a moment', soon burst and left the 'over-heated brain, totally incapable of mentally appreciating the rational enjoyments of "real life"'. How different was the study of history, 'Corneille' exclaimed. Though the study of history was at first 'irksome and prolix to the lover of romances, yet the mind will soon yield to the pleasure it affords: the intellect will rapidly strengthen and the love for works of *"sterling worth"* soon become paramount to the present unpropitious desire for mere delusive fiction'. The study of history, 'Corneille' concluded, would polish the intellect, bring forth 'the brilliant flashes of some sparkling genius, unpolluted with the fictitious wit of the novelist', and make 'TRUTH' fashionable, and 'SINCERITY' pleasing.[483]

The 'Gossip' concurred with the extraordinary power of novels, but again condemned their pernicious excesses. These 'works of the imagination commonly called *Novels*' confused and weakened the understanding – especially for young people with their 'ardent imaginations'. There were of course, good novels, 'Gossip' acquiesced. These represented 'human nature as it is'. 'The first beauty

of works of fancy', 'Gossip' concluded, 'is to keep as near the truth as possible'.[484]
Representations were not the problem, it was the over-active imagination which
created fictitious and pernicious scenarios.

Others pointed to the alleged pernicious consequences of 'Modern novels and
their effects'. 'Every town and village affords some instance of a ruined female,
who has fallen from the heights of purity to the lowest grade of human misery',
'Leander' noted. 'Pernicious' novels corrupted the youth with their emphasis on
emotion and love. Ironically, the author of this denunciation felt obliged to print
an example of these pernicious stories alongside his diatribe – a romantic fragment by 'Sighing Friend' – lest the reader not be familiar with the genre! 'Poor
Eliza!' was pursued by the 'beautiful M—' – 'ye Gods what an air!' she exclaimed.
'He talked of disinterested love – was ever man's words attended with such rapture!' she sighed. Later that evening he appeared at the door: 'I descended with
care and haste, and soon saw sufficient to convince me (though it was dark) that
he was irresistible, and would to heaven, I had been as impregnable – the sofa
stood near by – he told me a thousand tender things – "On his fair lips such
pleasing accents hung, that while he spoke, I thought an angel sung"'.[485] But we
never reach the end of the story. 'Sighing Friend' sighed off and left 'Leander' to
condemn novels written 'with an intent to capture the feelings' and lead women
to 'vice'.[486]

These critics focused on the power of novels to imagine new worlds and thus
destroy the moral fibre of the 'real' world. The subjective imagination, a world of
private systems, thus undermined the 'real' social order. But not all critics condemned the power of novels or saw them leading women to vice and infamy.
Indeed Anglo-Americans acclaimed novels' power precisely because they were
direct routes to the heart – precisely because they 'captured the feelings'. These
writers concurred that it was the very power of the novel to engage the imagination and feelings that gave them their truth-value. Put another way, the subjective
imagination was the source of truth.

The 'student of science', 'F.' noted, trusts his senses and not abstract results.
Likewise the philosopher rested his ideas upon observation, rather than the 'theories and errors' of the ages. In the same manner, novels and other fictions brought
moral truth to life – 'one real act of benevolence, one living instance of patriotic
self-devotion will kindle a vital fire, burning not merely within the heart, but
instantly revealing itself in glorious sympathetic actions'. Men did not act upon
abstract principles or ideas but upon practical results – illustrated by example.
Deep inside humanity – in part of the 'original constitution of man' he was sus-
ceptible to the '*impression* of examples'.

This was the 'immense moral power' of the novel, 'F.' argued. The novel's
practical example, joined with the 'distinct influence of the imagination, and the
uncounted sympathy' acted as a powerful force to virtue. 'We must confess', 'F.'

concluded, 'that the novel is, or may be, among the mightiest instruments for swaying the heart and guiding the lives of men'.[487]

Novels, argued 'TD', 'broke up the cold and debasing selfishness with which the souls of so large a portion of mankind are encrusted'. They exposed a 'vast class' to unknown emotional experiences – 'an interest in things outside themselves, and a perception of grandeur and beauty, of which otherwise they might have ever lived unconscious'. However, 'TD' saw real sympathy and pity as superior to the imitation – to be moved to tears at all was better than not. As such, novels were the 'teachers with the widest range'. They taught humanity the most essential lesson – sympathy. In this respect, 'excellent romances' worked best. They taught the reader how to 'feel tenderly and deeply for things in which he has no personal interest'.[488]

The idea that the unrealistic nature of romances worked against their moral effect was mistaken, 'TD' argued. The heightened imagined sentiments and/or feelings of romance had some basis in human experience. Furthermore, 'All the softenings of evil to the moral vision by the gentleness of fancy are proofs that evil itself shall perish'. Descriptions of virtue and noble acts 'expanded the imagination and made hearts gush with delight'. They led men to rediscover their feelings and 'awaken their sympathies'. Put briefly, novels improved humanity by speaking to the heart and warming their emotions.[489]

'R' too defended the 'unrealistic' nature of novels, and thus the power of subjectivity and the imagination against those 'authors who recommend an observance of nature, as the standard of propriety in all compositions'. 'No author', 'R' began, ever stayed close to nature. Stories bore no interest if they did not deviate from the norm in some manner. Citing a long list of 'classical' examples of this deviation, 'R' strove to explain the source of taste in literature. Taste, 'R' concluded, did not derive from that 'indefinable phrase, nature'. 'The truth is', he went on, 'that between the grossness of vulgar life and a perfectability unattainable by mortals, there is a sort of fairy ground, or what may well be denominated a middle nature. It is an imaginary existence, found in the heads of our poets or our painters, chiefly, in which mankind are sublimated from the feculences of earth, and still not perfect enough to be candidates for heaven. In this visionary world events are at the disposal of the Power which created it and that is the fancy.' Taste referred to this 'delicate and judicious combination of fancy and fact'. A man without fancy (imagination) was a man without taste – and could never enjoy a painting or a novel that strayed beyond the world of fact. The fancy was the great source of power for novels and other representations and a great source of moral virtue.[490] Novels were true lies.

Thus novels through their representations of distress and suffering kindled the imagination and feelings of the spectator, generating pleasure and sympathy. At the same time, however, the new subjectivity they engendered undermined and replaced objectively knowable standards ('true to nature') perceived as central to social cohesion, with social bonds based on the imagination. Increasingly in the 1810s and 1820s, and very clearly by the 1830s, these ideas on the imagination dominated Early Republic culture.[491]

A second powerful expression of the tension between truth and the imagination is explicit in the title and structure of many novels. Repeatedly early American novels insisted on their authenticity. No less than seventeen of fifty-seven novels published in the United States between 1789 and 1811 include a claim of truth in their title ('Founded on Truth', 'Founded on Incidents in Real Life', 'a Tale of Truth', 'Founded on Recent Facts' and variations thereupon) and/or are structured in epistolary format – as a series of truthful 'letters'.[492] Furthermore, hundreds of stories printed in the magazines as 'novels' were presented as 'A True Tale', 'A Story Founded on Truth', and so on.[493] These claims speak to the perceived need of the authors to present their material as non-fiction, untainted by the imagination. This too continued British phenomena. Daniel Defoe, arguably the first novelist, in his preface to *Moll Flanders* had his 'imagined' editor speak to the truth crisis implicit in novel writing. 'The World is so taken up of late with Novels and Romances', Defoe complained, 'that it will be hard for a private history to be taken of genuine'.[494]

The most famous early American novel, *Charlotte, A Tale of Truth* (1794), had its truth claims further validated by a fake headstone for Charlotte Temple in New York City's Trinity Churchyard, not far from the less popular and less visited Alexander Hamilton. Adoring fans visited the site and left tokens of their affection for the imagined victim of a Revolutionary rake late into the nineteenth century. Susanna Rowson insisted throughout her life that Charlotte Temple was real.[495] In the 1870s, Caroline Dall established a second imaginary provenance for the still-popular fictional character, and the character of a second novel, Eliza Wharton.[496] Hannah Foster's *The Coquette; or The History of Eliza Wharton* (1797) was also surrounded with intrigue with regard to the story's origins and veracity. Readers commonly attributed her story to the 'real-life' death of Elizabeth Whitman in a Massachusetts boarding house.[497] *The Coquette* is presented as a true story and is also structured as an epistolary novel. It is a series of letters between the tragic character seduced by a rake and her friends and lovers. This format, used in a number of early American novels and magazine stories, was by no means exclusive to these productions. No less a figure than Shaftesbury carefully planned and structured his philosophical treatises as letters to a patron, or as dialogues between friends, painfully aware that his audience desired 'truthful' narratives. For Shaftesbury this served two roles. First, it added veracity to the text. Second, it made the audience invisible to themselves and added to the spectatorial nature of their reading.[498]

Shaftesbury constructed many of his works in epistolary fashion with the aim to vanish the reader. The narrative does not address the reader and subsequently the reader, in this genre, is not there as an audience. He or she is an impartial spectator, peering in, unbeknownst to the principals, on the unfolding private scenario. In Shaftesbury's case, the scenario was the unfolding of a number of philosophical ideas. In Hannah Foster's case, the scenario was the tragic death of a young seduced woman. Both narratives partake of the reader's spectatorial position to affirm the truth-value of their narratives, and to appeal to the disinterested benevolence and/or sympathy implicit in the reader's spectatorial impartiality.

Although this was particularly obvious in the epistolary narrative, it was also implicit in the 'novel' as a genre. The whole structure of the novel, with its emphasis on everyday events, replicated the spectatorial emphasis found in all Moral Sense philosophy, but particularly in Shaftesbury and Smith.[499] In many ways, the 'spectator' is the embodiment of sympathy, and is central to understanding how the 'law' is writ upon the heart. This was, in part, the work of the novel – it both encouraged and was shaped by, the 'doubling' of self implicit in the 'Spectator'. The Spectator was for Americans in the Early Republic a form of conscience; it represented the internalization of social approbation. In their mind's eye Americans (and Britons) saw themselves in a perpetual social mirror that reflected the approval or disapproval of their peers. This was a central tenet of the new commercial and sociable society, based on a political economy of paper credit, and a religious moral system based on the heart.

An Imaginary Friend

Expressions of this spectatorial perspective began with Joseph Addison. His 'Spectator' was a fabricated character, a man everywhere in town, but known only to a few friends. The 'Spectator' thrust his head into Will's Coffee-House and listened to the politicians; he smoked his pipe at Child's Coffee-House and, while he 'seemed attentive to nothing but the *Post-Man*', listened in on every table in the room; he attended St James's Coffee-House to 'hear and improve'; in short, he was known at all the coffee-houses and theatres; he was even 'taken for a Merchant upon the *Exchange* for ten years now' and sometimes 'passed for a *Jew* in the Assembly of Stock-Jobbers at Jonathan's'. He was, in other words, everywhere but nowhere – invisible to all through a consistent presence and silence – he never opened his 'Lips but in my own Club' (the society of fictional friends Addison created). 'Thus', the 'Spectator' famously concluded, 'I live in the world, rather as a Spectator of Mankind, than as one of the species'.[500]

Shaftesbury, writing at around the same time as Addison, continued this spectatorial theme with an aesthetic version of moral approbation discussed at length in Chapter 2. Moral approbation was, for Shaftesbury, an aesthetic idea, qualified as 'beauty'. He also contributed directly to the Smith's impartial spectator, the culminating author in this tradition.

In his 'Advice to an Author', Shaftesbury pondered the paradox of advice. The popular maxim that 'as to what related to private Conduct, *No one was ever the better for* Advice', Shaftesbury postulated, was essentially correct for most kinds of advice. Free advice especially usually benefited the giver not the taker – it was an exhibition of wisdom at the expense of the recipient. Thus Shaftesbury was particularly reluctant to engage in advice-giving, even as he began his 'Advice to an Author' essay. His solution was to advise 'Self-Surgery' as a way to seek counsel. Speaking as an incredulous reader, Shaftesbury mocked the project: 'Who can thus multiply himself into *two Persons*, and be *his own subject?*' – 'Nothing is more common', Shaftesbury retorted to his own double, 'go to the poets ... Nothing is more common with them, than this sort of SOLILOQUY.'[501] What Shaftesbury suggested was that the self, to gain inner knowledge – and to know itself – had to speak to itself – or '*Self-Converse*'. 'Tis the hardest thing in the world to be a *good Thinker*', he concluded, 'without being a strong *Self-Examiner*, and *thorow-pac'd Dialogist*, in this solitary way'.[502]

To what end, however, did Shaftesbury advise this process? Turning to the issue of 'Morals' Shaftesbury recalled that the Ancients ascribed a '*Damon, Genius, Angel*, or *Guardian Spirit*' to every human. Were this 'literally true', Shaftesbury postulated, it would be 'highly serviceable'. No one would shun 'so Divine *a Guest*' – no one would deny the service of this '*Adviser*' or '*Guide*'. But, he continued, it is only a figure of speech. The Ancients meant no more than that 'we had each of us a Patient in *our-self*; that we were properly our own Subjects of Practice; and that we then become due Practitioners, when by Virtue of an intimate *Recess* we cou'd discover a certain *Duplicity* of Soul, and divide our-selves into *two Partys*'. To the extent that human beings were successful in this venture, Shaftesbury concluded, they advanced in 'Morals and True Wisdom'. Only through the '*vocal* Looking-Glass' of soliloquy – by 'Divid[ing] Your-Self' and 'Be[coming] Two', could inner peace and self-knowledge be achieved. Furthermore, to the extent that humans achieved inner peace and self-knowledge, they attained moral wisdom.[503] Thus for Shaftesbury, self-division and introspection were central to the moral life – they wrote moral law in the breast of man.

Both Hutcheson and Hume, who in their works mention a spectator or impartial spectator in the context of moral approbation, furthered the spectatorial perspective. No one, however, took the system as a far as Adam Smith. As discussed in Chapter 2, Smith's impartial spectator was central to his idea of sympathy. Human beings created new social bonds *vis-à-vis* an imaginative transference of place. Smith also pursued the impartial spectator idea in terms of self-approval, or conscience.

In the third part of his *Theory of Moral Sentiments*, 'Of the Foundation of our judgments concerning our own sentiments and conduct, and of the sense of duty', Smith explored the idea of conscience. The moral approbation of others, Smith argued, was not enough to bestow 'satisfaction'. 'If we are conscious that we do not deserve to be so favorably thought of', Smith maintained, 'and that, if the truth was known, we should be regarded with very opposite sentiments, our satisfaction is far from complete'. Instances of this sort, when the outward approval of the individual did not match his worth, Smith argued, were properly defined as vanity. The 'foolish liar' or 'coxcomb' who deceives the audience into praise indeed sees himself through their eyes, Smith concluded, but this 'superficial weakness and trivial folly hinder them from ever turning their eyes inwards, or from seeing themselves in that despicable point of view in which their own consciences should tell them that they would appear to every body, if the real truth should ever come to be known'.[504] Quite the opposite, Smith argued, we are satisfied with our actions even if they are unknown to others through the process of imagining their approbation were they 'better informed':

> The man who is conscious to himself that he has exactly observed those measures of conduct which experience informs him are generally agreeable, reflects with satisfaction on the propriety of his own behavior; when he views it in the light in which the impartial spectator would view it, he thoroughly enters into all the motives which influenced it; he looks back upon every part of it with pleasure and approbation, and tho' mankind should never be acquainted with what he has done, he regards himself not so much according to the light in which they actually regard him, as according to that, in which they would regard him were they better informed.

Likewise, Smith continued, 'detestable' criminals whose crimes were never even suspected suddenly confessed and faced execution in order to appease their conscience and secure some of the moral approbation of their fellows. What were the origins of these feelings, Smith queried? For Smith, the conscience was the impartial spectator in the breast of mankind – reflecting the eyes of society on the self and its actions. 'We examine [our conduct] as we imagine an impartial spectator would examine it.' Individuals, according to Smith, approved or disapproved of their own conduct 'by sympathy with the approbation of this supposed equitable judge'.[505] Smith's vision of morality and conscience was thus wedded to a vision of humanity in society. A human being alone on an island would be insensible to right and wrong, beauty and deformity. Our peace of mind depended on our ability to 'judge of ourselves as we judge others'. But 'in order to do this we must look at ourselves with the same eyes with which we look at others: we must imagine ourselves not the actors but the spectators of our character and conduct ...'[506]

This did not mean that God was out of the picture. Mankind was accountable to God in the long run. But in the everyday functioning of life an individual's beliefs and ideas were shaped in humanity – through the spectatorial perspective by which men judged others, were indeed judged by others and, in the final analysis, judged themselves. This was no easy task: 'He is a bold surgeon, they say, whose hand does not tremble when he performs an operation upon his own person', Smith conceded. Candidness and impartiality (Hutcheson called it disinterestedness) were the clues to this surgical exercise and were most difficult to engage.

Stewart, in his *Elements of the Philosophy of the Human Mind*, by and large agreed, though he found that an instinctive moral sense commanded the scheme. In his *Outline of Moral Philosophy*, however, he pointed to impartiality as the key to sympathy, and novels as proof of this spectatorial act of moral approbation. The 'emotions excited by characters exhibited in histories and novels, are sometimes still more powerful than what we experience from similar qualities displayed in the article of our own acquaintance'; Stewart declared, 'because the judgment is less likely to be warped by partiality or prejudice'.[507] To be disinterested or impartial heightened the power of sympathy.

The spectatorial perspective as outlined by the Scottish Moral Sense philosophers was thus crucial to sympathy and was enhanced by the reading of novels. It was also crucial to the knowledge of the self and the construction of conscience. The reading of novels was in effect a writing of the conscience; it was an act of self-narration and self-creation. Novels created an 'omniscient observer'.[508] 'Within fictional space-time – the ahistorical, out-of-time dimension of the reading process', Cathy Davidson concludes, 'there occurs a transubstantiation wherein the word becomes flesh, the text becomes the reader, the reader becomes the hero'.[509]

The impartial spectator and/or spectatorial perspective was implicit in the literature of sympathy discussed above. It was in the imagination that men envisioned the distress of others. It was in the imagination that men saw themselves through their peers' eyes, dispensing benevolence. The impartial spectator was also implicit in the self-narration found in diaries, journals and other narratives compiled mostly by young women during this period.[510] These narratives acted as a kind of impartial spectator or double for the practice of self-surgery. Eunice Callender filled her journal with her day-to-day observations in the language of the romantic novels that she spent too much time reading. Callender was familiar with the language of the 'sublime' – and she did not fail to use it in describing alewives from a fisherman's basket on the grass ('romantic'); moonbeams trembling over the water; a choir performance by young orphans ('the purest benevolence ... excited my compassion'); or a 'picturesque and romantic' walk on the beach. Listening to an address delivered to the Humane Society, she noted that she never was partial to this minister, but 'never did I hear such an energetic feeling address as this was, it was all passion and feeling'. She also 'feelingly' subscribed to the minister's sermon in the evening, who was a man of the 'most genuine sensibility'.[511]

Mehetable May Dawes likewise spent too much time on novels – and hoping that her 'romantic notions' might some time be realized. She addressed her journal to a friend who also kept a journal to eventually exchange. Nevertheless, she took the task as a project of self-exploration – quoting from the *Spectator* – she validated her journal as an exercise in self-knowledge: 'This kind of *self-examina-*

tion would give [the journal keeper] a true state of themselves, and incline them to consider seriously what they are about'.[512] For Dawes this seemed to work. Her plan for self-improvement included more and more reading – though often what she read did not seem to her educational. She protested her predilection to *The Coquette* – 'My head is filled with Eliza Wharton's adventures'. She even noted when it lay in her 'chamber' untouched for a day. She read *Ormond* in one sitting and was surprisingly familiar with Ossian – the faux-Celtic poet who inspired the German Romantics.[513] But what seemed to best suit her education was an inner dialogue. Worried about her frequent bouts with melancholy and 'fits', Dawes noted the relief she found in her 'invisible friend'. 'I have one comfort', she noted, 'I do think such fits are less frequent with me than they used to be – I believe I grow more reasonable – one cause is perhaps, because, I generally now at such time apply for comfort to an invisible friend'. Seemingly following Shaftesbury's advice, she concluded that 'people cannot live half so comfortably that are not in the habit of resorting to such an one on every occasion joyful or sorrowful – no other being can ever conceive of all our feelings as well as he that knows and searches the heart'.[514]

This sort of self-surgery was hardly particular to Dawes. Harriet Otis, though much more scholarly, was an avid journal keeper, and was also very aware of sentimental and 'sublime' narratives. She worried, however, about her need for 'mortification'. 'Christmas evg. Took myself to task', she entered in her journal. 'Ah why', she continued, 'does my mind need mortifications to make it reflect on itself without any mists of vanity and partiality to obstruct its vision?'[515] For Otis, impartiality was key to self-reflection, though she lamented the pathos that it seemed to require. As discussed above, she was familiar with the writing of Dugald Stewart and other moral philosophers and/or theorists of her day. She often used her journal to sound out her interpretations of their ideas. Elsewhere in the journal, however, she sounded much like a dramatic heroine of romantic fiction. Turning to record her thoughts after an evening of 'peaceful reflections' she suddenly grew sombre. 'Reperusing' an old 'dear little budget of notes which used to excite such lively sensations', she lamented her increasingly 'cold heart'. 'Earthly pleasures' had ceased to charm her – 'time has rent the flimsy veil, through which earthly delights seemed capable and worthy of causing [delight] – Imagination was that veil – realities now appear and I turn dissatisfied from them – my fate in this respect is not peculiar – all have experienced it – but peculiar is my ingratitude if with such innumerable causes of gratitude I suffer the spirit of repining to take place of youthful hope and ardor'.[516]

Otis's melancholy did not, however, last long. In July of 1817 she partook of an extended 'Journey Through Vermont'. Otis, according to her journal, spent much of the time gazing in rapture at the scenery. 'At Ringe [?] a pretty neat town we saw a prospect more sublime and extensive than any I have ever seen, a prospect extending as far as the eye can reach, terminated on every side in lofty mountains.'

But only a few days later, the vista left her speechless: 'How can I describe the rapturous admiration with which I caught the first glimpse of the Green Mts. Lifting their heads like dark clouds on the horizon'.

Otis shared the notions of the sublime and the picturesque found in popular theoretical texts. Tremendous prospects, ungraspable in their totality, were sublime. A winding road through the forest was enhanced by a 'rustic bridge thrown across' the river, which 'added to the picturesque effect of this sweet scene'. 'Picturesque' churches dotted the countryside. 'Picturesque' streams cut through 'sublime' rock cliffs.[517] Her lifting spirits confirm the observation of current poets and modern philosophers. Nature rejuvenated the modern bourgeois self – after a century of aesthetic and personality development, the idea of nature encompassed the providential order, sentiment and the imagination.

This world of sentiment and feelings accurately reflects the increased subjectivity that marked life during the Early Republic. Americans of this period thought and felt deeply about their emotions. They experienced religious worship in terms of the heart. They experienced moral feeling through the imagination. Sympathy was central to the construction of horizontal bonds between them. Sentiment was an integral part of the their new subjectivity – a subjectivity which, as Otis indicates, included new ideas on aesthetic value as well.

7 THE POLITICAL ECONOMY OF BEAUTY AND THE IMAGINATION

'Didn't I tell you so?' said Flask; 'yes you'll soon see this right whale's head hoisted opposite that parmacetti's.'

In good time, Flask's saying proved true. As before, the Pequod steeply leaned over towards the sperm whale's head, now, by the counterpoise of both heads, she regained her even keel; though sorely strained, you may well believe. So, when on one side you hoist in Locke's head, you go over that way; but now, on the other side, hoist in Kant's and you come back again; but in very poor plight.

Herman Melville, *Moby Dick*; quoted in M. H. Abrams, *The Mirror and the Lamp: Romantic Theory and the Critical Tradition* (Oxford: Oxford University Press, 1953), p. 47.

Questions about the nature of value were not confined to economic issues and morality. The erosion of empiricism or received value structures and the rise of subjectivity also affected aesthetic values. In this realm as well, the Scottish Moral Sense philosophers and Scottish Enlightenment thinkers contributed to an ongoing debate surrounding the nature of beauty and the related ideas of taste, the sublime and the picturesque.[518] There were almost as many angles to this lively eighteenth-century discourse as there were participants.[519] This chapter will, however, focus on one major point that seems to hold the key to this debate: the site and nature of beauty. Did beauty lie in the object, or in the subjective imagination of the artist and/or spectator? Or, put another way, was beauty intrinsic to objects and people, and thus a real value or external reality that could be defined, measured or otherwise categorized; or was it, *vis-à-vis* association, a function of the imagination? Again, the main conflict was between Lockean empiricism and moral sense humanism, transformed by Ahab's time into German idealism; or, as Herman Melville put it, the transition was from Locke to Kant, albeit, I will argue, through the Scots.[520]

This chapter argues that debates on the site and nature of beauty were the aesthetic counterparts of the debates on money and political economy. Anglo-American aesthetic theorists formulated a vision of beauty that increasingly relied on the internalization of value structures; on an epistemology of feelings opposed to empiricism.[521] Beauty was not, for these theorists, an empirically quantifiable quality. Furthermore, the basis for beauty was not the mimetic empiricism current in early eighteenth-century art and aesthetic theory. Instead, shapers and consumers of aesthetic objects and ideas perceived beauty as a function of the imagination.[522] The imagination, as Terry Eagleton argues, was 'the precious key releasing the empiricist subject from the prison-house of its perceptions'.[523] These changes bit deep into early modern culture and personality. A theocratic world objectively verifiable through the senses implied a fixed and shared social order. Human subjectivity threatened received and objectively verifiable value structures, and displaced the social order that 'reality' engendered.[524] Morally, the heart replaced the pulpit. Financially, paper, and the trust and confidence implied in paper-credit instruments, replaced silver. Aesthetically, the imagination displaced empirical reality. Objectively knowable standards of beauty disappeared as beauty found a new source in the self. This debate between intrinsic and nominal beauty, between empiricism and the imagination, often in the words of Continental and British thinkers, fascinated cosmopolitan aesthete Americans in the Early Republic – but also made its way into the larger population through poetry, novels and objects that derived their aesthetic value from an emotive epistemology.

Mimesis

The tension between the mimesis of the mirror and the expressionism of the lamp has classical roots. Aristotle espoused a mimetic theory of art. His *Poetics*, M. H. Abrams argues, 'maintains that the models and forms for artistic imitation are selected or abstracted from the objects of sense-perception'.[525] This was not, however, simply a superficial rendering of the object. Somehow, Aristotle maintained, the 'form' integral to the object in the physical world was recreated in the artistic work. Certainly, the work of art was a selective mirror. Nevertheless, all the 'forms' or 'qualities' that it reflected were 'inherent in the constitution of the external world'.[526]

The notion that art reflected a 'real' external world was familiar to Americans in the Early Republic. The March 1784 *Boston Magazine*, for example, published an excerpt from one of Joshua Reynolds's '*Academical Discourses*'. Reynolds, as both artist and theorist, was internationally influential. Early American painters such as Benjamin West, Gilbert Stuart and Washington Allston, all of whom at various points in their career read Reynolds's *Discourses* and/or corresponded with him, suffered in their efforts to adhere to his respected yet contradictory dictums.[527] Stuart, who painted Reynolds's portrait, eventually turned away from the master and may have even stooped to satire.[528] Nevertheless, as President of the Royal Academy, Reynolds held extraordinary influence on Anglo-American art and his *Discourses*, delivered from 1767 to 1790, mostly as addresses to the Royal Society, were tremendously influential.

The passage excerpted in the *Boston Magazine* was an essay on 'Genius and Taste' that criticized the 'inflated' language of some 'towering talkers' who Sir Joshua claimed, seemingly parodying the language of the sublime, 'were never warmed by that Promethean fire which animates the canvas and vivifies the marble'. Fully immersed in the continuing crisis of money in Britain, Reynolds compared contemporary aesthetic opinions to 'the current coin in its circulation, we are obliged to take it without weighing or examining'. As outlined in the *Boston Magazine* article, Sir Joshua's preference in art was definitely for the empirical – and thus for the 'true'. 'The natural appetite or taste for the human mind, is for truth', he declared.

> It is the very same taste that relishes a demonstration in geometry, that is pleased with the resemblance of a picture to an original, and touched with the harmony of music. All these have unalterable and fixed foundations in nature and are therefore equally investigated by reason, and known by study ... A picture that is unlike is false. Disproportionate ordinance of parts is not right because it cannot be true, until it ceases to be a contradiction to assert, that the parts have no relation to the whole. Colouring is true where it is naturally adapted to the eye, from brightness, from softness, from harmony, from resemblance, because they agree with their object NATURE, and are therefore true, as mathematical demonstration.[529]

Elsewhere Reynolds advocated a certain Neo-Platonism, but quickly couched it in empiricism.[530] He remarked that 'beauty exists only in the mind', yet still saw that beauty as firmly founded on earthly and material ideas.[531]

The Scottish Common Sense philosopher Thomas Reid buttressed this effort to maintain the seat of beauty in the object. As discussed above, Reid reacted to Hume's scepticism by constructing a counter, so-called Common Sense, philosophy. Borrowing from Hutcheson, Smith and others, Reid contradicted the epistemological confusion elicited by Hume's radical relativism with 'common sense' notions. Hume had questioned the human ability to know reality, and hence the existence of reality. If all knowledge comes either through the senses and/or is innate or instinctive, then there existed no objectively verifiable proof of reality. All of our evidence was subjective. Reid dismissed these speculations as sophistry. Men knew because they knew – God would not have so designed men's senses as to trick them.[532] In his *Essays on the Intellectual Powers of Man*, sections of which were excerpted in the *Massachusetts Magazine* of June 1790, he complained of the 'fashion among modern philosophers to resolve all our perceptions into mere feelings or sensations, in the person that perceives without anything corresponding to those feelings in the external object. According to those philosophers', Reid continued, 'there is no heat in the fire, no taste in a sapid body; the taste and the heat being only in the person that feels them. In like manner there is no beauty in any object whatsoever; it is only a sensation or feeling in the person that perceives it.' 'Beauty or deformity in an object', he concluded, 'results from its nature or structure. To perceive the beauty therefore we must perceive the nature or structure from which it results.'[533] Beauty was, for Reid, an external, received and empirically definable reality.

Numerous other commentators agreed. The *Encyclopedia or a Dictionary of Arts and Science*, published in Philadelphia in 1798, for example, broke beauty down into two 'kinds': intrinsic and relative. Intrinsic beauty was instantly recognized through an act of perception by the senses. Relative beauty required some 'understanding and reflection'; it was a function of utility. Utility beatified subjects void of intrinsic beauty. 'In a word, intrinsic beauty is ultimate; and relative beauty is that of means relating to some good end or purpose.' Both kinds of beauty were, however, located in the object.[534]

A competing aesthetic theory that located beauty not in the object but in the mind of the spectator and/or creator challenged beauty as an empirically and objectively verifiable idea. At first intimately associated with Neo-Platonic principles of harmony and a universal ideal, this notion of beauty evolved into the complete subjectivism of associationism.

Harmony

A competing theory of art and beauty based on a harmonious relationship between the inner self and universal ideals had equally established classical roots and ascended in the eighteenth century. Plato originally introduced what Abrams calls a 'Transcendental' theory of art. Objects of art derived from nature and the 'world of sense, but are ultimately trans-empirical, maintaining an independent existence in their own ideal space, and available only to the eye of the mind'.[535] Still Plato, like most classical thinkers, derided art as craft. It was his followers, Plotinus in particular, who 'elevated' art from craft and transformed mimesis into 'creation' and expression. Plotinus, Cicero and other Neo-Platonic thinkers maintained that the 'Idea' resides in the mind. True beauty 'is not available to the external senses, but only to thought and imagination'.[536]

Anthony Ashley Cooper, the third Earl of Shaftesbury, was the first of the eighteenth-century theorists to argue for an aestheticization of the social order; a harmony between aesthetic and moral principles based on universal ideals. Shaftesbury, as noted above, was one of the early Neo-Platonic thinkers. Neo-Platonic ideas maintained an *a priori* subject-oriented world where the *ideal* and the human were in alliance.[537] He clearly believed in absolute notions of wrong and right that he equated with beauty and deformity and harmony and dissonance. The mind, Shaftesbury argued, 'feels the Soft and Harsh, the Agreeable and Disagreeable, in the Affections; and finds a *Foul* and *Fair*, a *Harmonious* and a *Dissonant*, as really and truly here, as in any musical Numbers, or in the outward Forms or Representations of sensible Things. Nor can it with-hold its *Admiration* and *Exstasy*, its *Aversion* and *Scorn*, any more than to the other of these subjects. So that to deny the common and natural sense of a Sublime and Beautiful in things, will appear an Affectation merely, to any-one who considers duly of this affair.'[538] Still, for Shaftesbury, as Terry Eagleton agues, 'all moral action ... must be mediated through the affections and what is not done through affection is simply non-moral. Beauty, truth and goodness are ultimately at one: what is beautiful is harmonious, what is harmonious is true, and what is once true and beautiful is harmonious and good.'[539]

Francis Hutcheson followed Shaftesbury deep into these ideas. As noted above, Hutcheson saw his work as a defence of Shaftesbury against the doctrines of Bernard Mandeville's *Fable of the Bees*. Mandeville followed Hobbes and Locke in seeing human agency as hedonistic. A selfish mankind, emptied of benevolence, disgusted Hutcheson as it had Shaftesbury. It was an affront to the deity. Human beings were not only innately good; they also carried within them an affinity with the providential order, including the idea of 'beauty'.[540]

For Hutcheson, '*Beauty* is taken for *the idea rais'd in us*, and a *Sense* of Beauty for *our Power of receiving this Idea*'. Thus he clearly differentiated between the ideas of *beauty and harmony* and the 'Power of perceiving these Ideas'. Still, for Hutcheson, this perception depended upon an 'internal Sense' stimulated by objects. 'Objects are *immediately* the Occasions of this Pleasure of Beauty ... Yet there must be a *Sense* of Beauty, antecedent to Prospects even of this advantage', without which Sense, these Objects would not be thus *Advantageous* ....'[541] Furthermore, Hutcheson differentiated between two notions of beauty: '*Original* or *Comparative*; or, if any like the terms better, *Absolute*, or *Relative*'. By absolute he did not, however, mean that beauty was a quality in the object: 'Only let it be observ'd, that by *Absolute* or *Original* Beauty, is not understood any Quality suppos'd to be in the Object, which should of itself be beautiful, without relation to any Mind which perceives it: For Beauty, like other names of sensible Ideas, properly denotes the *Perception* of some Mind; so *Cold, Hot, Sweet, Bitter*, denote the Sensations in our Minds, to which perhaps there is no resemblance in the Objects which excite these Ideas in us, however, we generally imagine that there is something in the Object just like our Perception'.[542] Not only was beauty a function of the imagination, all other sensations existed only in the mind.[543]

Adam Smith also positioned beauty in the subject, albeit reluctantly. In his *Theory of Moral Sentiments*, after discussing for several pages the varieties of beauty in various parts of the world, Smith plaintively concluded that beauty was indeed relative, or a function of custom. 'Such is the system of this learned and ingenious father, concerning the nature of beauty'; he concluded, 'of which the whole charm, according to him, would thus seem to arise from its falling in with habits which custom had impressed upon the imagination ....'[544]

Shaftesbury, Hutcheson and Smith were important theorists in the development of an aesthetic based on harmony and the imagination. Nevertheless, their formulation of beauty still pointed to objectively knowable principles or standards; standards innate in humanity, but in harmony with a social and universal order. Even Smith's 'custom'-based beauty pointed to social consensus. A still more subjective idea of beauty developed alongside this theory and more forcefully highlighted the role of the imagination. In the Anglo-American world, Joseph Addison was, arguably, the first of the eighteenth-century aesthetic thinkers who highlighted the expressive imagination as the sole source of beauty.[545] This theory of art and beauty based on the 'desires, emotions and imagination' became dominant in the eighteenth century.

Imagination

For Addison, beauty was one of the pleasures of the imagination.[546] In a series of essays in the *Spectator* he introduced the idea to a large 'public sphere' coffee-house audience. The pleasures of the imagination were, for Addison, twofold. The primary pleasures of the imagination proceeded entirely 'from such Objects as are present to the Eye'. The secondary pleasures of the imagination 'flow from the ideas of visible objects, when the Objects are not actually before the Eye, but are called up into our Memories, or form'd into agreeable Visions of Things that are either Absent or Fictitious'.[547] Clearly the secondary pleasures were a form of whimsy – a fanciful construction existing primarily in the mind. Yet the primary pleasures of the imagination did not speak to qualities inherently beautiful or deformed in objects. 'There is not perhaps any real beauty or deformity more in one piece of matter than another', Addison argued, 'because we might have been so made, that whatsoever now appears loathsome to us, might have shown itself agreeable; but we find by Experience that there are several Modifications of Matter which the Mind, without any previous Consideration, pronounces at first sight beautiful or deformed'.[548]

Ultimately, for Addison, the ability of 'beautiful' objects to fill the imagination with pleasurable sensations was an integral part of God's design. It was a 'spell' that held our pleasurable existence in suspended animation. 'Things would make but a poor Appearance to the eye, if we saw them only in their proper figures and motions', he declared. 'We are everywhere entertained with pleasing Shows and Apparations, we discover imaginary glories in the heavens, and in the Earth, and see some of this Visionary beauty poured out upon the whole creation ... In short our souls are at present delightfully lost and bewildered in a pleasing delusion, and we walk about like the enchanted hero of a romance ... but upon the finishing of some secret spell, the fantastick scene breaks up, and the disconsolate Knight finds himself on a barren heath or in a solitary desert.'[549] Thus, though Addison argued strongly for divine design, he saw all beauty and pleasure as a function of the imagination – not inherent in an otherwise 'barren' or 'solitary' nature.

Americans read Addison into the nineteenth century.[550] Critics in Boston and Philadelphia praised, mimicked and reprinted his *Spectator* essays.[551] Hugh Blair's *Lecture on Rhetoric and Belles Lettres*, used by students at Harvard and elsewhere, used Addison's *Spectator* articles as lessons to imitate.[552] Shaftesbury, Hutcheson and Smith were also influential. Americans read their ideas in the original books, widely available in bookstores and circulating libraries, and excerpted in magazines. Nevertheless, no aesthetic theorist so fully embraced or promoted the pleasures of the imagination as Archibald Alison.[553] Alison's influential book, *Essays on the Nature and Principles of Taste*, was first published in Edinburgh in 1792, and subsequently reissued widely, including in Boston in 1812, and Hartford in the 1820s.[554] Furthermore, his ideas were widely promoted in popular magazines and encyclopaedias. His aesthetic ideology was the clearest and most prominent exegesis of beauty as a function of the imagination through the medium of association. Alison and numerous of his contemporaries espoused an ideal of beauty that was, as Abrams remarks, far removed 'from the doctrine most characteristic of [a] generation of critics, that the content of art has an internal origin, and that its shaping influences are not the Ideas or principles informing the cosmic structure, but the forces inherent in the emotions, the desires, and the evolving imaginative process of the artist himself'.[555] The diffusion of this new aesthetic 'undermined' the 'old necessarily conservative idea of the intrinsic beauty of objects' and replaced it with subjectivity.[556]

Expression

Alison clearly saw himself immersed in a debate with a tremendous intellectual genealogy. He divided previous ideas on beauty into two schools. The first of these included William Hogarth, Abbe Winkelman and Sir Joshua Reynolds. These thinkers, Alison argued, 'resolve[ed] the emotion of taste directly into an original law of our nature ...'. According to Alison, this argument took for granted a 'sense' (not unlike Hutcheson's) that recognized beauty instinctively. However, these thinkers concluded 'that the genuine object of the arts of taste, is to discover, and to imitate those qualities in every subject which the prescription of nature has thus made essentially either beautiful or sublime'. Beauty was a function of certain qualities in objects. These men were, according to Alison, 'artists and amateurs ... those whose habits of thought lead them to attend more to the causes of their emotions than to the nature of the emotions themselves'.[557]

The second school of thought, Alison argued, approached the problem from the other extreme. Here Alison positioned David Hume, Diderot and 'St. Austin' (Augustine?). These men rejected 'any new or peculiar sense, distinct from the common principles of our nature'. Instead, they supposed 'some *one* known and acknowledged principle or affection of mind, to be the foundation of all our emotions we receive from the objects of taste, and which resolves, therefore, all the various phenomena into some general law of our intellectual or moral constitution'. In turn, this was a more natural argument for 'retired and philosophic minds ... whose habits have led them to attend more to the nature of the emotions they felt, than to the causes which produced them'.[558] Alison's ideas clearly approximated yet differed from this latter group. In his mind at least, he provided a methodology or 'causes' for the emotions of beauty and sublimity in his association paradigm.

'The emotions of sublimity and beauty are uniformly ascribed', Alison began, 'both in popular and in philosophical language, to the imagination'. But how does this occur? What was 'the nature of that effect which is produced upon the imagination, by objects of sublimity or beauty?'.[559] For Alison, all beauty derived from what he called the 'train of thought' or associations which excited the imagination: 'When any object of sublimity or beauty is presented to the mind', he argued, 'I believe every man is conscious of a train of thought being immediately awakened in his imagination, analogous to the character or expression of the original object'. The object itself – or rather the perception of that object – did not 'do' anything. Rather, it was the imagination, 'and our fancy busied in all those trains of thought', which stimulated the emotions of sublimity and beauty.

Alison verified these propositions through a series of mental exercises. A man in grief or otherwise distracted, he argued, does not see the beauty of a 'beautiful scene in nature'. He is senseless to its power to excite his imagination. Likewise, professional critics and men of business also had dulled their imagination. 'To a young mind, on the contrary', Alison concluded, a beautiful scene in nature excites 'ideas of peace and innocence, and rural joy, and all the unblemished delights of solitude and contemplation ... [that] lead [the mind] almost insensibly along, in a kind of bewitching reverie, through all its store of pleasing or interesting conceptions'.[560] For Alison, beauty resided in the subject. It was not a function of actual qualities, but of the imagination's engagement and reverie.

American and British intellectuals hotly debated Alison's ideas. The 1812 Boston edition of the *Christian Observer* reviewed the new edition of Alison's book and concluded that he completely and correctly refuted the class of theorists who 'resolve taste into a distinct sense and beauty and sublimity into certain material qualities, as lines, colours, motions, etc'. Alison, according to the anonymous reviewer, demonstrated that 'the beauty or sublimity of any object is not to be ascribed to its material qualities, but to certain other qualities, of which these are the signs or expressions ...'. These signs or expressions stimulated the imagination to 'conceive of a train of ideas corresponding with these emotions'.[561]

In May 1818, F. W. Winthrop in the *North American Review* reviewed Francis Jeffrey's article on 'Beauty', which had appeared in the 1816 *Supplement to the*

Encyclopedia Britannica and which promoted Alison's association theory.[562] Winthrop complained of the effort to find an all-encompassing principle of beauty and cited Dugald Stewart's ideas as his guide. He contradicted Jeffrey's efforts to restrict associationism to memory and complicated Alison's ideas. 'Beautiful objects', he concluded, 'may engage our feelings in behalf of ourselves or of others, of beings, that exist or may be imagined, but some of them do one of these things and some another, and in various ways'. Furthermore, he was horrified by the implied relativism of absolute associationism. For Winthrop, Alison's association theory spoke to more than the idea of beauty. The subjectivism of associationism threatened reason, and the social order. What linked men together in objectively verifiable standards if the subjective imagination ruled? As Christine Holbo argues, 'the creative imagination thus implied the possibility of empirical chaos, individual autonomy and isolation, and social disorder'.[563] For Winthrop, the subjectivity of associationism represented a 'dangerous influence' that distorted the 'moral sensibilities'.

> In general, taste may be true or false, so far as judgment and knowledge are concerned, or as far as we undertake to determine the universality of the associations by which we ourselves are influenced. When we speak only of our own inclinations and feelings, they may be considered merely as odd and ridiculous, or natural and proper. If we are more interested in Coleridge, than in Milton, our taste may be ridiculed, but it can only be denominated false, in relation to some rules of art, or exercise of judgment. Arbitrary and individual associations may be equally powerful and interesting with those that are universal. But this can hardly be admitted as a reasonable motive for cherishing a want of conformity to the taste of others. If we wish to gain reputation by the public display of any liberal accomplishment we must throw off everything that is particular and accidental in this part of our constitution. If we would cultivate a high toned and innocent morality, it is still more necessary to shut the mind to the dangerous influences of those solitary prejudices, which corrupt and distort our moral sensibilities. Here to be singular is almost to be criminal; the sources of action are pure, and any new ingredient is too apt to render the waters turbid and bitter and noxious.[564]

Winthrop pointed to Dugald Stewart as the source of his ideas. It is, however, difficult to see where precisely the separation between Stewart and Jeffrey or Alison lay. Certainly, Alison was more adventurous in his language, yet Stewart quickly acquiesced to Alison on ideas referring to taste: 'Such of my readers as are acquainted with *An Essay on the Nature and Principles of Taste*, lately published by Mr. Alison', Stewart declared, 'will not be surprised that I decline the discussion of a subject which he has treated with so much ingenuity and elegance'.[565] Clearly, Stewart was familiar with Alison's ideas. He edited the six-volume supplement to the *Encyclopedia Britannica* in which Jeffrey's celebratory essay appeared, and either directly commissioned or approved the entry.[566]

Though critics have characterized Stewart as a Common Sense thinker and thus tied into to a Lockean realism, he strongly rejected Lockean notions of *tabula rasa*: 'the mind cannot, without the grossest absurdity, be considered in the light of a receptacle which is gradually furnished from without, by materials introduced by the channel of our sense, nor in that of a *tabula rasa,* upon which copies or resemblances of things external are imprinted ...'. The senses provided the material for knowledge, he acquiesced, nevertheless this did not lead to 'materialism'. Instead, Stewart argued, following Hutcheson, that 'the impression made on our sense by external objects, furnish the occasions on which the mind, by the laws of its constitution, is led to perceive the qualities of the material world, and to exert all the different modifications of thought of which it is capable'.[567] The 'laws of the mind's constitution' were central to beauty and pleasure – associations and impressions were not enough – something inside the mind also contributed to knowledge and pleasure.[568]

Stewart seems not to have undertaken the effort to weight these factors. Nevertheless, he did place a great deal of emphasis on the imagination. Indeed, the final chapters in his treatise on the human mind are exclusively devoted to it. The imagination was, for Stewart, the source of all art. Furthermore, in some of the arts, it played a dual role – it acted in both creation and perception. Both painting and poetry were acts of the imagination that relied on the imagination of the artist and the spectator for pleasure. Quixotically, he argued that landscape gardening, although clearly a function of the imagination in creation, required only the 'external' senses for enjoyment. Part of his logic here was that artists did not create land but merely moulded or shaped it. Poetry and painting, however, clearly relied on the imagination of the artist and that of the spectator to 'convey pleasurable feelings to the mind'. Stewart also saw the imagination as central to sympathy and sentiment.[569]

Other commentators were less circumscribed in their praise for and allegiance to Alison's ideas. The second American edition of the *Edinburgh Encyclopedia* published in New York in 1816, embraced Alison wholeheartedly through most of its article on beauty. The article investigated numerous aesthetic theories, beginning with Augustine who, according to the *Edinburgh Encyclopaedia*, saw beauty in 'unity of parts, or in perfect symmetry'. The penchant for symmetry and fitness of parts, also clearly discussed by Joshua Reynolds, was, however, the author(s) argued, a classical ideal. Edmund Burke, according to the authors, first undermined this ideal. He argued that 'beauty is no idea belonging to mensuration; nor has it anything to do with calculation and geometry'.[570] Nevertheless, for Burke, according to the authors, beauty was 'a quality in bodies acting mechanically upon the human mind, through the medium of the senses, and arising from ... smallness of size, smoothness, gradual variation of outline, delicacy and colour'. The authors, however, especially emphasized the place of Alison in these aesthetic debates. 'The insufficiency of all those systems that attempt to reduce beauty to certain permanent and invariable qualities in objects', the authors argued, 'has been very satisfactorily proved by Mr. Alison in his *Essays on the nature and Principles of Taste*. 'If these qualities [of matter]', the *Edinburgh Encyclopaedia* quoted Alison, 'are in themselves fitted to produce the emotions of beauty, (or, in other words, are in themselves beautiful,) I think it obvious that they must produce this emotion, independently of any association'.[571] Destroy the association, the *Edinburgh Encyclopedia* authors concluded, and the qualities vanish.

Overall the authors were satisfied that Alison clearly proved 'that the beauty of material objects does not result from any permanent qualities in the objects themselves, but from the expression of the objects, or 'from their being the signs or expressions of such qualities as are fitted by the constitution of our nature to produce emotion'.[572] Furthermore, the authors concluded, the source of these qualities is in the mind. To this effect they ended with a verse from Akenside's oft-quoted poem, *Pleasures of the Imagination*:[573]

> Mind, mind, alone! bear witness earth and heaven,
> The living fountains in itself contains
> Of beauteous and sublime. Here, hand in hand,
> Sit paramount the Graces. Here, enthroned,
> Celestial Venus with divinest airs,
> Invites the soul to never-fading joy.

The *Harvard Lyceum* concurred with the *Edinburgh Encyclopedia* authors in their respect for Akenside's famous poem. Akenside, they argued, pointed 'out the sources of that inexpressible charm, which ... poetick structures ... possessed. It was for him to trace their pleasing influence to actual principles, implanted by nature in the human mind.' Of course, it was Addison who 'first investigated with considerable success the properties and charackteristics of the imagination' upon which Akenside constructed his poetic tribute. The imagination, argued the *Lyceum* authors, was the source of pleasure and enjoyment. This, according to the authors, was Akenside's message. God had implanted a principle in man, 'by the operation of which we are led imperceptibly in the ways of truth and virtue'.[574]

Twenty years later, according to an anonymous fancier in the *Boston Magazine*, the imagination fully dominated life and *belles-lettres* – indeed it acted as the aesthetic counterpart of the Moral Sense. The imagination was the source of pleasure, beauty and virtue. It was, for this anonymous author, the source of everything worthy in life. Life, according to this author, was like 'the flowing stream', constantly passing, or in 'perpetual motion'. 'The most abundant resources of his enjoyments must therefore exist in his anticipations and recollections.' The imagination was the source of these 'scenes of pleasure'. There were, 'to the imaginative man', no 'happier moments' than those spent alone, abandoned to 'his own fancy'. The imagination was the source of delight, melancholy and the sublime;

it was central to poetry, painting and sculpture; 'it exerted a strong influence on manners, pursuits and happiness of man'; 'the dear associations which bind us to life, arise mostly from the imaginative power'; it travelled back into the past and forward, 'in review of thousands of unborn generations', all for the delight of the subject.[575]

These ideas did not, however, simply exist in magazines and texts on taste and beauty. Indeed, in Boston, a new aesthetic of the imagination evolved in the work of the painter and theorist Washington Allston.

Washington Allston

For Allston, beauty was almost a wholly subjective function of the imagination. Beauty could not succumb to rules and formulas, and certainly was in no way related to Sir Joshua's 'mathematical demonstration', or a classical model. 'But there is scarcely a subject on which mankind are wider at variance, than on the beauty of their own species', Allston declared. 'Some will tax their memory, and resort to the schools for their supposed infallible *rules*; – forgetting, meanwhile, that ultimate tribunal to which their canon must itself appeal, the ever living principle which first evolved its truth and which now, as then, is not to be reasoned about, but *felt*.'[576]

Though Allston was hardly typical, in many ways he accurately represented the new subjectivity. Washington Allston was a Boston artist deeply immersed in the Anglo-American art world during the first quarter of the nineteenth century. Born in South Carolina in 1779, he made his home in Boston after attending Harvard. Through his Harvard friendships and marriage into the Dana and Channing families he was deeply immersed in Boston high culture. Interested in art at Harvard, upon graduation he moved to England where he studied at the Royal Academy with the influential royal court painter, Benjamin West, a fellow American. He also met and befriended the Romantics Samuel Taylor Coleridge and William Wordsworth. He travelled with Coleridge in Italy and for more than twenty-five years maintained a warm and intellectually stimulating friendship with him. Allston's portrait of Coleridge survives at the Boston Museum of Fine Art. In his posthumously published *Lectures on Art*, he warmly acknowledged his intellectual debt to the Romantic poet and critic. 'To no other man do I owe so much intellectually, as to Mr. Coleridge', Allston claimed. '[W]hen I recall some of our walks under the pines of the Villa Borghese', he reminisced, 'I am almost tempted to dream that I have once listened to Plato in the groves of the Academy.'[577]

Allston, however, was not just a painter; he was also an art theorist, novelist and poet, and his ideas on art and beauty demonstrate the influence of Shaftesbury; the Scots David Hume, Francis Hutcheson and Archibald Alison; and the German thinkers Kant and Jacobi.[578] In his *Lectures on Art* and in his personal papers he reveals a sophisticated knowledge and engagement with contemporary aesthetic theory, philosophy and religion. He was immersed in the art culture of the Early Republic, and his subjectivity is consistent with those changes.

Allston expressed a fundamentally Scottish/Hutchesonian belief in innate or instinctive principles – an interior life. However, he recast those principles in terms of the new subjectivity. The 'mighty intellects of the past', he began, have taught us 'to look into the mysterious chambers of our being, – the abode of the spirit';

> and not a little, indeed, if what we are there permitted to know shall have brought with it the conviction, that we are not abandoned to a blind empiricism, to waste life in guesses, and to guess at last that we have all our lives been guessing wrong, – but, unapproachable though it be to the subordinate Understanding, that we have still within an abiding Interpreter, which cannot be gainsaid, which makes our duty to God and man as clear as the light, which ever guards the fountain of all true pleasures, nay, which holds in subjection the last high gift of the Creator, that imaginative faculty which his exalted creature, made in his image, might mould at will, from his most marvelous world, yet unborn forms, even forms of beauty, grandeur, and majesty, having all of truth but his own divine prerogative, – the *mystery of life*.[579]

God had internalized the higher faculties in man. Man was endowed with an 'abiding Interpreter' who held the keys to truth and beauty, and who held in 'subjection the last high gift of the Creator' – the imagination. The imagination served God's purpose in empowering his 'exalted creature' to mould 'yet unborn forms, even forms of beauty, grandeur and majesty' – and at the same time deified humanity; it allowed for an intimacy with the highest act, creation. As Charles Taylor argues, the artist as creator 'doesn't imitate nature so much as he imitates the author of nature'.[580]

Furthermore, for Allston, though man took his material as the 'most marvelous world' – the pleasures of his creation were clearly a function of internal sensation. He echoed both Francis Hutcheson and Dugald Stewart by arguing that objects, sounds, nature, did not in and of themselves 'contain' beauty, but rather occasioned it:

> When the senses, as the medium of communication, have conveyed to the mind either the sounds or images, their function ceases. So also with respect to the objects: their end is attained, at least as to us, when the sounds or images are thus transmitted, which, so far as they are concerned, must for ever remain the same within as without the mind. For where the ultimate end is not in mere bodily sensation, neither the senses nor the objects possess, of themselves, the *tertium aliquid*, whether the pleasure we feel be in a beautiful animal or in according sounds, neither the one nor the other is really the cause, but simply the *occasion*.[581]

Allston also expressed Scottish humanist ideas in his firm belief in the existence of one overriding idea – harmony. For Allston, pleasurable emotions 'have their true source in One Intuitive Universal Principle or living Power, and the three Ideas of Beauty, Truth and Holiness, which we assume to represent the *perfect* in the physical, intellectual and moral worlds, are but the several realized phases of this sovereign principle which we shall call *Harmony*'.[582]

Beauty, truth, and holiness constituted '*Harmony*'. Yet they were doubtless 'pre-existing Ideas, being in the living constituents of an immortal spirit, [and needed] but the slightest breath, of some outward condition of the true and good – a simple problem, or a kind act – to awake them, as it were from their unconscious sleep, and start them for eternity'.[583] But even '*Harmony*' as an 'external characteristic' was only knowable subjectively. 'All objects that give pleasure to the mind', he wrote, 'must first become subordinated to this subjective principle; that is, they must reflect back, as *realized*, this principle to the mind. This realization', he concluded, 'is not a matter of induction produced by the intervention of the reflective faculties, but is intuitively recognized by the mind'.[584] Put briefly, as Doreen Hunter notes, Allston was caught between two worlds. Firmly invested in the 'quest for univer-sally valid truths', he also clearly believed that the 'truth is discovered not by the understanding and common sense but by the imagination'.[585] Allston's literary pro-duction paled besides his painting, and it is in his painted works that we see most

Figure 1: Washington Allston, *Moonlight* (1819). Oil on canvas, 63.82 x 90.8 cm. Courtesy of the Museum of Fine Arts, Boston (21.1429). William Sturgis Bigelow Collection.

clearly his aesthetic ideas. Barbara Novak in her discussion of nineteenth century American painting notes that it was Allston who introduced the imagination and sentiment into American art. American romanticism, as expressed by Allston, in Novak's words, 'emerged ... at the extreme of a dialectic between fact and antifact, in which the palpable finds its antithesis in the impalpable, the seen and touched in the remembered and distilled'.[586] His images derived, in her words, 'more directly from the imagination, untempered by the immediate confrontation with fact'. This is clear, Novak argues, from paintings like *Moonlight* (Figure 1), which, in her words, display 'his lyric emphasis on sustained mood', and correspond to his imaginative dream-like reconstructions of places and events.[587]

It is also, however, as David Bjelajac has recently argued, clear from his controversial *Elijah in the Desert* (Figure 2).[588] As Bjelajac notes, the painting's reception was a terrible disappointment to Allston. Though his English followers raved over the imposing work, Boston's Unitarian Brahmins were not ready to accept its strong imaginative representations. Allston, fresh from an impressionable trip to the Louvre, was clearly affected by the Venetian Renaissance painters whose work he later claimed 'left the subject to be made up by the spectator'. Though Bjelajac emphasizes the religious and social connotations of *Elijah*, I would argue that it fits well into contemporary aesthetic arguments as well. *Elijah*, as the contemporary art critic and Unitarian minister William Ware noted, 'neglected the general

Figure 2: Washington Allston, *Elijah in the Desert* (1818). Oil on canvas, 125.09 x 184.78 cm. Courtesy of the Museum of Fine Arts, Boston (70.1). Gift of Mrs Samuel and Miss Alice Hooper.

truth of nature'. 'There may be such a tree as this of Mr. Allston', Ware declared, 'with just such roots; but if there is, none but the natives of the country know the fact, or naturalists, whose business it is to be acquainted with it through their science. And to make it a principle object in a great work of art is to degrade the art to the rank of a print in Goldsmith's *Animated Nature*. It was painting a mere whim; the whole tree, roots, branches and all, a mere whim, a *capriccio*.'[589] Ware, I suspect, chose the word *capriccio* carefully. Italian and English eighteenth-century *Capricci* landscapes merged real and imaginary elements.[590] Clearly, as far as some of Boston's art patrons were concerned, *Elijah* was far too imaginative.

These and other paintings suggest that, as Nathalia Wright notes, 'the chief characteristic of Allston's painting ... is its subjectivity. He was the first American painter to transcend external forms and project the visions within his own mind.'[591] Allston wrote sparingly on another subject central to contemporary art, literature and aesthetics – the sublime. The sublime and the picturesque were a powerful narrative of the imagination in the late eighteenth- and early nineteenth-century Anglo-American world.

The Sublime and the Picturesque

The sublime played a particular role for Allston. He saw the relationship of man to the world as anthropocentric: 'In the preceding discussion [on beauty, truth and holiness], we have considered the outward world only in its immediate relation to Man, and the Human Being as the predetermined centre to which it was designed to converge.' The sublime differed from this pattern. 'As the subject, however, of what are called sublime emotions, he holds a different position; for the centre here is not himself, nor, indeed can he approach it within conceivable distance ....' Indeed, for Allston, the sublime was an outward principle of 'Infinite Harmony' that corresponded to the one 'principle in ourselves ... by which to recognize any corresponding emotion – namely the principle of Harmony'.[592] The sublime emotion arose when an object prompted the mind 'beyond its prescribed limits, whether carrying it back to the primitive past, the incomprehensible beginning, or sending it into the future, to the unknown end, the ever-present Idea of the mighty author of all these mysteries must still be implied, though we think not of it. It is this Idea, or rather its influence, whether we be conscious of it or not, which we hold to be the source of every sublime emotion.'[593] Sublime objects somehow resembled or were analogous to the 'Infinite Idea'. This relationship gave sublime objects their 'unattainable, *ever-stimulating ... ever-eluding*' characteristics.[594]

The ideas of the sublime and/or the picturesque (sometimes conflated) were at the centre of the debate on beauty; they were particularly strong examples of the role that the imagination and thus the new subjectivity suddenly played in aesthetic theory and practice.[595] The sublime and the picturesque were in effect aesthetic categories that derived all of their value from the imagination. Sublime and picturesque objects were not objects of objective beauty, but were instead wholly a function of this new imaginative aesthetic.[596] Furthermore, debates on the nature of the sublime partook of the epistemological dilemma at the centre of the debates on economic and moral value. Artists and theorists agreed on a sublime that resembled Allston's idea – it had to overwhelm: awe, size and magnificence; sheer raw and natural power, were all central concepts in the theories of the sublime. Yet the source of these feelings differed. Numerous critics argued for a 'real' sublime to counter the pernicious 'false' sublime of the imagination.

For Dr Ladd, as excerpted in the *American Museum*, the sublime was emblematic of a crisis in style that he found in modern authors. 'From the union of the florid and bombastic manner', he concluded, 'is formed the style which at present obtains'. 'This we would choose to call, by way of distinction, the frothy manner; and is what modern writers have in idea, when they speak of a sublime; a style as far different from sublimity in writing, as tinsel is different from bullion; or as the mock majesty of the theatre differs from the grandeur of the imperial magnificence.' This false sublime of 'Johnson, Hervey, Akenside and Shaftesbury ... perverted our taste, corrupted our style, and weakened by the glitter of false ornaments, the native energy of the true English manner'. Furthermore, he found in the criticism of Hugh Blair, a corrective to 'this corrupt taste'.[597]

Blair, according to Ladd, argued for simplicity in the sublime. 'Persons are apt to imagine, that magnificent words, accumulated epithets, and a certain swelling kind of expression, by rising above what is usual or vulgar, contributes to, or even forms, the sublime. Nothing can be more false', Blair/Ladd concluded. The most striking example of the sublime was biblical: 'God said, let there be light, and there was light'. The sublime lay in the matter, not in the signs; in the substance, not the expression; it was an objective reality, not a subjective emotion.[598]

The anonymous author excerpted in the *Boston Magazine* agreed with Dr Ladd. 'The foundation of the Sublime in Composition must always be laid in the nature of the object described; except it be such an object, if presented to our sight, if exhibited to us in reality, would excite ideas of that elevating, that awful, and magnificent kind, which we call sublime: the description, however finely drawn, is not entitled to be placed under this class.'[599] Sublime composition succeeded or failed relative to its faithfulness to the sublime object. Too 'frigid', it 'degraded' an 'object or sentiment, which is sublime in itself, by a mean conception of it'. Too bombastic, it elevated an 'object out of its rank' or exalted a sublime object 'beyond all natural and just bounds'.[600]

A competing vision of the sublime and the picturesque derived from Alison. Examples of picturesque objects were, according to Alison: 'An old tower in the middle of a wood, a bridge flung across a chasm between rocks, a cottage in a precipice'. He took for granted that these objects had powerful associational value and suggested an additional train of conceptions. 'No objects are remarked as picturesque', Alison concluded, 'which do not strike the imagination by themselves'.[601]

It was, however, William Gilpin in his 1791 *Remarks on Forest Scenery*, and in his subsequent travel books, who presented a vision of the picturesque that, in my reading, most accurately reflects American ideas during the Early Republic period.[602] Gilpin avoided the polemics associated with the debate between the sublime, beauty and the picturesque – for him the picturesque was simply an aestheticized landscape that, in sometimes unclear ways, stimulated the imagination. This often included 'picturesque' rotten tree trunks or other forms of decayed nature, ruins of buildings, particularly castles and abbeys, and other rustic or decayed sights.

Gilpin's essays, in particular his *Essay on Picturesque Travel* excerpted in the *New York Magazine*, were instructional manuals for ways of seeing – or perhaps more accurately, ways of feeling.[603]

> We are most delighted when some grand scene ... strikes us beyond the power of thought – when the *vox facibus hoeret,* and every mental operation is suspended. In this pause of intellect, this *deliquim* of the soul, an enthusiastic sensation of pleasure overspreads it, previous to any examination by the rules of art. The general idea of the scene makes an impression, before any appeal is made to judgment. We rather *feel* than *survey* it.

Gilpin's ideas demanded the active role of the imagination. Only the imagination, he argued, could translate the inspiration of the artist. Furthermore, the imagination was a sort of 'camera obscura, only with this difference, that the camera represents objects as they really are'. The imagination had a freer range to create and recreate objects from fancy or nature. 'The imagination', Gilpin argued 'can plant hills; can form rivers, and lakes in vallies; can build castles and abbeys; and if it can find not other amusement, can dilate itself in vast ideas of space'.

Richard Payne Knight's more authoritative voice seconded many of these ideas relying on the work of Alison. The picturesque, the sublime and beauty were, according to Knight, interrelated. Sublimity was simply a stronger emotional response than beauty, and picturesque objects, *vis-à-vis* association, excited both these emotions. Emotions were, however, the basis for these evaluations. Feelings determined the nature of the aesthetic judgment.[604]

The sublime and the picturesque signified a fundamental change in the nature of self in the western world. Nature had for a long time been the source of human value – aesthetic value in nature through mimesis; natural economic value in objects, like silver; and moral value, in the natural law. With the picturesque, nature was aestheticized. The inside was turned out and nature recast to resemble the imagination. The whole penchant for landscape painting in Britain, France, the United States and Germany is a function of these changes in personality. Natural phenomena ceased to be defined 'by the order of nature in it self or by the order of the Ideas which they embody'. They were 'defined through the effects of the phenomena on us, in the reactions they awaken. The affinity between nature and ourselves is now mediated not by an objective rational order but by the way that nature resonates in us. Our attunement with nature no longer consists in a recognition of ontic hierarchy, but in being able to release the echo within ourselves.'[605] Americans familiarized themselves with this new aesthetic through their magazines.[606] In the Boston magazines, they read of '*Picturesque Views of London*', a '*Picturesque survey of water, wood, and mountain scenery*', a '*Picturesque voyage round Great Britain*' or '*A description of the principal picturesque beauties of the isle of Wight*'.[607] But Americans everywhere enjoyed this new aesthetic in a variety of forms.

A good example of this contemporary expression of the sublime and the picturesque is the work of Joshua Shaw as interpreted by the engraver Samuel Hill in *Picturesque Views of American Scenery*, published by Mathew Carey in Philadelphia in 1820 (Figures 3 and 4).[608] This was the first of a number of picturesque books that followed a British tradition. Shaw and Hill, both British immigrants, were familiar with the theory and literature of the picturesque. *Picturesque Views* presented Shaw's paintings – as engraved by Hill – opposite (we can assume) Mathew Carey's prose.

Figure 3: Frontispiece to Joshua Shaw, *Picturesque Views of America*, engraved by Samuel Hill. Courtesy of the Winterthur Library, Printed Book and Periodical Collection.

The nature of this early American picturesque is obvious in the text and print of *View on Spirit Creek, Georgia* (Figure 4). The text accompanying the engraving reads: 'At the moment at which the present sketch was taken the aspect of the heaven seemed to correspond with the gloom of the scenery. Black and solemn clouds overhung the observer's head, rain had begun to fall in broad and heavy drops, the wind roared through the forest, and the rumbling of distant thunder might have been mistaken by the "belated cottager" for the hoarse threatening of the spirit of the stream.'[609]

View on Spirit Creek, Georgia was clearly an effort to unite picturesque imagery and narrative to engage the imagination and excite the emotions of sublimity and beauty. Some of the language and choice of subjects indeed could have been taken directly from Alison's work. More importantly, however, it spoke directly to the subjective imagination of the 'Spectator'. Indeed, it called for participation and co-creation.[610] With these views, Edward Nygreen has argued, Shaw brought a 'highly developed romantic strain of landscape to America'.[611]

Carey's book was part of a new appreciation of the picturesque aesthetic in America – which included numerous publications, as well as an American Grand Tour of Jefferson's Natural Bridge, tours of Niagara Falls, and other natural wonders.[612] Shaw's work as engraved by Hill, hand coloured by anonymous artists and published by Carey, was part of many fine homes. Boston's 'Brahmin' merchants as well as the Athenaeum proudly displayed Washington Allston's work.[613] But Americans experienced the aesthetic ideal of the imagination beyond the range of

Figure 4: Joshua Shaw, *View on Spirit Creek, Georgia*, engraved by Samuel Hill. Courtesy of the Winterthur Library, Printed Book and Periodical Collection.

Figure 5: *The Massachusetts Magazine* (June 1795). Courtesy of the Winterthur Library, Printed Book and Periodical Collection.

Allston's paintings and the Shaw/Hill prints. Many of the passages quoted above were from the *Massachusetts Magazine* – a monthly Boston based magazine that published sentimental stories, poetry, excerpts from British and French magazines and all manner of other articles of interest to cosmopolitan Bostonians.

These magazines also usually published a plate that accompanied a story. These plates, combined with a lively literature of sentiment, were clearly meant to stimulate the imagination, evoking sympathy, sentiment and the 'echo within'. Both the plates and the narratives by and large depended on standard picturesque and so-called rustic tropes in order to produce the desired emotional response.

Figure 5 repeats the 'danger of nature' theme: 'In general, we may observe', Blair concludes in his discussion of the sublime, 'that great power and force exerted, always raise sublime ideas and perhaps the most copious source of these is derived from this quarter. Hence the grandeur of earthquakes; and burning mountains; of great conflagrations; of the stormy ocean, and overflowing waters; of tempests of wind; of thunder and lightning; and of all the uncommon violence of the elements.'[614]

Nor were these sorts of narratives limited to magazines. For many readers this was lived experience. Eunice Callender recorded one such day in her diary entry of Thursday 31 May 1808. Out in the country with some friends, Eunice was caught in a violent storm. 'Never before were my ideas more sublimed than at that time', she declared. She described the steep inaccessible hill behind their shelter and the boundless prospect of hill and slate in front, in the language of the picturesque. Her understanding of nature reflected a modern emotional consumption of nature – not the ontic hierarchy that Shakespeare or other authors demonstrated. Eunice, for example, failed to see in the rolling thunder and lightning the disorder that Shakespeare projected in Macbeth, in which the violence of the storm and other natural and 'unnatural' phenomenon foreshadow and reflect the violence and disorder in Duncan's household.[615] For Eunice, the 'majestic thunder bursting directly over our heads, or rolling off on deep and solemn [illegible] and the lighting brightly quivering through the clouds, the rain fast flowing, all gave birth to the most sublime ideas'. She consumed her thunder as an aesthetic experience, and described the events as a function of her emotions – indeed the storm gave rise to 'sublime' emotions completely detached from 'foul weather'. Her sublime idea was a daydream where she was a hermit, 'living secluded, as we are told that hermits have in ancient times', and conversing only with the birds.[616] Clearly, for the nineteen-year-old Eunice, the beautiful, sublime and picturesque were a function of the imagination and experienced through emotions; Eunice and other Americans in the Early Republic clearly partook of a new emotional landscape.[617]

The *Massachusetts Magazine*, other examples like it and sentimental illustrated pocketbooks such as Isaiah Thomas's *Beauties of the Muses* (Figure 6), had relatively large readerships, and were also available in the circulating libraries. But the dissemination of an aesthetic of the imagination was not limited to painting or print culture. Indeed, an aesthetic of the imagination was central to the consumption-driven demand that inspired the flurry of goods associated with the consumption patterns of this period; through association, the imagination attached value to objects and awakened desire.[618]

Goods are Good

[In imagination] the appetites and desires are fabricated ... If I can stop the mischief here and prevent false coinage, I am safe.
    Anthony Ashley Cooper, third Earl of Shaftesbury.[619]

Aesthetic, moral and economic values came together in consumption. As discussed in Chapter 5, the culture of sentiment confirmed the source of moral value in feelings and emotions. Moreover, the consumption of those feelings and emotions produced pleasure. Shaftesbury begat this tradition with his emphasis on innate feelings. But Shaftesbury did not apply his logic solely to moral value – he also saw aesthetic value as deeply intertwined with his emotion-based ethics. For Shaftesbury, 'that what is beautiful is harmonious and proportionable; what is harmonious and proportionable is true; and what is at once both beautiful and true is, of consequence agreeable

Figure 6: *Beauties of the Muses* (Worcester, MA, 1793). Courtesy of the Winterthur Library, Printed Book and Periodical Collection.

and good'.[620] Thus Shaftesbury clearly linked goodness to beauty – and thus to goods. Though he articulated an aesthetic of harmony he left the door open to later theorists who detached both beauty and goodness from objective standards and seated them in the subjective imagination. The consumption of goods in this construction was not a functional or instrumental relationship – rather, the sentimentalist consumed not the goods but the feeling evoked by those goods.[621]

Certainly Adam Smith saw it that way. In an essay on beauty from his *Theory of Moral Sentiments*, excerpted in the March 1790 *Universal Asylum and Columbian Magazine*, he argued for a 'utility'-based theory of beauty. 'The conveniancy of a house', he declared, 'gives pleasure to the spectator as well as its regularity ... That the fitness of any system or machine to produce the end for which it was intended, bestows a certain propriety and beauty upon the whole, and renders the very thought and contemplation of it agreeable, is so very obvious that nobody has overlooked it.' Smith's 'conveniancy' clearly resembled the 'relative' beauty explicated in the Philadelphia *Encyclopaedia*.[622] But, for Smith, this was not the end of the story. More surprisingly, in his opinion, the actual 'fitness' or utility had been aestheticized. '[T]he fitness, this happy contrivance of any production of art [is] often ... more valued, than the very end for which it was intended.' Put another way, the potential utility of objects generated more pleasure than their use. This valuation was the special function of the imagination: 'Our imagination, which in pain and sorrow seems to confined and cooped up within our persons, in times of ease and prosperity expands itself to everything around us'.[623]

For Smith, the engagement of the imagination with goods was part of the providential, or natural order. Suddenly, Smith argued, the 'pleasures of wealth and greatness ... strike the imagination as something grand and beautiful and noble'. Capacity lost all proportion to desire. Yet, 'it is well that nature imposes upon us in this manner'. This 'deception' spurs mankind on to industry and civilization. The rich through the 'gratification of their own vain and insatiable desires ... are led by an invisible hand to make nearly the same distribution of the necessaries of life, which would have been made, had the earth been divided into equal portions among all its inhabitants'.[624]

The consumption of feelings evoked by goods in contrast to the consumption of goods proper is key to understanding the wave of household furnishings decorated in the picturesque style during this period. Household furnishings such as worktables and screens that used sentimental and picturesque motifs to advantage are good examples of this aesthetic. Figure 7 is a New England Empire worktable decorated with a scene from Laurence Sterne's *A Sentimental Journey*. Painted

Figure 7: New England work table, 1815–25. Maple, pine, basswood and brass, OH: 30.37'; OW: 17.62'; OW: 17.25'. Courtesy of the Winterthur Museum.

Figure 8: English pole screen, 1800–25. Canvas and wood, OH: 62.25'. Courtesy of the Winterthur Museum. Bequest of Mrs Waldron Phoenix Belknap.

furniture was exceedingly fashionable in the first few decades of the nineteenth century. Many of these tables derived from the women's academies that flourished in this period.[625] Though there is some debate on the subject, historians of furniture have generally assumed the young women of the academies painted these images, and otherwise decorated furniture as part of their genteel education. The side surfaces of this table are covered in castle ruins and other picturesque and sentimental motifs. The tabletop is decorated with a scene from a novel by Angelika Kaufman's *Maria*. John Brewer, in his *Pleasures of the Imagination*, notes that images from Kaufmann's *Maria* and Goldsmith's *The Vicar of Wakefield*, had widespread circulation both as magazine and furniture prints, as well as other material goods.[626] They also circulated as prints in the popular magazines of the day. The *Massachusetts Magazine*, for example, featured prints from both of these novels.[627]

'Fancy Furniture', which as Dean Fales has noted reached the height of fashion and consumption in the first quarter of the nineteenth century, also expressed this new imaginative aesthetic.[628] In the eighteenth and early nineteenth centuries the word 'fancy' meant the 'imagination'. Alison and Addison both often used fancy in place of the imagination. Ads for painted or fancy furniture announced 'real' views and 'fancy' landscapes. The New York side chairs below clearly demonstrate the picturesque aesthetic on the painted chair backs (Figures 9 and 10). These chairs and other objects, such as porcelain, were often decorated with landscapes that borrowed from the picturesque tropes of classical antiquities, ruined castles, bridges and other aestheticized and imagined landscapes.[629]

The constant repetition of the 'ruins' trope clearly appealed to the imagination. Antiquities, Archibald Alison wrote, allowed the spectator to indulge 'in the imagination of living in a world, which, by a very natural kind of prejudice, we are always willing to believe was both wiser and better than the present'. Through relics and other objects that recalled antiquity, the values associated with periods long gone were resurrected and reconstructed in the imagination: 'the gallantry, the heroism, the patriotism of antiquity, rise again before his view, softened by the obscurity in which they are involved, and rendered more seducing to the imagination by that obscurity itself, which while it mingles a sentiment of regret amidst his pursuits, serves at the same time to stimulate his fancy to fill up, by its own creation, those long intervals of time of which history has preserved no record'.[630]

Other objects combined this imagined nostalgia with the new aestheticized nature. Imagined waterfalls, thatched-roof cottages and ponds with caves marked reverse painted mirrors, porcelain bowls and pole screens such as the example below (Figure 8).[631]

Decoration thus trumped design. The value of the object was less a function of its inherent design qualities – its objective reality – and more a function of the associations attached to the images and style and the feelings evoked by them. In this way goods were good. They were part of a larger culture of feeling that placed economic, moral and aesthetic value inside mankind; values ceased to be an objectively verifiable reality and became part of the new subjectivity – a function of the emotions and feelings of the spectator.

Figure 9: Detail back of New York side chairs, 1810–20. Tulip, ash, soft maple, OH: 34'; OW: 18.75'; OD: 20.5'. Courtesy of the Winterthur Museum.

Figure 10: New York side chairs, 1810–20. Tulip, ash, soft maple. Courtesy of the Winterthur Museum.

CONCLUSION: SENSE SUBORDINATED TO THE MIND

Perhaps it may be wondered that I should treat at the same time the question of property of all our riches, and that of all our sentiments, and thus mingle economy and morality; but, when we penetrate to their fundamental basis, it does not appear to me possible to separate either these two order of things or their study. In proportion as we advance, the objects separate and subdivide themselves, and it becomes necessary to examine them separately; but in their principles they are intimately united. We should not have the property of any of our goods whatsoever if we had not that of our wants, which is nothing but that of our sentiments; and all these properties are inevitably derived, from the sentiment of personality, from the consciousness of our *self.*

> Count Destutt Tracy, *A Treatise of Political Economy*, trans. by Thomas Jefferson (Georgetown, 1817), p. 52.

This book began with a discussion of Locke's insistence on the intrinsic value of silver-as-money. I interpreted Locke's notion of intrinsic value through his epistemology, and thus his theology. This emphasis highlighted Locke's strong theocratic message and his single-minded rejection of 'any conception of the causal processes of human belief as a self-subsistent locus of value'.[632] In Locke's mind, human values usurped theocratic systems yet failed to establish social consensus, cohesion and order – even individual purpose. Thus for Locke a social order founded on anthropocentric values and institutions was 'a castle in the air', or, to paraphrase Ware's objection to Allston's painting, a mere whim, or *capriccio*.

Shaftesbury and the Scottish Moral Sense philosophers challenged these ideas and constructed a vision of humanity directly attuned to the moral good in the universe and based solely on feelings. The Scottish philosophers' sociology of human life placed humanity *in history* – their institutions and personality evolved over time; experience and needs determined the nature of the social order. Human beings built their societies and the moral, aesthetic and economic value structures that dominated their lives. These ideas expressed a profound confidence in

159

human activity. Smith in particular expounded a 'self-regulating system' of morality, production and exchange that connected human beings' ordinary activities to the 'interlocking providential order of nature' – the *summum bonum*.[633] The guiding principles in all these activities, according to the Scots, were feelings – beliefs – ideas.[634]

In this way, the argument about the location of value in money touched on the mainsprings to human life. The question was not just where value in money lay – in silver, or in confidence – but the question of where all value structures or knowledge lay – as external and received entities or systems, or as internalized and thus subjective ideas; as divinely ordained entities or human creations. It was the very idea that human action, institutions, ideas, and feelings created human life and spontaneously generated order and harmony that undermined empiricism. It was precisely this vision of a social order that Locke established himself against.[635]

These debates resonated through Early Republic Boston. In the post-Revolutionary period, the necessity of reconstructing society and economy took on particular importance. Innovative economic institutions that created economic value developed during the Revolution – and by the late 1820s mushroomed to multiply the potential of the young nation. On a bank-to-bank level, the value of the instruments they issued reflected the confidence men had in the issuing institutions. In the aggregate, however, bank notes rode on the confidence men had in the country and in themselves. The imagined tremendous potential that surrounded them combined with the ceaseless needs of commerce to legitimize consistently larger and larger volumes of a currency only tenuously tied to intrinsic notions of value. This increased subjectivity in economic value transformed human personality, as reflected in changes to aesthetic and moral value structures.

These fractures were clear in the debates on monetary, aesthetic and moral value. Persistent advocates of silver or real commodity value perceived the creation of value in paper as a crime against the natural order – not the aestheticized nature of the sentimentalists – but the nature of the early modern natural law thinkers – the natural laws of reason established by the deity. As Witherspoon plaintively asked, how could you possibly exchange a sign for a thing? There was no reason in that logic. An equal part silver always equalled an equal part silver, Locke declared. Who could conceive of trading a silver coin for bullion of greater or lesser weight than that which the coin contained? These empiricists could not conceive that value might be imagined and not at all related to a commodity.

These conflicts shaped and expressed the debates over moral value in Boston. Arminian and Scottish Enlightenment theories of human perfectibility converged in Boston's liberal Unitarian religion and challenged orthodox beliefs as confirmed by the scriptures. As orthodox minister Moses Stuart asked, how could you discount scripture on the basis of human reasoning? Revelation was divine –

miracles confirmed the existence of a 'real' God. Still, Channing and many other Unitarians chose to travel inward to find the source of divinity. Morality derived less and less from external sources like the pulpit and more and more from human narratives, and the narrative within, the conscience. Human beings in effect housed the source of the good and engaged divine providence '*inside*'. Feelings determined what was right and wrong. Furthermore, this subjectivity found its most eloquent expression not in the sermons of the age, but in the popular fiction and sentimental culture that captivated readers during this period.

Novels and/or other works of fiction did not, however, go uncontested. Again, the challenge to fictitious or imagined narratives centred on their 'unreal' value. Novels, critics claimed, created private systems that undermined social norms and led women to infamy by stirring their emotions. Many Americans, however, voted with their eyes and devoured romantic tales, seduction novels and the magazines that serialized them. Furthermore, they privileged the feelings derived from novels and thus their epistemological foundation.

Aesthetic theory spoke even more clearly to the social and epistemological implications of the new subjectivity. The construction of an imagination-based aesthetic threatened the consensus culture of the senses. Early modern human beings could more or less trust in the shared external reality communicated through the senses. Beauty and deformity were obvious to the early modern mind. The internalization of these standards threatened the social order with a private system and thus chaos. Subjectivity was a 'solitary prejudice' that 'corrupted and distorted' our moral sensibilities. 'Here to be singular is almost to be criminal', F. W. Winthrop concluded, 'the sources of action are pure, and any new ingredient is too apt to render the waters turbid and bitter and noxious'.[636] Still, by the 1820s Allston and others internalized 'the sources of action' with no sense that they endangered society – rather their feeling was the opposite; they created truth. The artist created an '*alter et idem* ... being of the nature of the true inasmuch as it is an exponent of the mode in which it exists in the mind that projects it ....'[637] Thus men turned inward for the truth – in economic, moral and aesthetic value; they reconstructed value structures based on received and external authority with a subjectivity based on feelings.

Finally, this book began with a question: how did men reconcile the loss of their ancient virtue to commerce? Pocock's answer, *manners*, might have been Otis's response as well. For the bourgeoisie of Otis's generation, 'virtue was redefined ... with the aid of a concept of manners ... Commerce, leisure, cultivation and – it was soon perceived with momentous consequences – the division and diversification of labour combined to bring this about; and if he could no longer engage directly in the activity and equality of ruling and being ruled, but had to depute his government and defence to specialized and professional representatives, he was more than compensated for his loss of antique virtue by an indefinite and perhaps infinite enrichment of his personality, the product of the multiplying relationships with both things and persons in which he became progressively involved.'[638]

Pocock's answer is in effect an attempt to measure the consequences of modernity. Man had lost his martial and political personality – and what had he gained? Was the new subject self, living in an interdependent economy and society constructed on the principles of sentiment and sociability – a society dominated by his relationship with others and goods – worth the loss of ancient *virtue*? Throughout his life, Otis, and indeed most white Americans living in the Early Republic period, answered in the affirmative. Their lives had been enriched by the new subjectivity, sociability and consumption that marked their personalities and society. They preferred the 'artificial' world they imagined to the 'real' world the deity endowed them. Washington Allston spoke eloquently of these changes:

> Next to the development of our moral nature, to have subordinated the sense to the mind is the highest triumph of the civilized state. Were it possible to embody the present complicated scheme of society, so as to bring it before us as a visible object, there is perhaps nothing in the world of sense that would so fill us with wonder; for what is there in nature that may not fall within its limits? And yet how small a portion of this stupendous fabric will be found to have any direct, much less exclusive relation to the actual wants of the body! It might seem, indeed, to an unreflecting observer that our physical necessities, which, truly estimated, are few and simple, have rather been increased than diminished by the civilized man. But this is not true; for if a wider duty is imposed on the senses, it is only to minister to the increased demands of the imagination, which is now so mingled with our every-day concerns, even with our dress, houses, and furniture, that except with the brutalized, the purely sensuous wants might almost be said to have become extinct; with the cultivated and refined, they are at least so modified as to be no longer prominent.[639]

NOTES

1. Harrison Gray Otis to Sally Otis, 3 December 1797, Harrison Gray Otis Papers, Massachusetts Historical Society.
2. Harrison Gray Otis to Sally Otis, 23 December 1797, Harrison Gray Otis Papers.
3. Laommi Baldwin relates an excellent example of the babble of notes. In 1805, the General Court passed a law prohibiting the circulation of 'personal notes'. So dire was the need for change that merchants and retailers simply wrote out personal notes for small sums like fifty cents. These circulated locally amidst the bills from Vermont, New Hampshire and Rhode Island. These sort of experiments were not unknown elsewhere. Laommi Baldwin, *Thoughts on the Study of Political Economy* (Boston, 1809), p. 52. The Winterthur Museum houses an 1814 note from the 'Original Fringe and Worsted Yarn Warehouse' for fifty cents in goods or Philadelphia bank notes (item number 74.156.2A).
4. These ideas are developed further in Chapter 4. Hammond details the confused state of affairs relative to capital, deposits and liabilities. Bray Hammond, *Banks and Politics in America: From the Revolution to the Civil War* (Princeton: Princeton University Press, 1957, 1985), pp. 80–5, 134–43.
5. Janet Riesman, 'The Origins of American Political Economy, 1690–1781' (PhD Dissertation, Brown University, 1983), p. 140.
6. Howard Bodenhorn, *State Banking in Early America: A New Economic History* (New York: Oxford University Press, 2003).
7. Erick Bollmann, *Paragraph on Banks* (Philadelphia, 1810), p. 44; Samuel Blodget, *Economica: A Statistical Manual for the United States of America* (1806; New York: Augustus M. Kelley, 1964), p. 12.
8. J. G. A Pocock, 'The Mobility of Property and the Rise of Eighteenth Century Sociology', in *Virtue, Commerce and History* (Cambridge: Cambridge University Press, 1985), pp. 103–25; p. 103.
9. J. G. A. Pocock, *The Machiavellian Moment: Florentine Political Thought in the Atlantic Republic Tradition* (Princeton: Princeton University Press, 1975).
10. Fernand Braudel, *Civilization and Capitalism, 15th–18th Century, Volume 1, The Structures of Everyday Life: The Limits of the Possible*, trans. Sian Reynolds (London: Harper & Row, 1981), p. 473. Braudel writes: 'But the innovation of the Bank of England was that it added to the functions of deposit and clearing banks those of a deliberately organized issuing bank, capable of offering ample credit in notes (whose total amount far exceeded actual deposits). By doing this, said Law, it did the greatest

good to trade and the state, because it "increased the quantity of money"' (Braudel cites John Law, 'Premier memoire sur les banques', in *Oeuvres contenant les principes sur le Numeraire, le Commerce, le Credit et les Banques, avec des notes* (Paris, 1790), p. 197).

11. Pocock, 'The Mobility of Property', p. 112.

12. Alfred Sohn-Rethel, *Intellectual and Manual Labour: A Critique of Epistemology* (New York: Macmillan, 1978), p. 7. Sohn-Rethel pushes Marx's logic and argues that the 'conceptual basis of cognition is logically and historically conditioned by the basic formation of the social synthesis of its epoch'. For Sohn-Rethel, the 'constituent elements of the exchange abstraction unmistakably resemble the conceptual elements of the cognitive faculty emerging with the growth of commodity production' (p. 6). Throughout the text he argues for a causal relationship between commodity abstraction, money and epistemology. Sohn-Rethel, however, develops the argument into a critique of the epistemological bifurcation of labour. See also Sohn-Rethel's discussion of Marx's 'Historical Materialism'. According to Sohn-Rethel, Marx argues that 'history, by being channeled through human society, brings forth mental rather than physical alterations in man, developments like language, conscious reflection, faculties of knowledge together with those of error and human self-delusion and even possibly also of a social self-realization of man' (p. 75). This description fits my reading of the Scottish project (as discussed below). See also Ronald L. Meek, 'The Scottish Contribution to Marxist Sociology', *Economics and Ideology and Other Essays* (London: Chapman & Hall, 1967), pp. 34–50; and Marc Shell, *Money, Language and Thought: Literary and Philosophical Economies from the Medieval to the Modern Era* (Berkeley: University of California Press, 1982). Joyce Appleby makes a similar if less complicated argument: 'Cultural institutions rest on a particular economic base, and when the base shifts or disappears venerable institutions can collapse without warning, throwing into larger relief the inseparable union of the ideal and the material': Joyce Oldham Appleby, *Inheriting the Revolution: The First Generation of Americans* (Cambridge, MA: Harvard University Press, 2000), p. 19.

13. For an interesting confirmation of many of these ideas, see Ralph Lerner, 'Commerce and Character: The Anglo-American as a New-Model Man', *William and Mary Quarterly*, 3rd series, 36:1 (January 1979), pp. 3–26.

14. J. G. A. Pocock, 'Virtues, Rights and Manners: A Model for Historians of Political Thought', in *Virtue, Commerce and History*, pp. 37–50; p. 48.

15. J. G. A. Pocock, 'Cambridge Paradigms and Scotch Philosophers: A Study of the Relations between the Civic Humanist and Civil Jurisprudential Interpretation of Eighteenth Century Thought', in Istvan Hont and Michael Ignatieff (eds), *Wealth and Virtue: The Shaping of Political Economy in the Scottish Enlightenment* (Cambridge: Cambridge University Press, 1983), pp. 235–53.

16. I have self-consciously borrowed the phrase 'unified conceptual framework' from a recent review of Bernard Bailyn's work: Linda Colley, 'The Sea Around Us', *New York Review of Books*, 22 June 2006, pp. 43–5. Colley in turn borrowed the phrase from J. H. Elliott's description of Fernand Braudel's work, 'Atlantic History: A Circumnavigation', in David Armitage and Michael J. Braddick (eds), *The British Atlantic World, 1500–1800* (New York: Palgrave Macmillan, 2002), pp. 233–4.

17. Samuel Taylor Coleridge refers to the 'trichotomy of economic, aesthetic and moral value'; quoted in Kurt Heinzelman, *The Economics of the Imagination* (Amherst: University of Massachusetts, 1980), p. 22.

18. In this sense, this book engages Appleby's call to seat capitalism in the larger cultural and intellectual context: Joyce Oldham Appleby, 'The Vexed Story of Capitalism told by American Historians', *Journal of the Early Republic*, 21 (Spring 2001), pp. 1–18. As Appleby argues, 'capitalism caused a crisis of meaning wherever it acquired sufficient momentum to push aside obstacles to innovation' (p. 16). For a call to expand the domain of economic history, see Deirdre N. McCloskey, '*Bourgeois Virtue* and the History of P and S', *Journal of Economic History*, 58:2 (June 1998), pp. 297–317.

19. Corneille, 'The Album, No. 1: Novel Reading', *Boston Weekly Magazine* (3 April 1824), p. 53.

20. John Locke, *Further Considerations Concerning the Value of Money* (1695), in *John Locke on Money*, ed. Patrick Hyde Kelly, 2 vols (New York: Oxford University Press, 1991), vol. 2, p. 411.

21. See Joyce Oldham Appleby, 'Locke, Liberalism and the Natural Law of Money', *Past and Present*, 71 (May 1976), pp. 43–69; Joyce Oldham Appleby, *Economic Thought and Ideology in Seventeenth-Century England* (Princeton: Princeton University Press, 1978); Peter Laslett, 'John Locke, the Great Recoinage, and the Origins of the Board of Trade: 1695–1698', *William and Mary Quarterly*, 3rd series, 14:3 (July 1957), pp. 370–402; William Letwin, *The Origins of Scientific Economics* (London: Methuen, 1963), pp. 159–95; Terence Hutchison, *Before Adam Smith: The Emergence of Political Economy, 1662–1776* (London: Basil Blackwell, 1988); Ming-Hsun Li, *The Great Recoinage of 1696–1699* (London: Weidenfeld & Nicholson, 1963); Douglas Vickers, *Studies in the Theory of Money, 1690–1776* (Philadelphia: Chilton, 1959); J. Keith Horsefield, *British Monetary Experiments, 1650–1710* (Cambridge, MA: Harvard University Press, 1960).

22. Andrea Finkelstein, *Harmony and the Balance: An Intellectual History of Seventeenth-Century English Economic Thought* (Ann Arbor: University of Michigan Press, 2000), p. 151.

23. John Locke, *Two Treatises of Government* (1690), ed. Peter Laslett (Cambridge: Cambridge University Press, 1967), pp. ii, 50; quoted in Stephen Buckle, *Natural Law and the Theory of Property: Grotius to Hume* (Oxford: Clarendon Press, 1991), p. 154.

24. Finkelstein, *Harmony and the Balance*, p. 155.

25. For a discussion of Locke's theological voluntarism, see John Dunn, 'From Applied Theology to Social Analysis: The Break Between John Locke and the Scottish Enlightenment', in Istvan Hont and Michael Ignatieff (eds), *Wealth and Virtue: The Shaping of Political Economy in the Scottish Enlightenment* (Cambridge: Cambridge University Press, 1983), pp. 119–36; Buckle, *Natural Law and the Theory of Property*, pp. 130–3; and Charles Taylor, *Sources of the Self: The Making of the Modern Identity* (Cambridge, MA: Harvard University Press, 1989). 'Following the predominant view in the Puritan strand of Christian spirituality', Taylor concludes, 'Locke inclined to theological voluntarism' (p. 235).

26. John Locke, *An Essay Concerning Human Understanding* (1690), ed. John Yolton (New York: Dutton, 1964), book 1, Introduction, section 4.

27. 'Morality', Hume wrote to Francis Hutcheson, 'according to your opinion as well as mine is determin'd merely by sentiment, it regards only human nature & human life. This has been often urg'd against you & the consequences are very momentous': Hume to Hutcheson; quoted in Richard F. Teichgraeber III, *Free Trade and Moral Philosophy: Rethinking the Sources of Adam Smith's Wealth of Nations* (Durham, NC: Duke University Press, 1986), p. 80. See also Pocock, 'The Mobility of Property'.

28. Dunn, 'From Applied Theology to Social Analysis', p. 123.

29. Ibid., pp. 122–4. Dunn reaches the profound conclusion that Locke's ideas represent a self-conscious 'refusal of the future as it was to come to be'. Furthermore, he concludes that for modern human beings this future has turned out poorly. 'The development of a purely internal conception of rational agency has left human individuals impressively disenchanted and undeceived. But it has also left them increasingly on their own and devoid of rational direction in social or political action, prisoners of games of self-destruction to which, on these terms, there may well be no rational solutions. It is easier now to see the connections between these menaces. If there is indeed nothing to human existence, individually and socially but opinion, it will certainly be bad news if opinion ever falters.' Dunn concludes with a heartfelt admonition that the 'anguish' Locke protected us against will one day 'be truly ours when we at last learn to feel what now we know' (p. 135).

30. Appleby, *Economic Thought and Ideology*; Laslett, 'John Locke'; Letwin, *The Origins of Scientific Economics*; Hutchison, *Before Adam Smith*; Li, *The Great Recoinage*; Vickers, *Studies in the Theory of Money*; Horsefield, *British Monetary Experiments*.

31. Appleby discusses these complicated issues at length. Put briefly, the different prices for silver and gold created an incentive to melt down silver for export and import gold to 'buy up cheap silver coin': Appleby, 'Locke, Liberalism and the Natural Law of Money', pp. 45–6.

32. For the importance of the Bank of England see Pocock, 'The Mobility of Property', p. 108.

33. Patrick Hyde Kelly, 'Introduction', in *John Locke on Money*, ed. Patrick Hyde Kelly, 2 vols (Oxford: Oxford University Press, 1991), vol. 1, pp. 1–121; p. 66. Kelly notes that the immediate recoinage diminished the amount of silver coin by £2.5 million. Isaac Newton estimated the long-term consequences of the monetary crisis to be much more substantial. He estimated the loss of silver bullion at £5.75 million. Kelly's own research suggests that, between 1693 and 1698, England's silver coin fluctuated from £11 million (December 1693) to £5.1 million (June 1696) to £7.7 million (December 1698): ibid., p. 110, and Table 1, pp. 112–13.

34. William Lowndes, *A Report Containing an Essay for the Amendment of the Silver Coins* (London, 1695).

35. Lowndes, *A Report*, pp. 56–9; Kelly, 'Introduction', p. 24.

36. Ibid., pp. 71–5; Finkelstein, *Harmony and the Balance*, pp. 147–9.

37. John Dunn, *Locke* (New York: Oxford University Press, 1984).

38. Laslett, 'John Locke'.

39. Finkelstein, *Harmony and the Balance*, p. 150. Finkelstein argues that, given Locke's university training and the similarities in many of their arguments, he was 'surely' familiar with the Scholastic thinkers (p. 314, n. 11).

40. Nicole Oresme, *Tractatus de Origine, Natura, Jura, et Mutacionibus Monetarum* ([c. 1605]), ch. xiii; quoted in Timothy J. Reiss and Roger H. Hinderliter, 'Money and Value in the Sixteenth Century: The Monete Cudende Ratio of Nicholas Copernicus', *Journal of the History of Ideas*, 40:2 (April–June 1979), pp. 293–313; p. 296. See also Raymond De Roover, 'Scholastic Economics: Survival and Lasting Influence from the Sixteenth Century to Adam Smith', *Quarterly Journal of Economics*, 69:2 (May 1955), pp. 161–90.

41. Locke, *Further Considerations*, pp. 410–11.

42. Adam Smith also pointed to Locke's mercantilism as the source of his identification of money and treasure, and his denigration of consumption. See Buckle, *Natural Law and the Theory of Property*, p. 156.

43. John Locke, *Some Considerations of the Consequences of the Lowering of the Interest and Raising the Value of Money* (1696), in *John Locke on Money*, ed. Kelly, vol. 1, pp. 231–2.

44. For an analysis of Locke's trade ideas see Hutchison, *Before Adam Smith*, p. 65.

45. Locke, *Further Considerations*, p. 421. Locke's notion that merchants entered into contracts on the basis of weight engaged yet another monetary controversy. See Thomas Guggenheim, *Preclassical Monetary Theories* (New York: Pinter, 1989), pp. 23–8. Andrea Finkelstein also speaks to this issue, noting that merchants contracted and paid in currency ('monys of account') but that other transactions took place by weight: Finkelstein, *The Harmony and the Balance*, p. 151.

46. Guggenheim, *Preclassical Monetary Theories*, p. 27.

47. Finkelstein, *Harmony and the Balance*, pp. 102, 156.

48. Finkelstein quotes Locke: '... when any man snatches for himself as much as he can, he takes away from another man's heap the amount he adds to his own, and it is impossible for anyone to grow rich except at the expense of someone else': John Locke, *Essays on the Law of Nature*, trans. W. von Leyden, corrected reprint of 1954 edn (Oxford: Clarendon Press, 1958), p. 211; quoted in Finkelstein, *Harmony and the Balance*, p. 166.

49. G. L. S. Shackle, *Epistemics and Economics* (Cambridge: Cambridge University Press, 1972), p. 11.

50. Nicholas Barbon, *A Discourse on Trade* (London, 1690), pp. 20, 23, 27.

51. Nicholas Barbon, *A Discourse Concerning Coining the New Money Lighter in Answer to Mr. Lock's Considerations about Raising the Value of Money* (London, 1696), p. 36.

52. Ibid., p. 4.

53. Ibid., p. 48.

54. Andrea Finkelstein, 'Nicholas Barbon and the Quality of Infinity', *History of Political Economy*, 32:1 (Spring 2000), pp. 83–102. Appleby develops these ideas fully in *Economic Thought and Ideology*, pp. 199–217.

55. Laslett, 'John Locke', p. 397; Buckle, *Natural Law and the Theory of Property*, p. 156.

56. Finkelstein, *Harmony and the Balance*, p. 151.

57. John Locke *Two Treatises of Government*, pp. ii, 50; quoted in Buckle, *Natural Law and the Theory of Property*, p. 154. See also Constantine George Caffentzis, *Clipped Coins, Abused Words and Civil Government: John Locke's Philosophy of Money* (New York: Autonomedia, 1989). Caffentzis argues that Locke recognized that money was

imaginary and thus a 'mixed mode'. Money as such was an 'unnatural connection ... an unnecessary and fancied desire ...' (p. 138). Hence, Caffentzis argues, Locke strained to reconstruct money as an immutable substance.

58. See Buckle, *Natural Law and the Theory of Property*, p. 156. Buckle notes that Locke's theory of money in the *Two Treatises* allows him to sidestep thorny equality of distribution issues that arise from spoilage, the 'right of necessity', and the so-called 'enough, and as good', clause. For Locke, Buckle argues, a money economy, provides for the labourer without property and in a way legitimizes the unequal distribution of goods and property. See also Finkelstein, *Harmony and the Balance*, pp. 150–1.

59. Locke wrote: 'The *intrinsick* value of silver consider'd as Money, is that estimate which common consent has placed on it, whereby it is made Equivalent to all other things, and consequently is the universal Barter or Exchange which men give and receive for other things ...'. One possible explanation for this obvious contradiction is that Locke here refers to his notion, developed in the *Essay*, that men arrived at some common agreement on the basic qualities of all substances. Locke, *Further Considerations*, pp. 410–11. Tully comments on this. According to Tully, Locke argues that 'Adam and his friends' agreed on the basic characteristics that identified gold. These agreed-upon characteristics then became the 'norm in accordance with which nature is ranked by the language community (3.6.51)': James Tully, *A Discourse on Property: John Locke and his Adversaries* (Cambridge: Cambridge University Press, 1980), p. 15 (all references in Tully are to *An Essay Concerning Human Understanding*).

60. Finkelstein also ties in Locke's ideas on money to his contract theory. For Locke, Finkelstein argues, 'the intrinsic value of money was one of the pillars supporting civil society': Finkelstein, *Harmony and the Balance*, pp. 150–1.

61. Buckle, *Natural Law and the Theory of Property*, p. 128. For Locke and the divine law as the natural law, see ibid., pp. 125–38. On Locke and the relationship of 'natural law' to money, see Appleby, 'Locke, Liberalism, and the Natural Law of Money'. Briefly stated, Appleby and others argue that the rise of 'natural' ideas on money and the economy are linked with the rise of liberalism and that Locke played a central role in both of these developments. They thus assume a great deal of continuity between Locke and the political economists of the eighteenth century. My own reading differs significantly. Locke's understanding of the 'natural law' was antithetical to subsequent notions of the 'natural law' used by the Scottish political economists. In a number of texts, including his *An Essay Concerning Human Understanding*, Locke followed in the Pufendorf natural law tradition, emphasizing a theocratic 'law of nature' extrinsic to human beings. It was the divine law revealed to man through reason – but it was very clearly extrinsic and theistic. For thinkers like Hume and Adam Smith, the 'law of nature' was psychological and or sociological. It was an anthropocentric explanation of human behaviour, not a series of laws that bound humanity. This is an important difference. The entire source of the law changed and with it much of the meaning. The language remained the same and there was some continuity, but the consequences changed radically. In his analysis Buckle tries to emphasize the continuity between Locke and the Scottish thinkers with limited success (see review by T. J. Hochstrasser, 'Early Modern Natural Law Theories and Their Contexts', *Historical Journal*, 38:2 (June 1995), pp. 487–90). He does, however, acknowledge the difficulty of that endeavour – noting that he has to show how Hutcheson and the Scots

who followed used Lockean ideas to un-Lockean ends: Buckle, *Natural Law and the Theory of Property*, pp. 191–6. Charles Taylor develops at length the difference between these two sources of the 'natural law': Taylor, *Sources of the Self*, pp. 224–48, 327, 337–51. David Levy notes that Hume specifically eschewed any continuity in terms of the 'natural law'. According to Levy, 'Hume's opposition to any teleological connotations given to the word 'natural' is clear in his letters to Francis Hutcheson in July 1739: 'I cannot agree to your sense of *Natural*. Tis founded on final Causes; which is a Consideration, that appears to me pretty much uncertain and unphilosophical. For pray, what is the End of Man? Is he created for Happiness or Virtue? For this Life or for the next? For himself or for his Maker? Your definition of *Natural* depends upon solving these Questions, which are endless & quite wide of my Purpose. I have never call'd Justice unnatural, but only artificial ...': *The Letters of David Hume*, ed. J. Y. T. Greig, 2 vols (Oxford: Clarendon Press, 1932), vol. 1, p. 33; quoted in David Levy, 'Adam Smith's "Natural Law" and Contractual Society', *Journal of the History of Ideas*, 39:4 (October–December 1978), pp. 665–74; pp. 665–6. See also Knud Haakonssen, *Natural Law and Moral Philosophy: From Grotius to the Scottish Enlightenment* (Cambridge: Cambridge University Press, 1996). Haakonssen notes that the 'last three decades of the seventeenth century and the early years of the eighteenth century' saw an 'intense battle' between a theocratic and voluntarist natural law and the Scottish anthropocentric natural law of the heart. 'At issue was the old problem of whether natural law had moral force for humanity solely because it was God's will or whether in addition it had independent moral authority with us. Few disputed that natural law *existed* because of God's will; the question was rather whether or not there were moral values shared by God and humanity which entailed the moral obligations of natural law independently of our regard for God's willing this to be so' (p. 6). See also T. J. Hochstrasser, *Natural Law Theories in the Early Enlightenment* (Cambridge: Cambridge University Press, 2000), p. 2.

62. Dunn, *Locke*, p. 61. Dunn notes that this was Locke's argument against those sceptical of the binding force of natural law.

63. Locke, *An Essay Concerning Human Understanding* (1690); see below.

64. For a debate on Locke's contribution to the Enlightenment, see Isaac Kramnick, 'Republican Revisionism Revisited', *American Historical Review*, 87:3 (June 1982), pp. 629–64. Though Kramnick eloquently defends Locke's contributions to eighteenth-century Enlightenment thought, in this analysis I follow a slightly different interpretation, offered by Tully, *A Discourse on Property*; Dunn, *Locke*; Taylor, *Sources of the Self*; and Buckle, *Natural Law and the Theory of Property*.

65. The fixation with limits and boundaries runs through the *Essay* and was a feature of seventeenth-century thought. See Finkelstein, *Harmony and the Balance*, p. 2; Buckle, *Natural Law and the Theory of Property*, pp. 126–38.

66. Locke, *An Essay Concerning Human Understanding*, book 1, Introduction, section 4.

67. Ibid., book 1, Introduction, section 5.

68. Taylor, *Sources of the Self*, p. 230.

69. For a discussion of the relationship of science to Puritan theology in the seventeenth century, see Edward B. Davis, 'Christianity and Early Modern Science: The Foster Thesis Revisited', in David N. Livingstone, D. G. Hart and Mark A. Noll (eds),

Evangelicals and Science in Historical Perspective (New York: Oxford University Press, 1999), pp. 75–99. Davis's essay is a discussion of the so-called 'Foster Thesis'. In a series of articles M. B. Foster argued that empiricism is a logical necessity of Calvin's theological voluntarism: see M. B. Foster, 'The Christian Doctrine of Creation and the Rise of Modern Natural Science', *Mind*, 43 (1934), pp. 446–68; 'Christian Theology and Modern Science of Nature', *Mind*, 44 (1935), pp. 439–66; and 45 (1936), pp. 1–27.

70. Locke, *An Essay Concerning Human Understanding*, book 1, ch. 2, section 1.
71. Taylor, *Sources of the Self*, pp. 161, 231–2. As Taylor concludes, 'In the end, a mechanistic universe was the only one compatible with a God whose sovereignty was defined in terms of the endless freedom of fiat' (p. 161).
72. Locke, *An Essay Concerning Human Understanding*, book 1, ch. 4, section 21 (emphasis and punctuation in original).
73. Ibid., book 2, ch. 1, section 2.
74. Dunn, *Locke*, p. 73.
75. Locke, *An Essay Concerning Human Understanding*, book 2, ch. 31, section 3.
76. Ibid., book 2, ch. 31, section 3. For a full discussion of 'Mixed Modes' and 'Relations', see Tully, *A Discourse on Property*, pp. 10–15.
77. Ibid., p. 13.
78. On the complicated relationship of property, knowledge and creation, see ibid., pp. 22, 35. 'The Dominion of Man', Locke concluded, 'in this little World of his own Understanding, being muchwhat the same, as it is in the great World of visible things; wherein his Power, however managed by Art and Skill, reached no farther than to compound and divide the Materials, that are made to his Hand; but can do nothing toward the making the least Particle of new Matter, or destroying one Atome of what is already in Being': Locke, *An Essay Concerning Human Understanding*, book 2, ch. 2, section 2.
79. Tully, *A Discourse on Property*, p. 15. According to Tully: 'Locke asks his readers to imagine what happens to Adam's general term *zahab* [Adam's term for gold] in common use. If men were to refer *zahab* to the combination of qualities they were able to find in their own particular sample, each man would be speaking of a different species, since there is an endless number of qualities that can be found in any particular substance (3.6.48). All would be reduced to Babel (3.6.28). Therefore an agreement is made amongst Adam and his friends to count a few "leading qualities" as essential to being a member of a natural kind and to constitute nature into kinds on this basis (3.6.49). The idea of gold, enumerating a few easily observable qualities is turned into a norm in accordance with which nature is ranked by the language community (3.6.51)': Tully, *A Discourse on Property*, p. 15 (all references in Tully are to *An Essay Concerning Human Understanding*).
80. Locke, *An Essay Concerning Human Understanding*, book 2, ch. 31, section 9.
81. Ibid., book 2, ch. 23, section 12.
82. Finkelstein, *Harmony and the Balance*, pp. 166–7.
83. Paracelsus, *Paracelsus: Selected Writings*, ed. Jolande Jacobi (London: Routledge & Kegan Paul, 1951); quoted in J. B. Jackson, *The Necessity for Ruins* (Amherst: University of Massachusetts, 1980), p. 41 (no page given in citation).

84. For the opposite position, see Nathan Tarcov, *Locke's Education for Liberty* (Chicago: University of Chicago Press, 1984); and Peter A. Schouls, *Reasoned Freedom: John Locke and the Enlightenment* (Ithaca: Cornell University Press, 1992). Perhaps Mark Goldie is correct when he suggests, 'Locke scholarship invariably mirrors present concerns. Locke is totemic and is made to endorse our own values': Mark Goldie, 'Review of *Locke's Education for Liberty*', *Journal of Modern History*, 58:1 (March 1986), pp. 300–1.

85. John Locke, *An Essay Concerning Human Understanding*, book 2, ch. 21, section 49; quoted in W. Stark, *The Ideal Foundations of Economic Thought* (London: Routledge & Kegan Paul Limited, 1943, 1948), p. 8.

86. Locke, *An Essay Concerning Human Understanding*, book 2, ch. 21, section 49; quoted in Stark, *The Ideal Foundations*, p. 9.

87. Tully, *A Discourse on Property*, p. 25.

88. Locke, *Essays on the Law of Nature*, p. 211; quoted in Finkelstein, *Harmony and the Balance*, p. 166. This is a common theme for empiricist-mercantilists. Francis Bacon, for example, argued that 'whatsoever is somewhere gotten is somewhere lost'; quoted in Jan De Vries, *The Economy of Europe in an Age of Crisis, 1600–1750* (Cambridge: Cambridge University Press, 1976), p. 177 (no citation given).

89. Locke, *An Essay Concerning Human Understanding*, book 3, ch. 5, section 49 (emphasis added to phrase 'Things without him').

90. Taylor, *Sources of the Self*, p. 230.

91. Foster; quoted in Davis, 'Christianity and Early Modern Science', p. 79.

92. Dunn, *Locke*, p. 82.

93. Ibid., p. 88; see also J. M. Dunn, '"Bright Enough for All Our Purposes": John Locke's Conception of a Civilized Society', *Notes and Records of the Royal Society of London*, 43:2, Science and Civilization Under William and Mary (July 1989), pp. 133–53 (emphasis added).

94. Finkelstein, *Harmony and the Balance*, p. 155.

95. Dunn, 'From Applied Theology to Social Analysis', pp. 122–3.

96. Ibid.; Teichgraeber, *Free Trade and Moral Philosophy*.

97. Ibid., p. 47.

98. Taylor, *Sources of the Self*, p. 248.

99. As Taylor notes, scholars have pointed to innate depravity as overall inconsistent with the idea of *tabula rasa*. My own view on this is that innate depravity does not bind God to action. If man is innately depraved, he may be forgiven or condemned. If he is innately good, it is hard for the deity to send him to eternal damnation without some trepidation.

100. James O. Hancey, 'John Locke and the Law of Nature', *Political Theory*, 4:4 (November 1976), pp. 439–54; p. 448.

101. John Smith; quoted in Taylor, *Sources of the Self*, p. 149.

102. Ibid., pp. 251–3.

103. Ibid., pp. 249–51.

104. Ibid., pp. 248–65.

105. Anthony Ashley Cooper, third Earl of Shaftesbury, *Characteristicks of Men, Manners, Opinions, Times*, 3 vols (1711; Farnborough: Gregg, 1968), vol. 2: *An Inquiry Concerning Virtue and Merit*, book 1, part 3, section 1, p. 43.

106. Taylor, *Sources of the Self*, p. 250.
107. Shaftesbury, *An Inquiry Concerning Virtue and Merit*, book 1, part 3, section 1, p. 43.
108. Buckle, *Natural Law and the Theory of Property*, p. 195.
109. Teichgraeber, *Free Trade and Moral Philosophy*, p. 38.
110. Taylor, *Sources of the Self*, p. 253.
111. Hutcheson, *An Inquiry into the Original of our Ideas of Beauty and Virtue; In Two Treatises* (1726; New York: Garland, 1971), p. 135.
112. Daniel Carey, 'Hutcheson's Moral Sense and the Problems of Innateness', *Journal of the History of Philosophy* (January 2000), pp. 103–10.
113. Hutcheson; quoted in Taylor, *Sources of the Self*, p. 261.
114. Hutcheson; quoted in Teichgraeber, *Free Trade and Moral Philosophy*, p. 42.
115. See Albert O. Hirschman, *The Passions and the Interests: Political Arguments for Capitalism Before its Triumph* (Princeton: Princeton University Press, 1977).
116. Teichgraeber, *Free Trade and Moral Philosophy*, p. 47.
117. Hutcheson, *An Inquiry into the Original*, p. 277.
118. Ibid., p. 286.
119. Buckle, *Natural Law and the Theory of Property*, pp. 42–4.
120. Hutcheson, *An Inquiry into the Original*, p. 285.
121. Teichgraeber, *Free Trade and Moral Philosophy*, p. 70.
122. Buckle, *Natural Law and the Theory of Property*, pp. 239, 291.
123. Taylor, *Sources of the Self*, p. 252.
124. Buckle, *Natural Law and the Theory of Property*, p. 297.
125. Hume to Hutcheson; quoted in Teichgraeber, *Free Trade and Moral Philosophy*, p. 80.
126. Taylor, *Sources of the Self*, pp. 343–5.
127. Teichgraeber, *Free Trade and Moral Philosophy*, p. 92. Knud Haakonssen notes 'to see justice in this way as an unintended consequence of individual human actions, must be one of the boldest moves in the history of philosophy of law': Knud Haakonssen, *The Science of a Legislator: The Natural Jurisprudence of David Hume and Adam Smith* (New York: Cambridge University Press, 1981), p. 21; quoted in Ronald Hamowy, *The Scottish Enlightenment and the Theory of Spontaneous Order* (Carbondale: Southern Illinois University Press, 1987), p. 11.
128. Tatsuya Sakamoto, 'Hume's Political Economy as a System of Manners', in Tatsuya Sakamoto and Hideo Tanaka (eds), *The Rise of Political Economy in the Scottish Enlightenment* (London and New York: Routledge, 2003), pp. 86–102; p. 98.
129. David Hume, 'Of Money', in *Writings on Economics*, ed. Eugene Rotwin (Madison: University of Wisconsin Press, 1955), pp. 33, 37.
130. S. G. Checkland, *Scottish Banking: A History, 1695–1973* (Glasgow and London: Collins, 1975), p. 251.
131. Hume, 'Of Money', pp. 35, 68.
132. David Hume; quoted in Checkland, *Scottish Banking*, pp. 247–74.
133. Sakamoto, 'Hume's Political Economy', p. 99.
134. Furthermore, as Carl Wennerlind argues, many of Hume's ideas on property and exchange lead to a fiduciary theory of money. In the same manner that property derived from 'conventions', Wennerlind argues, in his *Treatise on Human Nature*

Hume described the development of a non-barter economy on the basis of symbols that maintained a system of promises and obligations between strangers. This symbolic system is for Wennerlind the description of a fiduciary system not unlike that created by bank notes or other forms of paper credit: Carl Wennerlind, 'The Link Between David Hume's *Treatise of Human Nature* and his Fiduciary Theory of Money', *History of Political Economy*, 33:1 (2001), pp. 139–60. In the same vein, Margaret Schabas has argued for the influence of natural history in Hume's monetary ideas – specifically the contemporary notion of 'electric fluid' in Hume's essay 'Of Money': Margaret Schabas, 'David Hume on Experimental Natural Philosophy, Money and Fluids', *History of Political Economy*, 33:3 (2001), pp. 411–35.

135. Adam Smith, *The Theory of Moral Sentiments* (1759; New York: Garland, 1971), p. 3.

136. Charles L. Griswold, Jr, *Adam Smith and the Virtues of the Enlightenment* (Cambridge: Cambridge University Press, 1999), p. 144.

137. Emma Rothschild, *Economic Sentiments: Adam Smith, Condorcet and the Enlightenment* (Cambridge, MA: Harvard University Press, 2001), p. 9.

138. Hamowy, *The Scottish Enlightenment*, p. 14.

139. Teichgraeber, *Free Trade and Moral Philosophy*, p. 153.

140. There is, however, a tremendous controversy regarding Smith's ideas on value. Recent economic historians such as Terence Hutchison have echoed earlier criticisms of Smith. According to these scholars, Smith set back the idea of subjective value in his analysis – especially in the construction of his so-called labour theory of value. This is, in my opinion, a misreading of Smith. As Schumpeter points out, Smith divided the 'real' or 'natural' price of a good into rent, labour and profit, in the context of equilibrium theory. He delineated the costs of the factors of production that went into making any product. These determined a 'natural' price because a price below the aggregate of these items would result in no product. Smith also clearly discussed the 'market' price of a product as a function of demand – and thus subjective. Again, however, even here his concern was equilibrium. Thus if demand exceeded supply, bidders would raise the price of a product above its 'natural' price, provide incentives for others to enter the market, and thus decrease the price of a product until the 'natural' price was once again met. For Smith, the market price was *de facto* desire-driven – indeed his whole system depends on it. He was clearly not oblivious to desire in the *Theory of Moral Sentiments*; for example, he evocatively discussed the impact of the imagination on desire and the role that desire played in the stimulation of demand and the economy overall: 'Our imagination, which in pain and sorrow seems to be confined and cooped up within our own persons, in times of ease and prosperity expands itself to every thing around us. We are then charmed with the beauty of that accommodation which reigns in the palaces and oeconomy of the great; and admire how everything is adapted to promote their ease, to prevent their wants, to gratify their wishes, and to amuse and entertain their most frivolous desires. If we consider the real satisfaction which all these things are capable of affording, by itself and separated from the beauty of that arrangement which is fitted to promote it, it will always appear in the highest degree contemptible and trifling. But we rarely view it in this abstract and philosophical light. We naturally confound it in our imagination with the order, the regular and harmonious movement of the system, the machine or

oeconomy by means of which it is produced. The pleasures of wealth and greatness when considered in this complex view, strike the imagination as something grand and beautiful and noble, of which the attainment is well worth all the toil and anxiety which we are so apt to bestow upon it. And it is well that nature imposes upon us in this manner. It is this deception which rouses and keeps in continual motion the industry of mankind.' Certainly, Smith depreciates the 'baubles' that man desires after – but he does so clearly in the context of man's engagement with these objects in their imaginations. See Hutchison, *Before Adam Smith*, p. 353; and Joseph A. Schumpeter, *History of Economic Analysis* (New York: Oxford University Press, 1954), pp. 188–9, 308–9.

141. Hamowy, *The Scottish Enlightenment*, p. 19.

142. Rothschild, *Economic Sentiments*, p. 9.

143. Free banking as I am using it refers to the unregulated banking practices common to Scotland in the eighteenth century. This includes free entry into and exit from banking and the unregulated issue of convertible notes. Lawrence White, *Free Banking in Britain* (Cambridge: Cambridge University Press, 1984).

144. Adam Smith, *The Wealth of Nations* (1776; New York: Modern Library, 2000), book 2, ch. 2, pp. 358–9.

145. Overall see ibid., book 2, ch. 2: 'Money', and book 5, ch. 3, part 5; see also Adam Smith, *Lectures on Justice, Police, Revenue and Arms* (1763), ed. Edward Cannan (1896; New York: Augustus M. Kelley, 1964).

146. Smith used Scottish banking practice as an example for most of his ideas: Smith, *The Wealth of Nations*, book 2, ch. 2.

147. Charles W. Munn, *The Scottish Provincial Banking Companies, 1747–1864* (Edinburgh: Donald, 1981), p. 143.

148. White, *Free Banking in Britain*, pp. 29–30.

149. Teichgraeber, *Free Trade and Moral Philosophy*, p. 11.

150. Taylor, *Sources of the Self*, p. 284.

151. Riesman, 'The Origins of American Political Economy', pp. 168–222.

152. Cathy Matson, 'American Political Economy in the Constitutional Decade', in *The United States Constitution: The First Two Hundred Years* (New York: Manchester University Press, 1989), pp. 16–35.

153. Joyce Oldham Appleby, *Capitalism and a New Social Order: The Republican Vision of the 1790s* (New York: New York University Press, 1984).

154. Taylor, *Sources of the Self*, especially, part 3: 'The Affirmation of Everyday Life'.

155. John E. Crowley, *The Privileges of Independence: Neomercantilism and the American Revolution* (Baltimore: Johns Hopkins University Press, 1993).

156. See Riesman, 'The Origins of American Political Economy', pp. 1–15.

157. See Edwin J. Perkins, *American Public Finance and Financial Services, 1700–1815* (Columbus: Ohio State University Press, 1994), esp. ch. 5: 'Wartime Finance'.

158. Janet Riesman, 'Money, Credit and the Federalist Political Economy', in Richard Beeman and Edward Carter II (eds), *Beyond Confederation: Origins of the Constitution and the American National Identity* (Chapel Hill: University of North Carolina Press, 1987), pp. 128–61; p. 132.

159. Riesman, 'The Origins of American Political Economy', pp. 30–2, 364, 390; Riesman, 'Money, Credit and the Federalist Political Economy', p. 135.

160. J. Van Fenstermaker, *The Development of American Commercial Banking: 1782–1837* (Kent: Kent State Bureau of Economic and Business Research, 1965), pp. 5–6.

161. Riesman, 'Money, Credit and the Federalist Political Economy'. Riesman seems surprised by the introduction of specie-backed paper instruments. They were, of course, common in Britain. Scottish and English banks, including the Bank of England, used convertible bank notes through the eighteenth century. For the development of banks in general see Hammond, *Banks and Politics in America*.

162. Pocock, 'The Mobility of Property', p. 112.

163. Riesman, 'The Origins of American Political Economy', pp. 39, 30.

164. For the association of bank notes with 'paper', see the anonymous articles 'Banks and Bank Notes' (21 September and 5 October 1816, 21 June 1817); 'Bank Notes Not Money' (31 May 1817); 'Banking – General Remarks' (25 April 1818); 'The Paper System' nos 1–7 (25 April–20 June 1818); and 'Common Sewer of Speculation' (12 December 1818), *Niles' Weekly Register*.

165. See Chapter 4 for a full discussion of banking in Boston during the Early Republic. Hammond, *Banks and Politics in America*, pp. 188–9.

166. See, for example, the discussion in the *Cyclopedia* on 'intrinsic' and 'extrinsic' value: Abraham Rees (ed.), 'Money', *The Cyclopaedia; or Universal Dictionary of Arts, Sciences and Literature*, 41 vols (Philadelphia, 1810–24), vol. 24.

167. Peter J. Diamond, 'Witherspoon, William Smith and the Scottish Philosophy in Revolutionary America', in Richard B. Sher and Jeffrey R. Smitten (eds), *Scotland and America in the Age of Enlightenment* (Princeton: Princeton University Press, 1990), pp. 115–32.

168. John Witherspoon, *Essay on Money as a Medium of Commerce* (Philadelphia, 1786), pp. 2–9.

169. As with many other commentators in these debates, he loosely followed a four-stages theory of civilization. Ronald Hamowy comments on the pervasiveness of these ideas for eighteenth-century thinkers: Ronald Hamowy, *The Scottish Enlightenment*, p. 15. See also Pocock, 'The Mobility of Property', p. 116. The four-stage theory placed human agency at the centre of history. This development is of course a tremendous change and suggests that even an intrinsic-theorist like Witherspoon saw human agency as central to value.

170. Witherspoon, *Essay on Money*, pp. 13–16.

171. Joseph Dorfman, *The Economic Mind in American Civilization* (New York: Viking Press, 1946–59), p. 299.

172. James Sullivan, *The Path to Riches* (Boston, 1792).

173. Ibid., p. 41. Sullivan quotes at length from 'a pamphlet written by Dr. Price, on the nature of civil liberty, in the year 1776'. I assume he is referring to Richard Price, *Observations on the Nature of Civil Liberty, the Principles of Government, and the Justice and Policy of the War with America: To which is Added, an Appendix, containing a State of the National Debt, an Estimate of the Money Drawn from the Public by the Taxes, and an Account of the National Income and Expenditure since the Last War* (Philadelphia, 1776). See Riesman, 'Money, Credit, and Federalist Political Economy', for a discussion of the American fascination with Dr Price (p. 144).

174. Sullivan, *The Path to Riches*, p. 25.

175. Ibid., p. 51.

176. Ibid., pp. 53, 1.
177. Ibid., p. 71.
178. Nestor, 'Thoughts on Paper Money', *American Museum* (July 1787), p. 40.
179. For example, in his emotional pamphlet published after the 1819 financial panic, Benjamin Davies condemned banks and the banking system as unnatural and pernicious to the social order. The banking system, according to Davies, allowed rich men to replace gold and silver with paper, to their benefit and the detriment of the poor. 'These inequalities in the laws of man', Davies declared, have 'destroyed the equality of the law of nature, which she has wisely designed for the just harmony of her works'. Davies subscribed to a limited and finite quantity theory of money. Thus the increase in paper-credit instruments had simply raised the price level much to the detriment of ordinary working people without access to bank stock: 'it must likewise be no less evident, that the Bankers as certainly rob every other man in society, by circulating their notes, as by levying a tax, or by putting their hands into peoples' pockets, and taking out a part of their money', Davies concluded. For Davies all banks were a manner of theft and were the scourge of humanity. 'Money', he quoted an anonymous source, 'when considered as the fruit of many years industry, as the reward of labour, sweat and toil, as the widow's dowry and the children's portion, and as the means of obtaining the necessaries, and alleviating the afflictions of life, and making old age a scene of rest, has something in it sacred, that is not to be sported with, or trusted to the airy bubble of paper currency': Benjamin Davies, *The Bank Torpedo* (New York, 1819), pp. 11, 53.
180. Riesman, 'Money, Credit, and Federalist Political Economy', p. 160.
181. The four points were: '1. That it carries gold and silver out of the province ... 2. That the merchants trading to America have suffered and lost by it ... 3. That the restriction of it has had a beneficial effect in New England ... 4. That every medium of trade should have an intrinsic value, which paper money has not ... 5. That debtors in the assemblies make paper money with fraudulent views ... 6. That in the middle colonies, where the credit of the paper-money has been supported, the bills have never kept to their nominal value, in circulation': Benjamin Franklin, 'Remarks and Facts relative to the American Paper Money' (London, 1764), *American Museum* (July 1787), p. 17.
182. Nicholas Barbon originally espoused a utility theory of value in *A Discourse Concerning Coining*.
183. Barbon also pointed to iron's greater utility value to make his point: ibid., p. 6.
184. Franklin, 'Remarks and Facts relative to the American Paper Money', pp. 20–1.
185. Dorfman, *The Economic Mind*, p. 224.
186. Barton quoted liberally from Robert Wallace, *Characteristics of the Present Political State of Great Britain* (Dublin, 1758; French trans. Le Haye, 1763).
187. William Barton, *Observations on the Nature and Use of Paper Credit* (Philadelphia, 1781), p. 7.
188. See also Rees (ed.), 'Money'. The idea that the extrinsic value of silver might differ from its intrinsic value was highly debated: 'There is, in fact, not the least occasion for bringing in this analogy to prove that money, in its character of money must possess value: that is implied in the very meaning of the term; nothing can facilitate the interchange of commodities; nothing can be exchanged itself for any other commod-

ity which does not possess value. But a much more important and difficult question remains to be noticed, discussed and solved. Is it essential to the character and uses of money that the commodity of which it is formed should possess value independent of its application as such? Another question arises out of this, or rather is involved in it. Can the value of any commodity, when used as money, be greater than it possessed when not applied to this purpose?': Barton, *Observations on the Nature and Use of Paper Credit*, p. 7.

189. William Barton, *The True Interest of the United States and Particularly of Pennsylvania Considered* (Philadelphia, 1786), pp. 2–3; and in the *American Museum*, July 1787, p. 4 (emphasis in original).

190. Sir James Steuart was no friend of an unregulated banking system. He envisioned and promoted a regulated flow of specie and bank notes. In his *Inquiry into the Principles of Political Oeconomy* (London, 1767), he argued strongly for a public bank that performed the functions of a central bank and bought gold and silver on the market to maintain specie reserves. Furthermore, under Steuart's plan, the tax system of the state was intimately connected to the currency. Nevertheless, Steuart's bank would also emit paper on land security and thus '[throw] solid property into circulation', and he envisioned a system of paper credit based on 'solid property ... melted down'.

191. For a discussion of Barton's political position, see Riesman, 'Money, Credit, and Federalist Political Economy', pp. 158–60. Riesman argues that Barton's ideas represented the Anti-Federalist emphasis on internal productivity. She notes, however, that Federalists also espoused more moderate versions of the same ideas and the role of money.

192. Perkins, *American Public Finance*, p. 250.

193. Joseph Dorfman, *The Economic Mind*, p. 487.

194. Bollmann, *Paragraph on Banks*, p. 21.

195. Ibid., p. 35. Bollmann correctly notes that only the first instalments of the bank's capital were ever paid in specie. Subsequent payments might be made in the notes of other banks, in the notes of the United States Bank itself, or in treasury stock. Thus, though the capital of the bank was $10 million divided into $7.5 million in 6 per cent stock and $2.5 million in specie, only $675,000 in specie was ever likely to have made it into the vaults.

196. Ibid., p. 44.

197. Ibid., p. 49.

198. Bollmann wrote the pamphlet in the midst of plans to charter the Second Bank of the United States, but there is no indication he wrote to that issue. The pamphlet was written from London: Dorfman, *The Economic Mind*, p. 497.

199. Erick Bollmann, *Plan of an Improved System of the Money-Concerns of the Union* (Philadelphia, 1816).

200. James Swan, *An Address to the President, Senate and House of Representatives, of the United States, on The Means of Creating a National Paper by Loan Offices, which shall Replace that of Discredited Banks, and Supersede the Use of Gold and Silver Coin* (Boston, 1819). Riesman notes that plans for land banks and/or labour banks spoke to the confusion in the nature of money and enjoyed popularity in the mid-eighteenth century: Riesman, 'The Origins of Political Economy', p. 185.

201. Anon., 'Extract from an Address to the Representatives of the People of Virginia', *American Museum* (July 1787), pp. 34–5.

202. Anon., 'Queries and Replies relative to Paper Money', *American Museum* (July 1787), pp. 35–6.

203. Anon., 'Supplement to the Pennsylvania Gazette: Considerations on the Bank of North America', *Pennsylvania Gazette* (7 September 1785). The author is quoting the Scottish political economist James Steuart.

204. See Condy Raguet, *An Inquiry into the Causes of the Present State of the Circulating Medium of the United States* (Philadelphia, 1815); also, for lengthy review essays of political economy, including the nature of wealth and money, see Anon., Review of Adam Smith, *An Inquiry into the Nature and Causes of Wealth* (French trans., 2nd edn, Paris 1822), *Boston Journal of Philosophy and the Arts* (July 1824), pp. 65–81; 'The Principles of Political Economy' nos I–XXII, *United States Literary Gazette* (October 1825–March 1826); Review of 'Essay on Money', Supplement to the *Encyclopedia Britannica*, vol. 5, part 2 (Edinburgh, 1822), *New York Review and Athenaeum Magazine* (September 1825), pp. 264–83; see also the articles on 'Money' and 'Political Economy', in Rees (ed.), *The Cyclopedia*, vols 24, 29; and the articles on 'Bank' and 'Political Economy', in *New Edinburgh Encyclopedia*, 2nd American edn (New York, 1817), pp. 39–77.

205. Blodget, *Economica*, p. 12.

206. Witherspoon, *Essay on Money*, p. 23.

207. Barton, *Observations on the Nature and Use of Paper Credit*.

208. Ibid., p. 14. Here Barton cited Sir William Blackstone as authority.

209. Ibid., p. 15. Here Barton is quoting Parliamentary Bullion Commission, 327.

210. Smith, *Lectures on Justice*, p. 199.

211. Riesman, 'The Origins of American Political Economy', p. 86. Riesman argues that eighteenth-century Britons recognized this idea long before Colonial Americans.

212. Appleby, *Capitalism and a New Social Order*, p. 82.

213. Riesman, 'The Origins of American Political Economy', pp. 1–15.

214. Margaret Ellen Newell, *From Dependency to Independence: Economic Revolution in Colonial New England* (Ithaca: Cornell University Press, 1998), pp. 111–80.

215. Riesman, 'The Origins of American Political Economy', p. 206.

216. Margaret Newell disputes Riesman's conclusion. After the Land Bank failure, she argues, colonists continued to exploit loopholes in the Currency Act. However, her own conclusions suggest that the Land Bank was indeed a pivotal point in New England economic practice and theory and that after the Land Bank failure, little effective innovation took place. Her own discussion of money and banks ends with the Land Bank failure. 'In the end', she concludes, 'the theories of paper money advocates imparted a crucial legacy to political and economic thought in New England ... These attitudes influenced New Englanders' reaction to the tightening of British economic regulations during the imperial crisis': Newell, *From Dependency to Independence*, pp. 234–5.

217. Appleby, *Capitalism and a New Social Order*, p. 88.

218. J. Gallison, Review of John Bristed's, *The Resources of the United States of America, or A View of the Agricultural, Commercial, Manufacturing, Financial, Political, Literary,*

Moral and Religious Capacity and Character of the American People, North American Review, 21 (December 1818), p. 402.

219. Norman A. Graebner, 'New England and the World, 1783–1791', in Conrad Edick Wright, *Massachusetts and the New Nation* (Boston: Massachusetts Historical Society, 1992), pp. 1–35.

220. Samuel Eliot Morison, *The Maritime History of Massachusetts* (Boston and New York: Houghton Mifflin Company, 1921), pp. 160–212.

221. Dorfman, *The Economic Mind*, p. 566; Kenneth V. Lundberg, 'Daniel Raymond: A Note', in Daniel Raymond, *The Elements of Political Economy* (1823; New York: Augustus M. Kelley, 1964).

222. James Maitland, Earl of Lauderdale, *An Inquiry into the Nature and Origin of Public Wealth, and into the Means and Causes of its Increase* (Edinburgh and London, 1804). Schumpeter refers to Lauderdale under the heading: 'Some of Those Who Also Ran', in *History of Economic Analysis*, p. 486. F. C. Gray referred to the Earl of Lauderdale sarcastically as that 'author of whom it has somewhere been said that he wrote a whole book to prove that he did not understand Adam Smith': Review of Daniel Raymond's *Thoughts on Political Economy, in two parts* (Baltimore, 1820), *North American Review*, 31, n.s. 6 (April 1821), p. 447.

223. See 'Political Economy', *New Edinburgh Encyclopedia*, for an explication of Adam Smith's ideas as understood by Americans.

224. Raymond, *The Elements of Political Economy*, p. 47.

225. Ibid., p. 47.

226. Ibid., pp. 35–9.

227. Ibid., pp. 230–53.

228. Ibid., p. 250.

229. Gray, Review of Raymond's *Thoughts on Political Economy*, p. 443.

230. Ibid., p. 445.

231. Anon., 'Essay on Money', *New York Review and Atheneum Magazine*, 1 (September 1825), p. 266.

232. [Caleb Cushing], 'Miscellanies – The Principles of Political Economy', *United State Literary Gazette* (October 1825–March 1826).

233. [Caleb Cushing], 'Principles of Political Economy', *United States Literary Gazette* (1 October 1825).

234. Ibid., p. 64.

235. Anon., Review of *Summary of the Practical Principles of Political Economy, with Observations on Smith's Wealth of Nations, and Say's Political Economy*, *North American Review* (October 1826), p. 465.

236. Joseph Dorfman, 'Introduction', in Thomas Cooper, *Lectures on the Elements of Political Economy* (1826; New York: Kelley, 1971), p. 9.

237. Appleby, *Capitalism and a New Social Order*, p. 88.

238. Dorfman, *The Economic Mind*, p. 534. There were rumours, according to Dorfman, that Cooper was an alcoholic.

239. Though numerous American political economists espoused Ricardian ideas they often misunderstood or simply ignored his maxims. Adam Smith and J. Say were more influential even among professed disciples of Ricardo: Dorfman, *The Economic Mind*, pp. 512–16.

240. Cooper, *Lectures on the Elements of Political Economy*, p. 199.
241. Ibid., pp. 160–5. For Bollmann's approval of Smith, see Dorfman, *The Economic Mind*, pp. 495–8.
242. Cooper, *Lectures on the Elements of Political Economy*, p. 281.
243. J. Porter, Review of Thomas Cooper's *Political Economy*, *North American Review* (October 1827), p. 416.
244. Ibid., p. 421.
245. Ibid., p. 420.
246. Willard Phillips, *A Manual of Political Economy* (1828; New York: Augustus M. Kelley, 1968), p. 11.
247. Ibid., p. 33.
248. Ibid., p. 7.
249. Dorfman, *The Economic Mind*, p. 596.
250. Ibid., p. 596.
251. *Intellectual Regale; or Ladies' TEA Tray* (8 July 1815), pp. 537–9.
252. 'I was ushered into being on the confines of Canada', began another such story in the Boston *Ladies Port Folio*. 'My father was the *noted* Stephen Burrows, a man who to this day holds a place on the waste of memory of many an honest New England farmer.' Stephen Burrows, having no 'parental affection for his offspring', sold the forged bank note narrating its story for one Spanish milled dollar. The note was exchanged as a forgery at a discount twice, gambled away twice, used to purchase a rump of beef, three tin pots, a shoe shine (with change), lost, found again – passed to a foolish Jack Tar, thrown away in anger, and finally found by a hapless poet who rode its false joy momentarily before mournfully burning it in his fireplace – 'but here I did not perish', concluded the forged note, 'for I flew up the chimney, and now I am traveling on the four winds of heaven alternately to the four quarters of the globe': *Ladies Port Folio* (22 January 1820), pp. 26–7. For the puffing and swelling of credit, see Joseph Addison, *Spectator*, 3 (3 March 1711); and Terry Mulcaire, 'Public Credit; or, the Feminization of Virtue in the Marketplace', *PMLA*, 114:5 (October 1999), pp. 1029–42.
253. See *The Bank Note or Lessons for Ladies: A Comedy in Five Acts as Performed at the Boston Theatre* (Boston, 1796). This romantic comedy about love, money and authenticity is saturated in the language of finance.
254. Richard Wright, *The Wealth of Nations Rediscovered* (Cambridge: Cambridge University Press, 2002). Wright argues that banking was the basis for the incredible growth of the American economy from 1780 to 1850.
255. Hammond, *Banks and Politics in America*, p. 183.
256. Ibid., p. 81.
257. Robert E. Wright, 'Banking and Politics in New York' (PhD Dissertation, SUNY Buffalo, 1996), p. 724.
258. Extracts From the Report of the Committee on the Bank of the United States', *Philanthropist*, 9:1 (1819), pp. 131, 130.
259. Hammond notes that only in 1837 did legislators restrict liabilities in proportion to specie reserves: Hammond, *Banks and Politics in America*, p. 136.
260. Bodenhorn discusses the practice of stock notes – paying in the capital for the bank with a discount or note from the bank – in *State Banking in Early America*, pp. 18–

20. See also the discussion below regarding the Glocester bank and the Second Bank of the United States.

261. The charter of the State Bank, for example, stipulated that 'deposits' were not liabilities: 'The Total amount of debts which the said corporation shall at any time owe, independently of its deposits; whether by bond, bill, note, or other contract, shall not exceed double the capital stock actually paid in, unless the contracting a greater debt shall have been previously authorized by a law of the Commonwealth': Massachusetts Senate, *An Act Establishing the State Bank* (Boston, 1810), pp. 9–10. As late as 1820, the *Boston Commercial Gazette* could boast of the 'deposits' in the Boston banks, seemingly unaware that the 'deposits' were liabilities: 'Bank Statements', *Boston Commercial Gazette* (3 February 1820).

262. Hammond, *Banks and Politics in America*, pp. 188–9. Hammond notes that contemporary confusion over the nature of deposits obscured the extent to which banks expanded the money supply. Furthermore, Hammond points out that bank capital was largely 'fictitious in the sense that it was legally supposed to be wholly in specie and in fact was not'. The changing nature of banking was also critical in this regard. Hammond notes that Alexander Hamilton followed the Bank of England charter in excluding 'deposits' as liabilities for the Bank of the United States. According to Hammond, however, Hamilton meant to exclude only 'real' deposits – specie put in the bank for safekeeping. As deposits generated by discounts became more and more critical to business the distinction was lost and liability restrictions on the Bank of the United States related only to note issues: ibid., p. 136.

263. The British banker Alexander Baring made this point to a Parliamentary Committee; quoted in ibid., p. 189.

264. On early paper money and banking see Newell, *From Dependency to Independence*.

265. In 1740 the British applied the 'Bubble Act', prohibiting the creation of joint-stock banking corporations in the colonies.

266. See Perkins, *American Public Finance*, pp. 106–37.

267. Hammond, *Banks and Politics in America*, p. 66.

268. N. S. B. Gras, *The Massachusetts First National Bank of Boston, 1784–1934* (Cambridge, MA: Harvard University Press, 1934), p. 14.

269. Charts 1 and 2 are derived from: Massachusetts Secretary, *A Correct Abstract of All the Statements by the Incorporated Banks in this Commonwealth from 1803 to January 1807* (Boston, 1807); Massachusetts Senate, *A True Abstract of the Statement of the Several Banks in the Commonwealth of Massachusetts. Rendered in January 1808* (Boston, 1808); Massachusetts Senate, *A True Abstract of the Statement of the Several Banks in the Commonwealth of Massachusetts. Rendered in January 1811 [to 1819]* (Boston, 1811–19).

270. All of the Boston banks except the State Bank converted their 'debts due' to 'debts due on interest' over this period. The Boston Bank on the other hand had all of its debt due on interest by 1811. The sources available are incomplete in this regard. The aggregate reports in Senate Document No. 38 differentiate between debts due and debts due on interest only between 1808 and 1814. Given the structure of discounts, my feeling is that this change represents 'accommodation loans' or renewed discounts. 'Discounts' subtracted the 'interest' from the loan at time of issue. There was thus no further interest to calculate. A loan rolled over (by definition, an accommodation

loan) would by necessity surpass its interest discount and begin to accumulate interest charges. Bodenhorn discusses this issue in some detail. It is clear that the early merchant-bankers sought to maintain a 'real-bills' discount policy. The evidence suggests, however, that accommodation loans, for stock speculation and other ventures, soon overwhelmed the bankers' intentions. Bodenhorn, *State Banking in Early America*, p. 54. As discussed below, the evidence from the Boston Bank suggests that the majority of its discounts were 'accommodation' loans or lines of credit.

271. Joseph G. Martin, *A Century of Finance: Martin's History of the Boston Stock and Money Markets, One Hundred Years, From January 1798 to 1898* (Boston, 1898), p. 94. Chart 3 and Table 3 are based on Martin's price data.

272. On the Boston Tontine Association see Joseph Stancliffe Davis, *Essays in the Earlier History of American Corporations* (Cambridge, MA: Harvard University Press, 1917), pp. 70–4.

273. David R. Weir, 'Tontines, Public Finance, and Revolution in France and England, 1688–1789', *Journal of Economic History*, 49:1 (March 1989), pp. 95–124; See also Robert M. Jennings, Donald F. Swanson and Andrew P. Trout, 'Alexander Hamilton's Tontine Proposal', *William and Mary Quarterly*, 3rd series, 45:1 (January 1988), pp. 107–15; and Donald F. Swanson and Andrew P. Trout, 'Alexander Hamilton, "the Celebrated Mr. Neckar", and Public Credit', *William and Mary Quarterly*, 3rd series, 47:3 (July 1990), pp. 422–30.

274. *Boston Gazette* (26 October 1792); quoted in Davis, *Essays in the Earlier History of American Corporations*, p. 71.

275. See note 269 above.

276. Martin, *A Century of Finance*, p. 97. See note 271 above.

277. Massachusetts General Court, *Acts and Laws of the Commonwealth of Massachusetts* (Boston, 1890), pp. 1803, 1804.

278. Ibid.; see also, Pauline Maier, 'The Revolutionary Origins of the American Corporation', *William and Mary Quarterly*, 3rd series, 50:1, Law and Society in Early America (June 1993), pp. 51–84; Naomi Lamoreaux, *Insider Lending: Banks, Personal Connections and Economic Development in Industrial New England* (New York: Cambridge University Press, 1994).

279. Letter from Harrison Gray Otis to the Boston Bank, 16 January 1826, Boston Bank Papers, 1796–1826, Massachusetts Historical Society.

280. Records of Banks of New England and New York, Boston Bank Records 1803–1813, Baker Library Collection, Harvard University. See entries for 1804.

281. See note 269 above.

282. Martin, *A Century of Finance*, p. 97. See note 271 above.

283. Massachusetts Secretary, *A Correct Abstract of all the Statements ... 1803 to January 1807*.

284. Massachusetts Senate, *Senate Document No. 38, Schedule Exhibiting the Conditions of the Banks in Massachusetts for every year, From 1803 to 1807, Inclusive* (Boston, 1837), pp. 5–7.

285. See for example, Anon., 'Course of Exchange for Bank Notes And Specie', *Cohen's Lottery Gazette and Register* (21 August 1818), p. 143.

286. Gilbert and Dean, *Names of the Banks in Massachusetts, New Hampshire ... Together with the Rates of Exchanging them for Specie* (Boston, 1815).

287. See Anon., 'Banks in Danger', *Salem Register* (2 April 1807).

288. Records of Banks of New England and New York, 16 and 26 September 1803.

289. Although Matthew Crocker has recently written about the 'Middling Interest' politics in Boston during this period, he missed the connection between 'Middling Interest' politics, renegade Federalists and the banks (Matthew Crocker, *The Magic of the Many: Josiah Quincy and the Rise of Mass Politics in Boston, 1800–1830* (Amherst: University of Massachusetts Press, 1999). For the still-definitive discussion of many of these issues, see Paul Goodman, *The Democratic-Republicans of Massachusetts: Politics in a Young Republic* (Cambridge, MA: Harvard University Press, 1964). For more on Dexter and the Boston Exchange Office, see Jane Kamensky, *The Exchange Artist: A Story of Paper, Bricks, and Ash in Early National America* (New York: Viking/Penguin, in press).

290. *Boston Gazette* (12 May 1803).

291. *Columbian Centinel* (18 June 1803).

292. *Independent Chronicle* (9 May 1803).

293. *Independent Chronicle* (4 April 1803).

294. *Columbian Centinel* (5 and 6 February 1803).

295. *Independent Chronicle* (12 May 1803).

296. *Boston Directory* (1805), pp. 141–6.

297. Richard D. Pierce (ed.), *The Records of the First Church in Boston* (Boston: Publications of the Colonial Society of Massachusetts, 1961).

298. Town of Boston, Town of Boston Tax Valuation Books, 1784 to 1822, Rare Book and Manuscript Room, Boston Public Library, Boston, Massachusetts.

299. *An Act to Incorporate the President, Trustees and Associates of the Boston Exchange Office, or Association Fund* (Boston, 1804).

300. *Independent Chronicle* (11 June 1804).

301. *The Changery, an Allegoric Memoir of the Boston Exchange Office: Or the Pernicious Progress of Bank Speculation Unveiled* (Boston, [1805?]). This interesting document suggests that the Exchange Office was begun by one group, 'the younger brethren', and seized by a second, 'the older brethren', when it became obvious there was money to be had in the business.

302. William L. Jenks, 'The First Bank in Michigan', *Michigan Historical Magazine*, 1 (July 1917), pp. 41–62.

303. Ibid., p. 48; Goodman, *The Democratic-Republicans of Massachusetts*, p. 175.

304. Fritz Redlich, *The Molding of American Banking: Men and Ideas* (New York: Johnson Reprint Corporation, 1968), pp. 40–1.

305. Jenks, 'The First Bank in Michigan', p. 54; Hammond, *Banks and Politics in America*, p. 175.

306. Records of Banks of New England and New York, 19 November 1804. The Boston Bank demanded collateral of $15,000 and wanted to charge 6 per cent interest.

307. *Columbian Centinel* (27 May 1807). By then references to the 'Office' in Boston were euphemisms for the Boston Exchange Office.

308. For a plan of the Annuity Fund, see 'Annuity Fund', *New-England Palladium* (12 December 1806). The act of incorporation was denied to Elbridge Gerry, William Eustis and others in the January session of the General Court, 1807. By late March of 1807, Dexter appears in the Annuity Fund advertisements calling upon interested

investors to meet and launch the fund without incorporation. See 'Massachusetts Annuity Fund', *Columbian Centinel* (18 March 1807).

309. In 1804, the *Boston Gazette* tried to claim the Exchange Office as a Federalist instrument: 'The friends of the Exchange Office are not such idiots to believe they obtained their object through the influence of the Democrats ... On the contrary they know that it was only through the exertions of a number of influential Federal characters, that they were gratified in their wishes ... The Democrats seized on the occasion to excite division among the Federalists; and to make friends to the Exchange Office dupes to their tricks': *Boston Gazette* (5 November 1804). However, less than a year later, under the headline 'The Middling Interest', the paper denounced the influence of the Exchange Office and the efforts of the Middling Interest to create a mixed list with Russell Sturgis as substitute for a Federalist candidate: 'Is all affection for the interests of the Exchange Office concentrated in the pliant bossom of RUSSELL STURGIS?': *Boston Gazette* (1 April 1805).

310. Boston's *Columbian Detector* reprinted the affirmation of William Colwell, the Farmers' Exchange Bank cashier. 'Banking Speculation: Farmers' Exchange Bank', *Columbian Detector* (9 May 1809). The deposition included testimony by Colwell and spelled out in lurid detail Dexter's desperate descent into economic collapse.

311. *Report of the Committee Appointed by the General Assembly of the State of Rhode Island and Providence Plantations at the February Session, A.D. 1809, to Inquire Into the Situation of the Farmers' Exchange Bank in Glocester* (Providence, 1809), pp. 6–7.

312. See Checkland, *Scottish Banking*, pp. 182–6; Hammond, *Banks and Politics in America*, p. 173.

313. Ibid., p. 173.

314. *Report of the Committee ... of the State of Rhode Island and Providence Plantations.*

315. Dexter convinced several family members to partake of his schemes at least briefly. His brother, Samuel Dexter, was a director for the Farmers' Exchange Bank. His celebrated uncle, the Hon. Samuel Dexter, appears in Boston advertisements as a director for the Boston Exchange Office.

316. Former stockholder Jesse Armstrong, whose son owned the store next to the bank and who often boarded in a room with a wall adjoining the bank testified to this nocturnal coming and going: ibid., p. 32.

317. Ibid., p. 53.

318. Ibid., p. 37.

319. Massachusetts Secretary, *A Correct Abstract of all the Statements ... from 1803 to January 1807.* In the Exchange Office case, liabilities being only deposits, since they were not allowed to print notes.

320. *Independent Chronicle* (27 June 1809).

321. *Boston Patriot* (29 June 1811). In a new feature titled 'British Bank Thermometer', the *Patriot* compared the 1811 crisis in British bank paper to the 1809 crisis engendered by the collapse of the Boston Exchange Office and its 'branches'.

322. *Omnium Gatherum* (November 1809), pp. 34–5.

323. *New England Galaxy* (5 July 1822).

324. Massachusetts General Court, *Report of the Committee Relative to Penobscot Bank* (Boston, 1811), p. 1. Emphasis in the original.

325. Massachusetts General Court, *Report of the Committee of Both Houses, on the Hallowell and Augusta Banks* (Boston, 1818), p. 3 and Appendix C.

326. Anon., 'Extracts from the Report of the Committee on the Bank of the United States', pp. 131, 130. See also *Boston Daily Advertiser* (25 January 1819).

327. Hammond, *Banks and Politics in America*, pp. 302–3. Hammond is paraphrasing Biddle's argument.

328. Massachusetts General Court, *The Committee Appointed on the Subject of the Banking System ... An Act Establishing a State Bank* (Boston, 14 January 1808).

329. Ibid., section 23.

330. See *Boston Gazette* (11 February 1808); *Boston Patriot* (24 June 1809). The *Essex Register* ran a series of articles supporting the proposed new bank on 27 February and 5, 9, 12 and 19 March 1808. Finally, for a condemnation of the final product, see Anon., 'The New STATE BANK', *Columbian Centinel* (31 August 1811).

331. Massachusetts General Court, *Report of the Committee of Both Houses, Appointed to Examine into the Doings of the State Bank* (Boston, 1814).

332. Warren Weber, Senior Research Officer with the Minneapolis Federal Treasury, has created a website that includes most of the data for Massachusetts banks, beyond that which is available in published sources: http://minneapolisfed.org/research/economists/wewproj.html.

333. Hammond, *Banks and Politics in America*, p. 182; Henry P. Kidder and Francis H. Peabody, 'Finance in Boston', in Justin Winsor (ed.), *The Memorial History of Boston*, 4 vols (Boston, 1881), vol. 4, pp. 151–78; p. 159.

334. Provident Institution for Savings, 'By-Laws', *At a Meeting of the Trustees* (31 December 1816); *Act of Incorporation* (Boston, 1817), p. 7.

335. Provident Institution for Savings, *At a Meeting of the Trustees*; *Act of Incorporation*. Overall, banks did not pay interest on deposits until the 1830s. The Massachusetts General Court explicitly prohibited this practice in 1834. As noted above, the Institute was not properly speaking a bank.

336. Provident Institution for Savings, *Brothers, or Consequences: A Story of What Happens Every Day, With an Account of Savings Banks* (Boston, 1823), pp. 60–1. See also, for savings institutes overall, Dudley P. Bailey, Jr, 'History of Massachusetts Savings Banks', *Banker's Magazine* (June 1876), pp. 963–74.

337. Weber, http://minneapolisfed.org/research/economists/wewproj.html.

338. Nathan Appleton, *Currency and Banking* (Boston, 1857, 1841); Hammond, *Banks and Politics in America*, p. 556.

339. Massachusetts Senate, *Senate Document No. 38*; J. Van Fenstermaker, John E. Filer and Robert Stanley Herren, 'Money Statistics of New England, 1785–1837', *Journal of Economic History*, 44:2, The Tasks of Economic History (June 1984), pp. 441–53; J. Van Fenstermaker, 'The Statistics of American Commercial Banking, 1782–1818', *Journal of Economic History*, 25:3 (September 1965), pp. 400–13.

340. Massachusetts Senate, *Senate Document No. 38*. This figure fluctuated substantially. With two fewer banks and approximately the same liabilities, the specie reserves were $1.1 million in 1824 and more than $700,000 in 1826.

341. Ibid., pp. 14–18. Again this figure fluctuated substantially. For example, in 1824 the ten Boston banks held more than $500,000 in Massachusetts country bank notes.

342. Ibid., pp. 23–30.

343. Winnifred Rothenberg, *From Market-Places to a Market Economy: The Transformation of Rural Massachusetts, 1750–1850* (Chicago: Chicago University Press, 1992); Wright, *The Wealth of Nations Rediscovered*.

344. Suffolk County Probate Court Record Books, 1790–1 and 1820–1, Boston Public Library.

345. Ibid., vol. 118, Probate Number 26214, p. 662.

346. Ibid., vol. 118, Probate Number 26220, p. 665. Her will can be found at p. 627.

347. Ibid., vol. 119, Probate Number 26279, p. 59.

348. Town of Boston Tax Valuation Books, 1784 to 1822.

349. Shareholders Lists, 16 January 1799; 'Correspondence', 6 March 1799, 7 May 1799, 13 May 1799; Secretary's Statement at Directors' Monthly Meeting, August and December 1799, Boston Marine Insurance Company Records, 1797–1839, Box 1, Massachusetts Historical Society. See Wright, *The Wealth of Nations Rediscovered*, for a discussion of the development of securities markets in this period.

350. Massachusetts Mutual Fire Insurance Co., 2 January 1801 and 6 August 1822, Records of Insurance Companies and Agents, 1781–1909, Baker Library, Harvard University.

351. Anon., 'Scripomania', *Universal Asylum and Columbian Magazine* (August 1791), pp. 141–2. See also Anon., *The Glass: or Speculation, A Poem* (New York, 1791). The last stanzas are as follows (p. 12):

> You've stretched the chord of credit 'till it cracks,
> And will keep pulling 'till it fairly breaks,
> Then down you'll fall and all your golden dreams,
> Like *South Sea bubbles, Mississippi Schemes,*
> And find at last, to your own cost and pain,
> *Its Strength existed only in your brain!*

352. Blodget, *Economica*, p. 12.

353. The dominant historiography on the Unitarian 'controversy' is still the work of Daniel Walker Howe in a number of texts but predominantly his *The Unitarian Conscience* (Cambridge, MA: Harvard University Press, 1970). In this and other texts, Howe insists that Scottish Common Sense dominated Unitarian ideas and largely worked to reconcile the tension between revealed religion and reason. My own reading of this controversy has gained much from Howe's work. I will, however, argue that the dominant trend in the Unitarian ideology was Scottish Moral Sense not Scottish Common Sense. Furthermore, the divergence of Scottish Common Sense from its Moral Sense origins has been, in my reading, much exaggerated. Thomas Reid and other Common Sense thinkers talked of 'reason' and 'rationalism', yet at the end of the day their reason greatly differed from Locke or Bacon's empiricism. Indeed, they based reason on intuitive knowledge, arguing that 'reality' was a 'common sense' idea obvious to all 'rational' men and women – endowed by God as part of their intuitive powers. If men trusted God, Reid argued, then we had to trust our sense and thus not doubt reality as postulated by 'idealists' such as Berkeley and Hume. There is, in my reading, very little of Locke's in this philosophy save for the consistent attribution. See Howe, *The Unitarian Conscience*; Daniel Walker Howe, *Making the American Self* (Cambridge, MA: Harvard University Press, 1997); and Daniel Walker Howe, 'The Cambridge Platonists of Old England and the Cambridge Platonists of New

England', in Conrad Edick Wright (ed.), *American Unitarianism, 1805–1865* (Boston: Northeastern University Press, 1989), pp. 87–120.

354. For examples of these international controversies as perceived in Boston, see the discussions on the English Predestinarian Controversy in the Boston edition of the *Christian Observer* (January 1820), pp. 32–49; and (May 1820), pp. 314–38. Also, for a description of the controversy in Geneva, Switzerland, see Anon., 'The Genevan Church', *Christian Disciple and Theological Review* (May/June 1821), pp. 214–30. According to the *Christian Disciple* in 1817, the theological debates in Geneva were so contentious that ministers and candidates to the ministry of the church had to swear an oath that they would never 'maintain either in an entire discourse, or in part of a discourse directed to that end, our views:

> 1st. Of the manner in which the divine nature is united to the person of Jesus Christ.
>
> 2dly. Of original sin.
>
> 3dly. Of the manner in which grace operates, or of effectual grace.
>
> 4thly. Of predestination.
>
> We promise finally, not to contest in our public discourses, the sentiments of any pastor or minister on these subjects. And we engage, whenever it is necessary to explain ourselves on any of them, to do it without enlarging, to avoid expressions unknown to the sacred writers, and to use, as far as possible, the terms which they employ (pp. 222–3).

355. For a good discussion of the 'Latitude Men', especially as they relate to the larger thesis under discussion, see R. S. Crane, 'Suggestions Toward a Genealogy of the 'Man of Feeling', *ELH*, 1:3 (December 1934), pp. 205–30.

356. Jonathan Edwards argued for a physical ability countered by a moral inability (predestination) to do good. This maintained the idea of 'saints' and 'sinners' while it opened up the possibility of free agency or will in the sinner. Norman Fiering and James D. German both see Edwards as reacting to the self-driven ethos of the eighteenth-century Moral Sense philosophers Shaftesbury, Hutcheson and Hume. According to these scholars, Edwards read them as legitimating the selfish impulse to benevolence without acknowledging their contribution to the idea he adopted – disinterested benevolence. See James D. German, 'The Social Utility of Wicked Self-Love: Calvinism, Capitalism, and Public Policy in Revolutionary New England', *Journal of American History*, 82:3 (December 1995), pp. 965–98; Norman S. Fiering, 'Irresistible Compassion: An Aspect of Eighteenth-Century Sympathy and Humanitarianism', *Journal of the History of Ideas*, 37:2 (April–June 1976), pp. 195–218. Interestingly, for Channing, disinterested benevolence was at the heart of his religious experience and ideas and he derived it from Hutcheson. See William Henry Channing, *The Life of William Ellery Channing* (Boston, 1880).

357. See Robert J. Wilson III, *The Benevolent Deity: Ebenezer Gay and the Rise of Rational Religion in New England, 1696–1787* (Philadelphia: University of Pennsylvania Press, 1984); The 'Liberal patriarch' label is from Howe, *The Unitarian Conscience*, p. 314.

358. Evelyn Marie Walsh, 'Effects of the Revolution upon the Town of Boston: Social, Economic, and Cultural' (PhD Dissertation, Brown University, 1964), p. 565.

359. There was, of course, a great deal of dissent on other issues during the Great Awakening. See Edwin S. Gaustad, 'The Theological Effects of the Great Awakening in New England', *Mississippi Valley Historical Review*, 40:4 (March 1954), pp. 681–706.

360. See Peter S. Field, *The Crisis of the Standing Order: Clerical Intellectuals and Cultural Authority in Massachusetts, 1780–1833* (Amherst: University of Massachusetts Press, 1998). In large part, the narrative that follows on the 'events' of the Unitarian controversy derives from Field's text.

361. Ibid., p. 50.

362. Field puts the materialist argument forth. No longer seemingly at providence's disposal, he argues, Boston's elite thus sought to control their religious worship as well. I am not sure that the religious tendencies of the 'Boston Brahmin' were so totally determined by their wealth. A more likely explanation, in my opinion, is that latitudinarian religious beliefs reflected larger cultural changes – overall marked by an increased cosmopolitanism. The institutional structure of Boston churches certainly provided the opportunity for these changes to develop quickly, yet it is hard to imagine that Boston's ministers and religion simply reflected the pecuniary interests and power of Bostonians.

363. David Shields, *Civil Tongues and Polite Letters in British America* (Chapel Hill: University of North Carolina Press, 1997); see also Norman S. Fiering, 'The Transatlantic Republic of Letters: A Note on the Circulation of Learned Periodicals to Early Eighteenth-Century America', *William and Mary Quarterly*, 3rd series, 33:4 (October 1976), pp. 642–60; and Phyllis Whitman Hunter, 'Ship of Wealth: Massachusetts Merchants, Foreign Goods, and the Transformation of Anglo-America, 1670–1760' (PhD Dissertation, William and Mary College, VA, 1996).

364. For British and Continental content in American popular magazines, see E. W. Pitcher, 'Fiction in the *Boston Magazine* (1783–1786): A Checklist with Notes and Sources', *William and Mary Quarterly*, 3rd series, 37:3 (July 1980), pp. 473–83.

365. Walsh, 'Effects of the Revolution upon the Town of Boston', p. 564.

366. William Ellery Channing Papers, Vote of the Meeting House on Federal Street, 21 April 1824, Massachusetts Historical Society.

367. Pierce (ed.), *The Records of the First Church in Boston*; *An Act to Incorporate the ... Boston Exchange Office* (Boston, 1804); *Historical Catalogue of the Old South Church* (Boston, 1883).

368. Walsh, 'Effects of the Revolution upon the Town of Boston', p. 577.

369. Massachusetts Senate, *A True Abstract ... January 1819*.

370. See Walsh, 'Effects of the Revolution upon the Town of Boston', p. 578; and Lawrence Buell, *New England Literary Culture: From Revolution Through Renaissance* (New York: Cambridge University Press, 1986), p. 38.

371. Gaustad, 'The Theological Effects of the Great Awakening in New England', p. 682.

372. As Robert J. Dinkin notes, the seating of Massachusetts's meeting-houses was always based in part on wealth. In most cases some sort of combination of 'Age, Honor, Usefulness; [and] real and personal estate' was used by a committee of elders to seat the house. Disputations often arose with regard to the seating, especially after the Revolution. Increasingly, Dinkin notes, pews were auctioned or sold off and *de facto* those willing to pay the most for a prominent pew – most often the rich – got the place

of honour. Robert J. Dinkin. 'Seating the Meeting House in Early Massachusetts', *New England Quarterly*, 43:3 (1970), pp. 450–64.

373. This narrative does not account for the different denominations present in Boston during this period. In 1776 there were five non-congregational churches in Boston, and by 1820 there were fifteen Baptist, Methodist and Universalist churches. As Anne C. Rose notes, much of this growth came from artisans and other middling men and their families, further concentrating the Boston merchant elites in the Unitarian churches. This trend should not, however, be exaggerated. Into the nineteenth century artisans continued to worship and own pews at many of Boston's elite churches. Ann C. Rose, 'Social Sources of Denominationalism Reconsidered: Post-Revolutionary Boston as a Case Study', *American Quarterly*, 38:2 (Summer 1986), pp. 243–64.

374. Buell, *New England Literary Culture*. Buell argues that it was Arminianism in both the Unitarian and Episcopalian denominations that encouraged free intellectual inquiry, expression and the arts (pp. 38–40). See also Paul Goodman, 'Ethics and Enterprise: The Values of a Boston Elite, 1800–1860', *American Quarterly*, 18:3 (Autumn 1966), pp. 437–51.

375. The Dorchester controversy derived from the conflict between John Codman, pastor of a Dorchester church, and his parishioners. The parishioners engaged him with full knowledge of his orthodox views. When he refused to exchange pulpits with Boston pastors – in large part because of their liberal religious opinions – he created a schism in the church that was only resolved when the liberal parishioners bought out Codman's orthodox supporters (Field, *The Crisis of the Standing Order*, pp. 180–9) The Dedham decision (*Baker* v. *Fales*, 1821) determined that church property belonged to parishioners not communicants. This placed many orthodox communicants at the mercy of the more liberal parishioners in a number of parish schisms across Massachusetts (ibid., pp. 210–12).

376. Anon., 'Farther Remarks on the Theological Institution in Andover, Occasioned by the Review of its Constitution and Statutes in the *Monthly Anthology*', *Panoplist*, (February 1809), pp. 413–25; and (March 1809), pp. 471–81; see (February 1809), p. 417.

377. Anon., *Review of The True Reasons on which the Election of a Hollis Professor of Divinity in Harvard College was Opposed at the Board of Overseers, Feb, 14, 1805* (Boston, March 1805), pp. 152–8.

378. Jedediah Morse, *The True Reasons on Which the Election of a Hollis Professor of Divinity in Harvard College was Opposed at the Board of Overseers* (Charlestown, 1805), pp. 14–17.

379. Field, *The Crisis of the Standing Order*, pp. 151–2.

380. Ibid., p. 201.

381. Anon., 'Review of the Constitution and Associate Statutes of the Theological Seminary in Andover; with a Sketch of its Rise and Progress', *Monthly Anthology* (November 1805). Field attributes this review to Samuel Cooper Thatcher. My copy has no attribution (and is the November not the March edition). Field, *The Crisis of the Standing Order*, p. 170.

382. 'Review of the Constitution and Associate Statutes', p. 603.

383. Moral agency was perhaps the most significant alteration made by Hopkinsinians to Calvinism. At the heart of Hopkins's efforts lay Edwards's differentiation between the moral and physical capacity not to sin. This differentiation was, in Edwards's scheme, a way to reconcile predestination and the election of saints with free will. Men were physically capable of choosing wrong or right but were morally 'handicapped' from making that choice. 'Moral inability was a voluntary indisposition, [but] it was also as intractable as if it arose from some physical compulsion.' Furthermore, it left the sinner totally at the mercy of God's 'free grace'. 'Atonement' referred to the idea that Christ died for the sins of man. The 'Old Calvinists' believed that Christ 'paid' the debt of the 'chosen'. Hopkinsinians argued that the atonement was general and not for the chosen alone. More importantly, they understood atonement not as a debt paid, which suggested a complete transaction, but as punishment for a law broken. Christ died for man's sins to maintain the dignity of the law – to uphold its authority. This in effect strengthened God's authority in a way that the debt model, by implying complete atonement, did not. 'Imputation' referred to the idea that Adam's sin caused man's innate depravity. Again this doctrine was the target of criticism for its sever- ity. Mankind was in effect punished for actions they did not undertake, although Hopkinsinians denied any causal connection. Adam had sinned and was responsible for those sins, but God had, as a result of Adam's actions decided to make his progeny sinful rather than not. Ultimately, however, God had the power to craft mankind as he chose – and questions of fairness were beside the point. Finally, Hopkinsinians denounced the idea of 'preparationism'. This referred to the idea that 'sinners' could perform duties (prayer and worship) by way of preparation for grace. The Hopkinsinians maintained that all acts of 'preparation performed before regenera- tion, such as attendance on the means of grace, were utterly sinful, did not fulfil any required duty, and aggravated the sinner's guilt'. Nevertheless, Hopkinsinians insisted these 'duties' be performed – even at the expense of accumulating sinfulness. William Breitenbach, 'The Consistent Calvinism of the New Divinity Movement', *William and Mary Quarterly*, 3rd series, 41:2 (April 1984), pp. 241–64.

384. See also Joseph A. Conforti, 'Samuel Hopkins and the New Divinity: Theology, Ethics, and Social Reform in Eighteenth-Century New England', *William and Mary Quarterly*, 3rd series, 34:4 (October 1977), pp. 572–89.

385. See 'Review of the Constitution and Associate Statutes', p. 607, for a full description of the 'hair-splitting' language adopted by the Hopkinsinians and Calvinists and the close reading of the text by the Unitarians.

386. Ibid., pp. 605–8.

387. Ibid., p. 612.

388. Ibid., p. 614.

389. Anon., 'Farther Remarks on the Theological Institution in Andover'.

390. Ibid., p. 481.

391. See Field, *The Crisis of the Standing Order*, pp. 170–9, for a discussion of the political intrigue behind the Park Street Church.

392. Edward D. Griffin, *A Sermon Preached Jan. 10, 1810, at the Dedication of the Church in Park Street, Boston* (Boston, 1810), p. 7.

393. Griffin remarked that the Unitarians were *'full of new wine'*: ibid., p. 27.

394. Anon., 'Review of a Sermon Preached 10 January 1810 at the dedication of the Church in Park-Street, Boston', *Monthly Anthology* (February 1810), p. 135.

395. William E. Channing, 'Unitarian Christianity: Discourse at the Ordination of the Rev. Jared Sparks, Baltimore, 1819', in *Unitarian Christianity and Other Essays*, ed. Irving H. Bartlett (New York: Liberal Arts Press, 1957).

396. Ibid., pp. 15–21, 22.

397. Ibid., p. 29.

398. Ibid., p. 4.

399. Channing here expresses a modern notion of time and anachronism. The world of archetypes – a world where, for example, 'the Virgin Mary might be dressed like a Tuscan merchant's daughter', relied on a 'sense of time as the locus for the recurrent embodiment of archetypes, not themselves temporally placed'. By developing this sense of historical anachronism Channing points to a changed sense of time – the progressive time best expressed in the novels of the period. Taylor, *Sources of the Self*, p. 287.

400. Channing, 'Unitarian Christianity', p. 6.

401. Ibid., p. 30.

402. Moses Stuart, *Letters to the Reverend William E. Channing Containing Remarks on his Sermon Recently Published at Baltimore* (Andover, 1819), p. 45. According to Channing, for example, 'This corruption of Christianity [the duality of Christ], alike repugnant to common sense and to the general strain of Scripture, is a remarkable proof of the power of a false philosophy in disfiguring the simple truth of Jesus': Channing, 'Unitarian Christianity', p. 16.

403. Stuart, *Letters*, p. 46.

404. Ibid., p. 47.

405. Ibid., p. 153.

406. Ibid., p. 168–70.

407. Ibid., p. 175.

408. Andrews Norton, Review of *Letters to the Rev. William E. Channing, Containing Remarks on his Sermon Recently Preached at Baltimore. By Moses Stuart* (1819), *Christian Disciple* (1819).

409. William E. Channing, 'The Moral Argument Against Calvinism' (1820), in *Unitarian Christianity and Other Essays*, pp. 39–59.

410. Channing, 'Likeness to God', in *Unitarian Christianity and Other Essays*, pp. 86–108; p. 92.

411. Ibid., p. 94.

412. Ibid., p. 104.

413. Howe, *The Unitarian Conscience*, p. 48.

414. Ibid., p. 39.

415. Alexander H. Everett, 'History of Intellectual Philosophy', in Perry Miller (ed.), *The Transcendentalists* (Cambridge, MA: Harvard University Press, 1950), pp. 26–33.

416. Howe, *The Unitarian Conscience*, p. 38.

417. Ibid., p. 49. See also Daniel Walker Howe, 'European Sources of Political Ideas in Jeffersonian America', *Reviews in American History*, 10:4, The Promise of American History: Progress and Prospects (December 1982), pp. 28–44.

418. Howe, *The Unitarian Conscience*, p. 94.

419. Ibid., p. 129.
420. See Jane Rendall, *The Origins of the Scottish Enlightenment* (London: Macmillan, 1978).
421. Teichgraeber, *Free Trade and Moral Philosophy*, p. 11.
422. Elsewhere, in almost identical essays, Howe acknowledges the influence of the Neo-Platonic tradition on New-England Unitarianism which was, Howe notes, 'consistently dualistic in metaphysics, affirming the existence of both mind and matter' – but, 'within this framework', consistently exalting 'mind over matter'. Channing, he argues, was the best example of this duality and the primacy of mind: 'From the very dawn of philosophy', Howe quotes Channing, 'there have been schools which have held that the material universe has no existence but in the mind that thinks it. I am far from assenting to these speculations. But I recur to them with pleasure, as indicating how readily the soul passes above matter, and as manifesting man's consciousness of the grandeur of his spiritual nature.' Indeed, according to Howe, this 'shared desire to accept the reality of both mind and matter while according mind priority over matter is what drew the New England Unitarians to the Cambridge Platonists. For both groups, mind was the active force in the universe, and, matter the passive': Howe, 'The Cambridge Platonists of Old and New England', pp. 94–5. Less than ten years later in a second version of this essay, he adds a paragraph to the passage quoted above. In this addition he argues that the 'mind over matter' idea the Unitarians and the Cambridge Platonists shared was analogous to the dominance of 'reason' over the 'passions'. 'The power of mind over matter was mirrored in the human character by the authority of reason over passion, for the passions represented what was merely animal in our nature. The impulse to subject matter to mind in the world at large was accompanied by the injunction to subject passion to reason in the world within': Howe, *Making the American Self*, p. 196. This seems to be completely at odds with Channing's exalted celebration of the mind as previously quoted by Howe. In this quote and elsewhere, Channing is clearly referring to matter in terms of the 'idealist' and 'materialist' metaphysical notion – not in terms of the 'passions'. In fact, the Scots and Channing did their best to legitimise the 'passions' or feelings as sources for moral virtue.
423. Taylor, *Sources of the Self*, p. 250.
424. Howe, *The Unitarian Conscience*, p. 12.
425. For a discussion of the Unitarian roots of New England romanticism, see Buell, *New England Literary Culture*, p. 44; and Lawrence J. Buell, 'Unitarian Aesthetics and Emerson's Poet-Priest', *American Quarterly*, 20:1 (Spring 1968), pp. 3–20.
426. Howe, *The Unitarian Conscience*, p. 199.
427. Norman S. Fiering notes that the new 'irresistible compassion' developed by the Scottish Moral Sense thinkers (Shaftesbury, Hutcheson, Hume and Smith) was in fact behind changes in the nature of religious worship. According to Fiering contemporaries perceived a contradiction between their own ideas on sympathy and 'traditional' Christian teaching on reprobation, hell and eternal punishment: 'If God had in fact given man involuntary compassionate responses, then God must be at least as compassionate as man'. These ideas, Fiering argues, derived from the Scots, were current in the United States (at Harvard) as early as the 1740s, and were also expressed by the Unitarian ministers, especially Channing. Fiering discounts the

"rational" objections to eternal punishment' for the 'affective': Fiering, 'Irresistible Compassion', pp. 216–18.

428. Channing, 'Likeness to God', p. 87; Howe, *The Unitarian Conscience*, p. 120.

429. Smith, *Theory of Moral Sentiments*, p. 457. An edition of Smith's seminal text was published in Boston in 1817 by Wells and Lilly, though various editions were readily available in all American cities.

430. William Henry Channing, *The Life of William Ellery Channing*, p. 32.

431. George P. Bradford, 'Philosophic Thought in Boston', in Winsor (ed.), *The Memorial History of Boston*, vol. 4, pp. 295–330; pp. 320–3. Bradford writes: 'We are informed by an intimate friend of Channing, who was very familiar with his thought, that he repudiated Locke's philosophy while in college, and accepted on moral and meta-physical questions the statements of Price in his *Dissertations on Matter and Spirit*, and of Hutcheson's moral philosophy. He recognized also a harmony between his own thought and that of the German systems of philosophy as reported by Madame de Stael. He acknowledged his obligation to the poetry of Wordsworth and Coleridge, and to the philosophy of the latter he considered himself specially and greatly indebted. He also read with pleasure Cousin's *Philosophy* and the writings of Carlyle, particularly his *Sartor Resartus*' (p. 302).

432. Hutcheson *An Inquiry into the Original*, pp. 150–1.

433. Ibid., pp. 302–3.

434. See Hutcheson's Preface for repeated attributions of these ideas to Shaftesbury.

435. Shaftesbury, *An Inquiry Concerning Virtue and Merit*, p. 75.

436. Ibid., p. 75.

437. Channing, 'Likeness to God', p. 97.

438. See the Review of the new edition of Akenside's poem in the *Monthly Anthology*, 3 (July 1806). See also Anon., 'Essay on Akenside's *Pleasures of the Imagination*', *Harvard Lyceum*, 1 (23 February 1811), pp. 392–400.

439. Anon., 'Self-love .... Benevolence', *Boston Spectator; Devoted to Politicks and Belles-Lettres* (19 February 1814), pp. 30–2.

440. Michael McKeon, *The Origins of the English Novel, 1660–1740* (Baltimore: Johns Hopkins University Press, 1987), discusses these changes in the context of the rise of the novel. For McKeon epistemological confusion derived from the conflict of Baconian and Aristotelian ideals, and pertained to 'questions of truth'. Socio-economic confusion and uncertainty spoke to 'questions of virtue'.

441. James Thompson, *Models of Value: Eighteenth-Century Political Economy and the Novel* (Durham, NC: Duke University Press, 1996).

442. On sentiment as the 'producer of society', see John Mullan, *Sentiment and Sociability* (Oxford: Oxford University Press, 1988), ch. 1: 'Sympathy and the Production of Society'.

443. The Investigator, No. VII, *Massachusetts Magazine* (July 1795), pp. 241–3.

444. Gordon S. Wood discusses the rise of 'sentiment' as an interpretive paradigm in his 'The American Love Boat', Review of Andrew Burstein's *Sentimental Democracy: The Evolution of America's Romantic Self-Image* (New York: Hill and Wang, 1999), *New York Review of Books* (7 October 1999), p. 41. Wood argues that sensibility was a reaction to the crisis of authority engendered by the Revolution, and was vital to the survival of the new Republic. Julie Ellison also sees the rise of eighteenth-century

sensibility in the crisis of authority during this period: '[In Cato] The virtuous son's dilemma suggests that sensibility is fundamental to both legitimising and to criticizing post-monarchical forms of power': Julie Ellison, 'Cato's Tears', *ELH*, 63:3 (Fall 1996), pp. 571–601; p. 582. Julia A. Stern's *The Plight of Feeling* argues that 'those eighteenth century novels best remembered for impassioned excess elaborate, in fictive form, a collective mourning over the violence of the Revolution and the pre-emption of liberty in the wake of the post-Revolutionary settlement. Such works, contemplate the possibility that the power of genuine sympathy could revivify a broadly inclusive vision of democracy.' While *Charlotte: A Tale of Truth* can arguably be read as a failed attempt to 'afford its readers a transparent vision of social relations that would radically extend the boundaries of the national body imagined in master narratives of the Founding', this does not explain the cross-Atlantic phenomena of sentiment. Julia A. Stern, *The Plight of Feeling: Sympathy and Dissent in the Early American Novel* (Chicago: University of Chicago Press, 1997), p. 2.

445. Ann Douglas argues that 'Sentimentalism ... attempts to deal with the phenomenon of cultural bifurcation by the manipulation of nostalgia ... The sentimentalization of theological and secular culture was an inevitable part of the self-evasion of a society both committed to laissez faire industrial expansion and disturbed by its consequences': Ann Douglas, *The Feminization of American Culture* (New York: Knopf, 1977), p. 12. Thomas L. Haskell argues that 'humanitarian sensibility', and the humanitarian reform movements that it spawned, including anti-slavery, were a function of changes the 'market wrought in perception or cognitive style. And it was primarily a change in cognitive style – specifically a change in the perception of causal connection and consequently a shift in the conventions of moral responsibility – that underlay the new constellation of attitudes and activities that we call humanitarianism': Thomas L. Haskell, 'Capitalism and the Origins of the Humanitarian Sensibility, Part 1', *American Historical Review* 90:2 (April 1985), pp. 339–61; p. 342. According to G. J. Barker-Benfield, the culture of sensibility was part of the English consumer revolution of the eighteenth century. 'It was in the interests of commerce', Barker-Benfield argues, 'that men cultivated politeness and sensibility, this tendency coinciding with the goals of the "reformation of manners"'. Furthermore, 'self-indulgence, the "luxury" of feeling, was at the heart of the culture of sensibility, and it was basic to the consumer psychology the polite and commercial economy required'. Barker-Benfield also notes, however, that sensibility 'expressed the attempt to solve' the perceived dilemma or contradiction of luxury and morality and was central to the reform impulse. G. J. Barker-Benfield, *The Culture of Sensibility: Sex and Society in Eighteenth Century Britain* (Chicago: University of Chicago Press, 1992), pp. xv, xvi, xxxii. More recently literary scholars have noted the connection between sentiment and capital: Gillian Skinner's analysis, *Sensibility and Economics in the Novel*, argues that the sentimental novel was replete with notions of wealth – who had it, what it was used for and what it meant. Skinner focuses on the sentimental novel's 'use of economic discourse and its engagement with economic debate'. Skinner, however, pays little attention to the origins of the idea of sentiment. Gillian Skinner, *Sensibility and Economics in the Novel, 1740–1800: The Price of a Tear* (New York: St Martin's Press, 1999), p. 14. Markman Ellis, in *The Politics of Sensibility* (Cambridge: Cambridge University Press, 1996), argues that 'it is fruitful [after Foucault] to think of these simultaneous uses

of the model of circulation in medical, economic, literary and cultural discourses as significant: one of episteme's "fundamental categories of analysis"' (p. 155). David Kaufmann has also argued for a relationship between the rise of classical economics and the novel: *The Business of Common Life: Novels and Classical Economics between Revolution and Reform* (Baltimore: Johns Hopkins University Press, 1995). As James Thompson notes, most of these discussions function on the level of content. His *Models of Value* emphasizes the crisis of values engendered by changes in the nature of money. My own analysis has clearly benefited from Thompson's formulation, though I have taken it in a significantly different direction. See Thompson's introduction for a historiographical discussion of the literature linking economics and the novel both in the United States and Britain. Clearly sentimental culture and/or the culture of sensibility was, in part, a reaction by rising middling men and women to the socio-economic changes they engendered.

446. American scholars have recently developed a voluminous literature on sentimental fiction. Most of the analyses, however, fail to deal with the issue of origins. Cathy N. Davidson, in her path-breaking study of sentimental fiction, 'attempts to explore early American novels as agents and products of social change'. Borrowing from Foucault, Derrida, Bahktin and others, Davidson positions sentimental fiction, and early American novels overall, as oppositional texts that were strongly condemned by the 'founding fathers' and other 'official' men. Furthermore she consciously chooses to analyse the early 'American' novel as a phenomenon of the Revolution, and thus unique: Cathy N. Davidson, *Revolution and the Word: The Rise of the Novel in America* (Oxford: Oxford University Press, 1986). My interpretation differs from both of these findings. Sentimental fiction was often opposed, but that opposition was incoherent and not class or interest-group based. The official subscribers list of the *Gentleman and Lady's Town and Country Magazine* was a 'Who's Who' of Boston, and included his Excellency, then-Governor John Hancock, future Lieutenant-Governor William Gray and numerous other notables. The Boston Library Society, an elite private library, was not so opposed to sentimental fiction that it did not carry the work of S. Rowson, Hannah Foster and numerous other sentimental authors (*A Catalogue of Books in the Boston Library. March 1, 1800* (Boston, 1800)). Furthermore, as Davidson notes, opposition to sentimental fiction was often expressed by anonymous authors in the same magazines that carried sentimental stories. To say the least, opposition to novels was inconsistent. She cites Jefferson as a vocal opponent of novels, yet her own footnotes reveal that he shaped his remarks to suit the audience. More conclusive, in my opinion, is Gordon Wood's observation that Jefferson always carried Sterne's *Sentimental Journey* when he travelled, and was always on the lookout for smaller travel versions ('The American Love Boat'). See also Lee Quimby's discussion of Jefferson in Lee Quimby, 'Thomas Jefferson, the Virtue of Aesthetics and the Aesthetics of Virtue', *American Historical Review*, 87:2 (April 1982), pp. 337–57. Davidson's efforts to isolate American fiction from its Anglo-American context also seem ill fated. As E. W. Pitcher's analysis indicates, the majority of stories published in the *Boston Magazine*, a representatively sentimental magazine, were of British origin: Pitcher, 'Fiction in the *Boston Magazine*'. Other analyses of sentimental fiction focus on the text, rather than the historical context in which that text was written. Jane Tompkins, in an excellent analysis of Brown's early

novel *Wieland*, uses historical evidence to interpret the text, but avoids the issue of origins. Jane Tompkins, *Sensational Designs: The Cultural Work of American Fiction, 1790–1860* (Oxford: Oxford University Press, 1985).

447. See Crane, 'Suggestions Toward a Genealogy of the "Man of Feeling"'. Crane argues that the roots of sensibility are in the latitudinarian divines who practiced a benevolent religion from 1660 to 1725; see also Maureen Harkin, 'Mackenzie's Man of Feeling: Embalming Sensibility', *ELH*, 61:2 (Summer 1994), pp. 317–40; also Gregg Camfield, 'The Moral Aesthetics of Sensibility: A Missing Key to Uncle Tom's Cabin', *Nineteenth-Century Literature*, 43:3 (December 1988), pp. 319–45. Camfield takes this discussion forward to Harriet Beecher Stowe but discusses at length the Scottish origin of her ideas. Another good discussion of origins is Chris Jones's *Radical Sensibility: Literature and Ideas in the 1790s* (London: Routledge, 1993). Jones argues that the French Revolution bifurcated 'sensibility'. After the French Revolution, according to Jones, 'the brittle consensus of eighteenth century benevolism had been broken and with it the optimistic idealism of the age' (p. 15). Jones deals specifically with British expressions of sensibility. My own analysis of the sources did not find the same bifurcation in the United States.

448. Fiering, 'Irresistible Compassion'.

449. Karen Haltunnen looks at this relationship in 'Humanitarianism and the Pornography of Pain in Anglo-American Culture', *American Historical Review*, 100:2 (April 1995), pp. 303–34. Haltunnen argues that into the 1790s numerous critics pointed to the 'pornographic' fixation that sensibility had on pain and suffering. As discussed below, although critics of the spectatorial consumption of sentiment did speak out, the sophisticated condemnation that Haltunnen examines was absent from the literature that I looked at. In Boston at least, Americans continued to identify sympathy and pleasure well into the 1820s. See also Louis I. Bredvold, *The Natural History of Sensibility* (Detroit: Wayne State University Press, 1962), esp. ch. 3, 'The Exaltation of Unhappiness'.

450. Shaftesbury, *An Inquiry Concerning Virtue and Merit*, p. 44.

451. Ibid., p. 101.

452. Ibid., p. 107.

453. Hutcheson, *An Inquiry into the Original*, p. 239.

454. Ibid., pp. 261–2.

455. Griswold, *Adam Smith*, p. 120. See also Mullan, *Sentiment and Sociability*, p. 45.

456. See 'Of the Pleasure of Mutual Sympathy', part 1, section 2, ch. 1, in *Theory of Moral Sentiments*.

457. Smith, *Theory of Moral Sentiments*, p. 64.

458. Teichgraeber, *Free Trade and Moral Philosophy*, p. 11.

459. Stewart's *Outlines of Moral Philosophy*, 3rd edn (Edinburgh, 1808) is one of the best explications of the Moral Sense. Likewise his *Elements of the Philosophy of the Human Mind* (London, 1792) is often at odds with Reid/Locke ideas. In this work Stewart develops a theory of the human mind. He breaks down his discussion into the various 'elements' of the mind: the Powers of External Perception, Attention, Conception, Abstraction, Association of Ideas, Memory and Imagination. The imagination also plays a strong role also in the chapter on Association. As noted in Chapter 7, in these discussions he also points to Archibald Alison as his guide – and Alison, as

discussed, argued for an increased subjectivity in aesthetic judgments. Stewart also spends a great deal of time discussing theatre, poetry and the arts overall in part 1 of his Association chapter, 'The Influence of Association in Regulating the Succession of Our Thoughts' (ch. 5, part 1), and in the chapter on the 'Imagination' (ch. 7). Locke on the other hand diminished the importance of both the imagination and the 'arts'. On Locke's 'disparaging' treatment of the imagination, see Alan R. White, *The Language of Imagination* (London: Basil Blackwell, 1990). Locke minced no words on the subject: 'Since wit and fancy finds easier entertainment in the world that dry truth and real knowledge, *figurative speeches*, and allusions in the language will hardly be admitted as *an* imperfection or *abuse* of it. I confess, in discourses where we seek rather pleasure and delight than information and improvement, such ornaments as are borrowed from them can scarce pass for faults. But yet if we would speak of things as they are, we must allow that all the art of rhetoric, beside order and clearness, all the artificial and figurative application of words eloquence hath invented, are for nothing else but to insinuate wrong *ideas*, move the passions and thereby mislead the judgments, and so indeed are perfect cheat; and therefore however laudable or allowable oratory may render them ... they are certainly in all discourses that pretend to inform or instruct, wholly to be avoided and, where truth and knowledge are concerned, cannot but be thought a great fault either in the language or person that makes use of them': Locke, *An Essay Concerning Human Understanding*, book 3, ch. 10; quoted in Quimby, 'Thomas Jefferson', p. 347. Here Locke did not even entertain the idea that discourses aimed at 'pleasure and delight' might lead to 'information and improvement'.

460. Stewart, *Elements of the Philosophy of the Human Mind*, pp. 501–2.

461. Stewart *Outlines of Moral Philosophy*, p. 147.

462. For the explosion of magazines in the post-Revolutionary period, see Frank Luther Mott, *A History of American Magazines* (Cambridge, MA: Harvard University Press, 1939). In Boston there were six short-lived publications between 1741 and 1774. In comparison, there were thirty-six magazines published in Boston between 1783 and 1825 (ibid., pp. 787–98). William Charvat notes that the Scottish *Edinburgh Review* and *Quarterly Review* each had a circulation of about 4,000 – singly equal to that of the *North American Review*. Someone like Stewart who edited the *Encyclopedia Britannica* was tremendously influential. William Charvat, *The Origins of American Critical Thought, 1810–1835* (Philadelphia: University of Pennsylvania Press, 1936; New York, A. S. Barnes, 1961), p. 29. Furthermore, whatever Americans missed in the foreign publications was usually reprinted in American magazines. E. W. Pitcher notes that a great number of the stories in Boston magazines derived from French and British journals: Pitcher, 'Fiction in the *Boston Magazine*'.

463. Circulating libraries greatly increased in number after the Revolution. For a discussion of circulating libraries, see Charles K. Bolton, 'Circulating Libraries in Boston, 1765–1865', *Proceedings of the Colonial Society of Massachusetts* (February 1907). Bolton notes that often women retailers added circulating libraries to their shops. These libraries carried all of the 'romance' novels – British and American – as well as magazines from Britain and the major American seaboard cities. They also stocked major works of moral philosophy, including the work of Shaftesbury, Hutcheson, Hume, Smith and Stewart. For an example of their selection, see *A Catalogue of Mein's*

Circulating Library; consisting of above twelve hundred volumes, in most branches of polite literature, arts and sciences (Boston, 1765); *New Select Catalogue of Benjamin Guild's Circulating Library, containing principally novels, voyages, travels, poetry, periodical publications, and books of entertainment, at the Boston Book-Store, no. 59, Cornhill* (Boston, 1789); *A Catalogue of Books for Sale or Circulation, by William P. Blake, at the Boston Book-Store, no. 59, Cornhill. Consisting of the most approved authors, in history, voyages, travels, lives, memoirs, antiquities, philosophy, novels, divinity, law, physic, surgery, chemistry, geography, husbandry, navigation, arts, sciences, architecture, miscellanies, poetry, plays, &c&c&c.* (Boston, 1793, 1796, 1798, 1800); *A Catalogue of Books in the Boston Library. March 1, 1800* (Boston, 1800); *Catalogue of Pelham's Circulating Library, no 59, Cornhill: consisting of a chosen assortment of books in the various branches of literature* (Boston, 1801); *A Catalogue of the New Circulating Library kept at no. 82, Newbury Street: to which is prefixed, the conditions of said library* (Boston, 1804); *Catalogue of the Boston Union Circulating Library and Reading Room* (Boston, 1815); *Catalogue of the Union Circulating Library, No. 3, School-Street* (Boston, 1806, 1810); *Catalogue of the Charlestown Circulating Library* (Charlestown 1815); *Catalogue of the Apprentices' Library in Boston: to be loaned gratis, under the superintendence of the Massachusetts Mechanic Association, to the mechanic, and all needy apprentices: with the names of the donors* (Boston, 1820); *Catalogue of the Suffolk Circulating Library, corner of Court and Brattle Streets, Boston: containing History – Biography – Voyages – Travels – Miscellanies – Magazine – Reviews – Novels – Tales – Romances and plays – alphabetically arranged* (Boston, 1822).

464. Harriet Otis, Diary Entry, Saturday 28 December 1811, Diary, 1811–14, Harrison Gray Otis Papers, Massachusetts Historical Society.

465. Benevolus, 'Thoughts on Benevolence', *Boston Magazine* (January 1786), pp. 26–7.

466. Investigator, No. VII, *Massachusetts Magazine* (July 1795), p. 242.

467. See for example, *Massachusetts Magazine* (April 1790 and July 1791).

468. Investigator, No. VII, p. 243.

469. Anon., 'Sentimental Scenes', *Massachusetts Magazine* (April 1795), p. 19.

470. Ibid., p. 21.

471. The contemporary popular literature on sentiment and benevolence is voluminous. See for example, in addition to works already cited, Anon., 'The Delights of Benevolence', *Massachusetts Magazine* (July 1795), pp. 206–11; Haley, 'Benevolence', *Massachusetts Magazine* (April 1796), p. 100; Anon., 'Benevolence: Or the Good Samaritan', *Massachusetts Magazine* (February 1789), pp. 76–8; Monzo, 'Benevolence: A Fragment', *Gentlemen and Ladies' Town and Country Magazine* (May 1789), pp. 191–2; Anon., 'Benevolence', *Something* (25 November 1809), p. 32; Anon., 'Benevolence', *Cabinet; a Repository of Polite Literature* (2 February 1811), pp. 73–5; Anon., 'Female Benevolence', *Boston Weekly Magazine* (31 May 1817), p. 134. Some of these were sentimental fragments – though most engaged the ideas at length. There was also a literature of religious benevolence: S. P., 'Benevolence and Gratitude', *Massachusetts Baptist Missionary Magazine* (June 1814), pp. 42–4; Anon., Review of *The Age of Benevolence: A Poem*, The *Gospel Advocate* (November 1822), pp. 353–6; Anon., 'Meditations on the Benevolence of God', *Weekly Monitor* (9 July 1817), pp. 52–4; Anon., 'On Charity as a Principle of Consistent Behavior, and Universal Benevolence', *Panoplist* (February 1817), pp. 54–61; Anon., 'Youthful

Benevolence', *Panoplist* (October 1806), pp. 223–4 (this story was so good it was reprinted again word for word nine years later in the *Weekly Monitor* (4 June 1817), p. 12); Anon., 'Singular Instance of Benevolence', *Polyanthos* (September 1814), pp. 292–5; Anon., 'Benevolence of Piety', *Polyanthos* (June 1812), p. 51. There was also a literature on the overlapping principle of sympathy and hundreds of 'sentimental fragments' and 'odes', tales, etc. See generally, *Gentleman and Lady's Town and Country Magazine* (1784) (this was later changed to *Gentlemen and Ladies'* (1789–90)), *Boston Magazine* (1783–6), *Boston Weekly Magazine* (1802–4), *Massachusetts Magazine* (two incarnations – 1789 and 1790–6), *Nightingale, or a Mélange of Literature* (1796), *American Apollo* (1792), *Something* (1809–10).

472. Benevolus, 'Thoughts on Benevolence', p. 26.

473. K—, 'Benevolence', *Boston Weekly Magazine* (15 October 1803), p. 206.

474. Anon., 'On Sympathy', *Massachusetts Magazine* (February 1791), p. 105.

475. H. Holley, 'On the Pleasure Derived from Witnessing Scenes of Distress', *North American Review* (November 1815), pp. 59–67; p 67.

476. Remarker, No. 30, *Monthly Anthology and Boston Review* (February 1808), pp. 88, 90–2. It is interesting that the *Review*, run mostly by Unitarian ministers, does not mention God. Indeed the whole article is a tribute to Moral Sense ideas.

477. Anon., 'Sensibility: A Mechanical Virtue', *Massachusetts Magazine* (November 1789), p. 668.

478. For an excellent discussion that situates these issues in their Anglo-American context, see Carla Mulford, 'Introduction', in Carla Mulford (ed.), *The Power of Sympathy and the Coquette* (New York: Penguin, 1996). For an interpretation that continues to emphasize the uniquely American and 'Republican' narrative, see Michael Warner, *The Letters of the Republic* (Cambridge, MA: Harvard University Press, 1990), esp. ch. VI, 'The Novel: Fantasies of Publicity'.

479. Terence Martin discusses these issues at length in *The Instructed Vision: Scottish Common Sense Philosophy and the Origins of American Fiction* (Indiana: Indiana University Press, 1961). According to Martin, New Englanders' 'Common Sense' inclinations led them to discount fiction and the imagination. Martin argues that 'Common Sense' philosopher Dugald Stewart distinguished between 'conception' and the 'imagination'. Conception spoke to memory, and the imagination combined 'qualities and circumstances from a variety of different objects, and by combing and disposing these, [formed] a new creation of its own'. Stewart, Martin argues, saw the imagination as a 'faculty which can create reality to its own taste, is dangerous and must be used with caution' (p. 95). Martin then marshals an impressive number of negative attacks on 'fiction' and concludes that, for Americans, 'the world of the imagination thus became in a special way a region of terror' (p. 107). Martin thus describes the creation of transcendentalism and romantic fiction in this climate of hostility as a series of unintended consequences. 'Thus it is not surprising that Thomas Reid with his intuitions of and epigraphs from Job could push an Emerson or a Thoreau toward idealism ... Thus as a reaction to Common Sense concepts and also because of them, a view of the imagination as a creative, dynamic and organic force bean to take form from the 1830s onward, even while the principles of Scottish realism were dominant in the colleges and throughout society' (p. 117). Later, Martin rehabilitates Stewart, arguing that he paid some attention to the 'apprehensive powers' of

the imagination – but not to the creative elements (the power of the artist). Martin is unfortunately 'Locked' into Howe's dilemma: how do we explain the rise of transcendentalism, sentiment and eventually romanticism through Common Sense? Both authors significantly misread Stewart. Martin quotes exclusively and selectively from one chapter that Stewart titled 'Inconveniences Resulting from an ill-regulated imagination'. There are four other chapters detailing the powers of the imagination and it is a central theme in the sections on Association and Memory. Furthermore, in ch. 7, section 2, Stewart addresses the role of the imagination for the artist. Quixotically, in a text that studies Emerson and the relationship of transcendentalism to epistemology, Martin makes no mention of Channing – his name does not once come up. Also, Martin never considers the insatiable thirst for novels in the midst of the alleged hostility he details. For Stewart, see *Elements of the Philosophy of the Human Mind*. For an example of the selective quotations compare Martin, *The Instructed Vision*, p. 95, and Stewart, *Elements of the Philosophy of the Human Mind*, ch. 7: 'Of Imagination', section 1: 'Analysis of Imagination', p. 475.

480. Anon., Review of *Self-Control* (Boston and Philadelphia, 1811), *General Repository and Review* (January 1812), pp. 191–2.

481. Ibid., p. 200.

482. Levi Frisbie, *Inaugural Address Delivered in the Chapel of the University of Cambridge, November 5, 1817* (Cambridge, MA, 1817), pp. 21–2.

483. Corneille, 'The Album, No. 1: Novel Reading', *Boston Weekly Magazine* (3 April 1824), p. 10 (emphasis added).

484. Gossip, No. XIII, 'Ficta Voluptatis causa sint proxima veris', *Boston Weekly Magazine* (22 January 1803), p. 53.

485. Leander, 'On Modern Novels and Their Effects', *Massachusetts Magazine* (November 1791), pp. 662–5.

486. Ibid., p. 665.

487. F., 'Novels', *Ladies' Magazine* (August 1828), p. 357.

488. TD, 'On British Novels and Romances', *Atheneum; or Spirit of the English Magazines* (15 June 1820), p. 319.

489. Ibid., p. 320, p. 324.

490. R, 'On Taste', *Monthly Anthology and Boston Review* (8 August 1808), pp. 411, 412, 414, 415.

491. The imagination is discussed at greater length in Chapter 7.

492. Lillie Deming Loshe, *The Early American Novel* (New York: Ungar, 1907), pp. 106–13.

493. For example, see Anon., 'Greenwich Hospital, A True Tale', *Boston Weekly Magazine* (3 April 1824), pp. 10–11; Anon., The Faithful Shepherd, A Story Founded on Truth', *Boston Magazine* (May 1784), pp. 265–8.

494. David Marshall, *The Figure of Theatre: Shaftesbury, Defoe, Adam Smith, and George Eliot* (New York: Columbia University Press, 1986), p. 21.

495. Cathy N. Davidson, 'The Life and Times of Charlotte Temple', in Cathy N. Davidson (ed.), *Reading in America* (Baltimore: Johns Hopkins University Press), pp. 157–79.

496. The second fictional biography of *Charlotte Temple* was Caroline Dall, *The Romance of the Association; or, One Last Glimpse of Charlotte Temple and Eliza Wharton* (Cambridge, MA, 1875).

497. See Cathy N. Davidson, 'Introduction', in Hannah W. Foster, *The Coquette* (New York: Oxford University Press, 1986), pp. vii–xx.

498. Marshall, *The Figure of Theatre*, p. 13. According to Marshall the purposeful effacing of the reader creates the theatrical and spectatorial context. Marshall looks closely at Shaftesbury's *Philosophical Regimen*, first published in 1900, a series of 'exercises', and at the unpublished notes for *Plastics: An Epistolary Excursion in the Original Progress and Power of Designatory Art*, in which he clearly and self-consciously discusses the structure of his texts and how to make philosophical narrative or dialogue seem to be a series of letters – even when they were clearly not. Marshall finds that the epistolary format was a rhetorical device that maintained the fiction of spectatorial distance by the reader. 'If the book is written for them', he concluded, 'it at least maintains the fiction that it was not written to them' (p. 25).

499. For a discussion of the emphasis of the everyday narrative and its relationship to identity, see Ian Watt, *The Rise of the Novel: Studies in Defoe, Richardson and Fielding* (Berkeley: University of California Press, 1962). Michael McKeon has greatly complicated that narrative, nevertheless it still, in my opinion, offers an excellent discussion of the novel as a genre. See McKeon, *The Origins of the English Novel*. See also Miranda Jane Burgess, 'The Work of Romance: The British Novel and Political Discourse' (PhD Dissertation, Boston University, 1995).

500. Joseph Addison, *Spectator*, 1 (Thursday 1 March 1711).

501. Shaftesbury, 'Advice to an Author', *Characteristicks*, vol. 1, part 1, section 1, p. 157.

502. Ibid., vol. 1, part 1, section 1, pp. 166, 168.

503. Ibid., vol. 1, part 1, section 1:2, p. 170.

504. Smith, *Theory of Moral Sentiments*, p. 248.

505. Ibid., p. 254.

506. Ibid., p. 257.

507. Stewart, *Outline of Moral Philosophy*, p. 118.

508. Taylor, *Sources of the Self*, pp. 288–9.

509. Davidson, 'The Life and Times of Charlotte Temple', p. 171.

510. See Anon., 'Hints on the Nature and Usefulness of Diaries', *Massachusetts Magazine* (May 1795), p. 72.

511. Eunice Callender, The Diary of Eunice Callender, May 1808–June 1809 (Boston, 1809). Eunice Callender Papers, Schlesinger Library, Radcliffe Institute, Harvard University.

512. M. M. Dawes, The Diary of M. M. Dawes (Boston, n.d.), p. 9, emphasis in original. May-Goddard Family Papers, Schlesinger Library, Radcliffe Institute, Harvard University.

513. On a particularly starry night Dawes was reminded of Ossian's poetry. Ossian was supposed to be a fourth-century Celtic poet whose poems were suddenly 'discovered' (i.e. created) in 1762. Ossianism, Louis Bredvold notes, 'burst like a storm all over Europe ... The Ossianic joy in grief was the attraction that drew Werther *away* from Homer, and the judgment of the young German poets of the *Storm and Stress* period was surely that the melancholy of Ossian stirred them in a way that Homer's sadness did not. The sentimentalists of the eighteenth century were discriminating readers, and they knew that Ossian was of their kind and Homer was not': Bredvold, *The Natural History of Sensibility*, pp. 60–7.

514. Dawes, The Diary of M. M. Dawes, Friday 28 February (n.y.), p. 72.
515. Harriet Otis, Diary Entry, 24 December 1811, Diary, 1811–1814, Harrison Gray Otis Papers, Massachusetts Historical Society.
516. Harriet Otis, Diary Entry, 18 July 1813.
517. Harriet Otis, Diary 1817; see also Kenneth John Myers, 'On the Cultural Construction of Landscape Experience: Contact to 1830', and Alan Wallach, 'Making a Picture of the View from Mount Holyoke', in David Miller (ed.), *American Iconology: New Approaches to Nineteenth Century Art and Literature* (New Haven, Yale University Press, 1993), pp. 58–80, 81–92, for a discussion of this picturesque mountain tourism.
518. There is also a lively secondary literature on these ideas. See, for example, Jerome Stolnitz, 'Beauty: Some Stages in the History of an Idea', *Journal of the History of Ideas*, 22:2 (April–June 1961), pp. 185–204; Camfield, 'The Moral Aesthetics of Sentimentality'; Preben Mortensen, 'Francis Hutcheson and the Problem of Conspicuous Consumption', *Journal of Aesthetic and Art Criticism*, 53:2 (Spring 1995), pp. 155–65; Peter Kivy, 'The "Sense" of Beauty and the Sense of "Art": Hutcheson's Place in the History and Practice of Aesthetics', *Journal of Aesthetics and Art Criticism*, 53:4 (Fall 1995), pp. 349–57; the essays in Ralph Cohen (ed.), *Studies in Eighteenth-Century British Art and Aesthetics* (Berkeley: University of California Press, 1985); Paul Mattick, Jr. (ed.), *Eighteenth-Century Aesthetics and the Reconstruction of Art* (Cambridge: Cambridge University Press, 1993); A. Philip McMahon, *Preface to an American Philosophy of Art* (Chicago: University of Chicago Press, 1945); Walter John Hipple, Jr, *The Beautiful, the Sublime, and the Picturesque in Eighteenth-Century British Aesthetic Theory* (Carbondale: Southern Illinois University Press, 1957); Ronald Paulson, *Breaking and Remaking: Aesthetic Practice in England, 1700–1820* (Brunswick: Rutgers University Press, 1989).
519. There were numerous debaters in eighteenth-century aesthetic theory. I will deal only with a few who were – admittedly in a teleological fashion – to my reading, important to the development of an aesthetic ideal in the Early Republic. Many of the debaters I have deliberately left out were indeed prominent, and many were even widely read in the United States. William Hogarth, for example, was tremendously influential in mid-eighteenth-century discussions. Likewise Burke's treatise on beauty and sublimity was and is an important component of any aesthetic history. I am, however, looking at aesthetic change from a very particular position – the erosion of empiricism and the development of an aesthetic of the imagination, particularly in the United States from 1780 to the 1830s. In terms of this goal and given my emphasis on Scottish commercial humanism elsewhere, I have chosen to look at Joshua Reynolds, Thomas Reid, Joseph Addison, Shaftesbury, Hutcheson, Smith, Stewart and Alison – as well as a number of select reviews or essays by anonymous writers in American magazines. Where possible I have used the material from these authors as excerpted in American magazines, or in American editions of their texts.
520. Kenneth Charles Hafertepe also argues for a Scottish influence on American aesthetics through to the advent of 'Romanticism', though from a slightly different perspective. See 'The Enlightened Sensibility: Scottish Philosophy in American Art and Architecture' (PhD Dissertation, University of Texas at Austin, 1986). Dabney Townsend argues the exact opposite position. According to Townsend, there was

continuity from Locke to Shaftesbury to Hume, and finally to Kant, who 'sums up the movement'. Townsend concedes that Shaftesbury, though he remains a 'traditional, and superficial thinker on these points', was a Neo-Platonic thinker, and thus held innate ideas. Still, for Townsend, Shaftesbury's ideas on taste were a function of experience and thus 'compatible with an empirical interpretation of much else that Shaftesbury says'. Francis Hutcheson, according to Townsend, 'misread' Shaftesbury and his defence of his ideas was 'misguided'. He ultimately 'fail[ed]' in his interpretation because there 'is no organ of internal sense'. It is not clear whether Townsend is arguing that Hutcheson's contemporaries came to believe there was no organ of internal sense or if Townsend is making a 'physiological' observation (i.e. Townsend is saying that Hutcheson is wrong because there is no organ of internal sense). Dabney Townsend, 'From Shaftesbury to Kant: The Development of the Concept of Aesthetic Experience', *Journal of the History of Ideas*, 48:2 (April–June 1987), pp. 287–305. For an opposing interpretation of Hutcheson, see Carey, 'Hutcheson's Moral Sense', pp. 103–10.

521. Terry Eagleton, *The Ideology of the Aesthetic* (London: Basil Blackwell, 1990). Eagleton argues that the construction of bourgeois culture in nineteenth-century Europe was really the aestheticization of culture. The Scottish Moral Sense philosophers aestheticized the 'whole of social life' and thus internalized previously external social value structures. For Eagleton this is at once a profoundly liberating moment in the history of humanity and yet it is, at the same time, a form of 'internalized repression'. My own reading of the sources owes much to Eagleton, though he does not focus on the American experience. Also, I am inclined to see aesthetic change not as the overwhelming principle that holds all the different cultural factors together, but rather as one of a number of structures that changes from mirror to lamp during this period (the others being political economy and morality). Furthermore, I am less inclined to see the internalization of value structures as a form of oppression.

522. See Miller (ed.), *American Iconology*; Edward J. Nygreen, *Views and Visions: American Landscapes Before 1830* (Washington: Corcoran Gallery, 1986); Bryan Jay Wolf, *Romantic Re-Vision: Culture and Consciousness in Nineteenth Century American Painting and Literature* (Chicago: University of Chicago Press, 1982).

523. Eagleton, *The Ideology of the Aesthetic*, p. 39.

524. For the relationship of Calvinist religion and sensational psychology, see John Morgan, 'The Puritan Thesis Revisited', and Edward B. Davis, 'Christianity and Early Modern Science: The Foster Thesis Revisited', in David G. Livingstone, D. G. Hart and Mark A. Noll (eds), *Evangelicals and Science in Historical Perspective* (Oxford: Oxford University Press, 1999), pp. 43–74, 75–99.

525. Abrams, *The Mirror and the Lamp*, p. 36.

526. Ibid., pp. 37, 42.

527. Barbara Novak, *American Painting of the Nineteenth Century* (New York: Vendome, 1969).

528. Susan Rather argues that Stuart satirized Reynolds in his portrait of him. See Susan Rather, 'Stuart and Reynolds: A Portrait of Change', *Eighteenth-Century Studies*, 27:1 (Autumn 1993), pp. 61–84.

529. Joshua Reynolds, 'On Genius and Taste', *Boston Magazine* (March 1784), pp. 169–71.

530. Though I position Reynolds defending empiricism, towards the end of his life he also turned to the imagination. He began his *Discourses* in 1769 focusing on 'classical concepts such as imitation, decorum and "general nature"'. By his thirteenth *Discourse* he embraced the imagination as the 'residence of truth'. Reynolds, James Engell argues, was thus 'the first enlightenment thinker to formulate bluntly and without qualifications a belief becoming widespread: truth is attained through the imagination and, more specifically, through imaginative art. From this point, it was a short step for the high Romantics to conclude that truth in art can be truth of life, nature, and the cosmos, that imagination is the highest organ of philosophy, and that art is the only way to climax philosophical inquiry': James Engell, *The Creative Imagination: Enlightenment to Romanticism* (Cambridge, MA: Harvard University Press, 1981), p. 186. This seems to me overstated. The antinomian nature of the full-blown romantic imagination is missing from Reynolds and other 'enlightenment' theorists. Though it seems unfair to set up Reynolds as a 'straw' man for empiricism, this is the Reynolds that Bostonians read in 1784.

531. Abrams, *The Mirror and the Lamp*, p. 46.

532. Reid is discussed at greater length in Chapter 5. William Charvat quotes American Scottish Realist Samuel Miller's definition of Common Sense or Scottish Realism: '[Common Sense] consists in the doctrine that the mind perceives not merely the ideas or images of external objects but the external object themselves; that when they are presented to our senses, they produce certain impressions; that these impressions are followed by correspondent sensations; and these sensations by a perception of the existence and qualities of the objects about which the mind is employed, and that they possess the qualities which we witness not by a train of reasoning, by formal reflection or by association of ideas, but by a direct and necessary connection between the presence of such objects and our consequent perceptions. In short the distinguishing peculiarity of such metaphysics is an appeal from the delusive principles of the idealism of Berkeley and the scepticism of Hume to the common sense of mankind as a tribunal paramount to all subtleties of philosophy': Samuel Miller; quoted (with no reference) in Charvat, *The Origins of American Critical Thought*, p. 36.

533. Thomas Reid, 'An Essay on Taste', *Massachusetts Magazine* (June 1790).

534. Anon., 'Beauty', *Encyclopedia or a Dictionary of Arts and Science* (Philadelphia, 1798), vol. 5, n.p.

535. Abrams, *The Mirror and the Lamp*, p. 36.

536. Ibid., p. 43.

537. Taylor, *Sources of the Self*, p. 253.

538. Shaftesbury, *An Inquiry Concerning Virtue and Merit*.

539. Eagleton, *The Ideology of the Aesthetic*, p. 35.

540. For a fuller discussion of these ideas see Chapters 1 and 2.

541. Hutcheson, *An Inquiry into the Original*, pp. 12–13.

542. Ibid., p. 15.

543. Of course, in these ideas he resembles Locke. He differs from Locke in that the receiving mind is not 'empty'. As discussed in several chapters, this was an important difference that spoke to the very nature of humanity and the deity.

544. Smith, *Theory of Moral Sentiments*, pp. 383–4.

545. Hipple, *The Beautiful, the Sublime, and the Picturesque*; and Cohen (ed.), *Studies in Eighteenth-Century British Art and Aesthetics*.
546. Addison, *Spectator*, 411–21 (Saturday 21 June–Thursday 3 July 1712).
547. *Spectator*, 411 (Saturday 21 June 1712).
548. *Spectator*, 412 (Monday 23 June 1712).
549. *Spectator*, 413 (Tuesday 4 June 1712). Interestingly, Addison in this issue calls the reader's attention to Locke's *An Essay Concerning Human Understanding* and the discussion on colours and light as proof of his own ideas. This has been, in my opinion, a source of great error for historians who have taken the cue uncritically. Addison did borrow from Locke's sensational psychology – as did the Scottish Moral Sense philosophers. Locke, however, never denied the 'reality' of qualities in objects – but spoke only of our ability to perceive them. For Locke, secondary qualities were real: 'Because being nothing but the effects of certain Powers in Things, fitted and ordained by GOD, to produce such Sensations in us, they cannot but be correspondent, and adequate to those Powers: And we are sure they agree to the reality of Things': Locke, *An Essay Concerning Human Understanding*, book 2, ch. 31, section 3, p. 209. In my reading, this confusion speaks to the nature of these changes. Addison, only twenty-two years after Locke wrote the *Essay*, was able to read it outside of the Calvinist context in which it was written. See Chapters 1 and 2 for discussions of the Scottish/Locke divide. For Locke, see Dunn, 'From Applied Theology to Social Analysis'.
550. See for example, Anon., 'Essays on Rhetorick: Sublimity in Writing', *Boston Magazine* (November/December 1786), pp. 409–17.
551. See, for example, *Boston Spectator; devoted to Politicks and Belles-Lettres* (1814–15); and for a discussion of the Addison phenomena see, Anon., Review of Nathan Drake, M.D., *Essays, Biographical, Critical, and Historical, illustrative of the Tattler, Spectator, Guardian, Rambler, Adventurer, and Idler, and of the various periodical Papers which, in imitation of the Writings of Steele and Addison, have been published between the close of the Eighth volume of the Spectator, and the commencement of the Year 1809, Select Reviews, and Spirit of the Foreign Magazines* (December 1809), pp. 361–5.
552. Charvat, *The Origins of American Critical Thought*, p. 30. In a 1790s edition published in Philadelphia, no fewer then four chapters reprinted and discussed Addison's *Spectator* articles: Hugh Blair, *Lectures on Rhetoric and Belles Lettres* (Philadelphia, 1790), pp. 179–209.
553. See also Anon., 'Philosophy of Musical Composition', *Euterpeiad; or Musical Intelligencer, and Ladies Gazette* (June 1823), pp. 27–31: 'But the author who has gone the farthest into the development of the means by which music affects us, is Mr. Alison, in his beautiful *Essays on the nature and principles of taste*, and while he classifies the sentiments to which sounds address themselves, and endeavors to establish some of the principles upon which music, properly so called, addresses itself to the understanding and the heart, he gives much more to association than any of his predecessors, and thus divides the sounds and ideas, and emotions, they excite'.
554. Charvat, *The Origins of American Critical Thought*, p. 30.
555. Abrams, *The Mirror and the Lamp*, p. 46.
556. Charvat, *The Origins of American Critical Thought*, p. 48.

557. Archibald Alison, *Essays on the Nature and Principles of Taste* (1790; Hartford, 1821), p. vi.

558. Ibid., p. vi.

559. Ibid., p. 3.

560. Ibid., p. 27.

561. Anon., Review of Alison, *Essays on the Nature and Principles of Taste*, *Christian Observer* (February 1812), p. 93.

562. Jeffrey founded and edited the *Edinburgh Review*, read widely in the United States. Charvat, *The Origins of American Critical Thought*, pp. 53–5.

563. Christine Holbo, 'Imagination, Commerce, and the Politics of Associationism in Crevecoeur's *Letters from an American Farmer*', *Early American Literature*, 32:1 (1997), pp. 20–65; p. 24.

564. F. W. Winthrop, Review of *Supplement to the Encyclopedia Britannica: Article, 'Beauty'* (Edinburgh, December 1816), *North American Review* (May 1818), pp. 1–25.

565. Stewart, *Elements of the Philosophy of the Human Mind*, pp. 361–2.

566. Charvat, *The Origins of American Critical Thought*, p. 30.

567. Stewart, *Elements of the Philosophy of the Human Mind*, p. 99.

568. Ibid., pp. 99, 364.

569. Ibid., pp. 366, 501, Stewart discusses Sterne's *Sentimental Journey*. On p. 501 he discusses the role of the imagination as stimulated by novels like Sterne's in the construction of sympathy. See Chapter 6 for a full discussion of sentiment.

570. *Edinburgh Encyclopedia*, 2nd American edn (New York, 1816), p. 364.

571. Ibid., p. 366.

572. Ibid., p. 366.

573. Ibid., p. 370. Hugh Blair also used this poem in his *Lectures*, p. 24.

574. Anon., 'Essay on Akenside's *Pleasures of the Imagination*'.

575. Anon., 'The Pleasures of the Imagination', *Boston Literary Magazine* (May 1832), pp. 14–18.

576. Washington Allston, *Lectures on Art, and Poems*, ed. Richard Henry Dana, Jr (New York, 1850), p. 22. The *Lectures on Art* were written in the 1830s. Numerous poems and short stories published in this collection were written in the 1810s and 1820s. Allston died in 1843 and this collection of his work was posthumously edited and published.

577. Washington Allston; quoted by Richard Henry Dana, Jr in the 'Preface' to Allston, *Lectures on Art*.

578. Allston copied long excerpts from James Marsh's translation of Jacobi (one of the less prominent German Enlightenment thinkers). On the interesting Dr Marsh, see Peter Carafiol, *Transcendent Reason: James Marsh and the Forms of Romantic Thought* (Tallahassee: University Presses of Florida, 1982). Allston's excerpts are in the Washington Allston volumes, Dana Family Papers, Massachusetts Historical Society; Kant and other German Enlightenment thinkers were well known in Boston. Aaron Webster's *The Minor Encyclopedia or Cabinet of General Knowledge* (Boston, 1803) also concluded with Kant as authority: 'Professor Kant's definition [of beauty] is perhaps more satisfactory [than Burke's], though it can only be understood by apposite comparative illustrations. He says, "Beauty is the *regular* conformation of an object

of Nature of Art, in which the mind, *intuitively*, perceives this conformation without reflecting upon its ultimate design or purpose"' (p. 155).

579. Allston, *Lectures on Art*, p. 13.

580. Taylor, *Sources of the Self*, p. 377.

581. Allston, *Lectures on Art*, p. 13; For the Stewart and Hutcheson parallels see respective above discussions.

582. Allston, *Lectures on Art*, p. 16. For the pervasiveness of some of these ideas, see also Harmonicus, *Massachusetts Magazine* (December 1783), p. 65.

583. Allston, *Lectures on Art*, p. 45.

584. Washington Allston, 'Memorandum: Pure Intelligence', in Washington Allston volumes, Dana Family Papers (unpaginated, n.d.).

585. Doreen Hunter, 'America's First Romantics: Richard Henry Dana, Sr. and Washington Allston', *New England Quarterly*, 45:1 (March 1972), pp. 3–30; p. 6.

586. Novak, *American Painting*, p. 122.

587. Ibid., p. 124.

588. David Bjelajac, 'The Boston Elite's Resistance to Washington Allston's *Elijah in the Desert*', in Miller (ed.), *American Iconology*, pp. 39–57.

589. William Ware, *Lectures on the Works and Genius of Washington Allston* (Boston, 1852), pp. 80–90.

590. See John Dowling, 'The Crisis of the Spanish Enlightenment: Capricho 43 and Goya's Second Portrait of Jovellanos', *Eighteenth-Century Studies*, 18:3 (Spring 1985), pp. 331–59; John Dowling, 'Capricho as Style in Life, Literature, and Art From Zamora to Goya', *Eighteenth-Century Studies*, 10:4 (Summer 1977), pp. 413–33.

591. Nathalia Wright, 'Introduction', in Allston, *Lectures On Art*.

592. Allston, *Lectures on Art*, p. 52.

593. Ibid., p. 53.

594. Ibid., p. 54.

595. Dennis Berthold, 'Charles Brockden Brown, "Edgar Huntly", and the Origins of the American Picturesque', *William and Mary Quarterly*, 3rd series, 41:1 (January 1984), pp. 62–84.

596. See Rolf Toman (ed.), *Neoclassicism and Romanticism: Architecture, Sculpture, Painting, Drawing, 1750–1848* (London: Konemann, 2002).

597. Dr Ladd, 'Critical Reflections on Style' *American Museum* (June 1787), p. 534.

598. Blair's own definition was subtler and resembles Allston's: 'It is not easy to describe, in words, the precise impression which great and sublime objects make upon us, when we behold them; but every one has a conception of it. It consists in a kind of admiration and expansion of the mind; it raises the mind much above its ordinary state; and fills it with a degree of wonder and astonishment, which it cannot well express.' For Blair, 'burning mountains' and 'earthquakes' were especially full of 'grandeur'. Blair, *Lectures on Rhetoric*, pp. 20–1.

599. Anon., 'Essays on Rhetorick', p. 409.

600. Ibid., p. 413.

601. Alison, *Essays on the Nature and Principles of Taste*, p. 37; see also the graphic distinction between beauty and the picturesque by an anonymous author in the *Literary Magazine*: 'Variety and intricacy ... roughness, sudden variation, and a certain degree of irregularity, are ingredient in the picturesque; as smoothness, gradual variation,

and a certain degree of uniformity are in the beautiful'. The beautiful gave rise to lethargy and a pleasurable stupor. The picturesque provided different forms of stimulation. 'How different is that active pursuit of pleasure, when the fibers are braced by a keen air, in a wild, romantic situation; when the activity of the body keeps pace with that of the mind, and eagerly scales every rocky promontory, explores every new recess!': Anon., 'Distinctions Between the Beautiful and the Picturesque', *Literary Magazine, and American Register* (June 1806), pp. 439–40.

602. For an example of the discussion, see Anon., 'On a Taste for the Picturesque', *Lady's Monitor* (20 March 1802), pp. 245–7; and 'Picturesque Voyage Round Great Britain', *Athenaeum* (15 August 1818), pp. 361–6.

603. William Gilpin, 'An Essay on Picturesque Travel', *New York Magazine* (December 1793), p. 738.

604. Richard Payne Knight, *An Analytical Inquiry into the Principles of Taste* (London, 1805). For the Price, Repton and Knight controversy, see Anon., Review of Uvedale Price, 'An Essay on the Picturesque, as compared with the sublime and the beautiful: and on the studying of pictures, for the purpose of improving the landscape', and Review of Richard Payne Knight 'A Sketch from the landscape, a didactic poem', in the *American Monthly Review* (July 1795), pp. 232–40. This is clearly an interesting discussion of picturesque and sublime principles. But, as Berthold has argued, common usage of these words and ideas drew less from Knight and Price than from Gilpin. The in-house scandals of the British aesthetic elite were too pedantic for what became the accepted ideas of the sublime and the picturesque.

605. Taylor, *Sources of the Self*, p. 299.

606. Anon., 'On a Taste for the Picturesque', *Monthly Magazine, and American Review* (July 1800), pp. 11–14.

607. *Polyanthos* (March 1807), pp. 259–62; *Athenaeum* (15 April, 1 May 1817), pp. 67–77, pp. 143–53; *Athenaeum* (15 August 1818), pp. 361–6.

608. John Shaw, *Picturesque Views of America* (Philadelphia, 1820). Courtesy of the Winterthur Library, Printed Book and Periodical Collection.

609. Shaw, *Picturesque Views of America*.

610. Lee Quimby argues that Jefferson's florid descriptions of his Natural Bridge played the same role: 'As the aesthetic eye for his readers, Jefferson became their intermediary, providing a memorial of his own experience of nature's artwork so that his readers too might be exhilarated by the elevation of their senses, opine nature's creation, and then imagine – or, perhaps, co-create – the tranquility promised in the distant horizon. The aesthetic vision itself is thus fused with a call for participation': Quimby, 'Thomas Jefferson', p. 350.

611. Nygreen, *Views and Vision*.

612. See ibid.; and also Myers, 'On the Cultural Construction of Landscape Experience'; and Wallach, 'Making a Picture of the View from Mount Holyoke'.

613. The Brahmin merchants often allowed for the viewing of their Allston holdings. For example, when the South Carolina lawyer, banker and artist John S. Cogdell visited Allston in Boston, Allston took him round to view his paintings in private homes: John S. Cogdell, Diary, Courtesy of the Winterthur Library, Joseph Downs Collection of Manuscripts and Printed Ephemera.

614. Blair, *Lectures on Rhetoric*, p. 21.

615. Taylor uses the Macbeth analogy to describe the difference between earlier ideas of nature and the eighteenth-century changes: Taylor, *Sources of the Self*, p. 298.

616. The hermit trope was popular in British landscape design. Indeed, in the eighteenth century, landlords advertised for 'hermits' to live on their property at specific vista points, as part of the view. See Ann Bermingham, *Landscape and Ideology: The English Rustic Tradition, 1740–1860* (Berkeley: University of California Press, 1986). Though the landscape design narrative is intimately associated with the picturesque, it is beyond the scope of this discussion.

617. Diary of Eunice Callender.

618. See Colin Campbell, *The Romantic Ethic and the Spirit of Modern Consumerism* (Oxford: Basil Blackwell, 1987).

619. Shaftesbury, 'Advice to an Author'; quoted in Quimby, 'Thomas Jefferson', p. 342.

620. Shaftesbury is quoted in Campbell, *The Romantic Ethic*, p. 151.

621. Eagleton, *The Ideology of the Aesthetic*, p. 40.

622. Since Smith came first, it was his ideas the *Encyclopedia* followed.

623. Smith, *Theory of Moral Sentiments*, pp. 337–51; and *Universal Asylum and Columbian Magazine* (March 1790), pp. 161–3.

624. Ibid..

625. Kathleen Eagan Johnson, 'Painted Furniture in Female Academies', Winterthur Museum (Term Paper, Artifacts in American History, Winterthur Program in Early American Culture, n.d.).

626. John Brewer, *Pleasures of the Imagination* (New York: Farrar Strauss Giroux, 1997), p. 462.

627. *Massachusetts Magazine* (August 1793 and May 1794).

628. Dean Fales, *American Painted Furniture 1660–1880* (New York: Dutton, 1972).

629. See Nygreen, *Views and Vision*, pp. 44–5.

630. Alison, *Essays on the Nature and Principles of Taste*, p. 37.

631. For a discussion of these ideas, see John E. Crowley, *The Invention of Comfort: Sensibilities and Design in Early Modern Britain and America* (Baltimore: Johns Hopkins University Press, 2001).

632. Dunn, 'From Applied Theology to Social Analysis', p. 123.

633. Taylor, *Sources of the Self*, p. 287. Taylor argues that these ideas originated with the physiocrats and were taken over by Smith.

634. Dunn, 'From Applied Theology to Social Analysis', p. 121.

635. Ibid., pp. 122, 124. Dunn reaches the profound conclusion that Locke's ideas represent a self-conscious 'refusal of the future as it was to come to be': see note 29 above.

636. Winthrop, Review of … *'Beauty'*.

637. Washington Allston, 'Note on Originality – Reproduction', in Washington Allston volumes. Dana Family Papers (n.d.).

638. Pocock, 'Virtues, Rights and Manners', p. 48.

639. Allston, *Lectures on Art*, p. 9.

BIBLIOGRAPHY

Primary Sources

Alison, Archibald, *Essays on the Nature and Principles of Taste* (1790; Hartford, 1821).

Allston, Washington, *Lectures on Art, and Poems*, ed. Richard Henry Dana, Jr (New York, 1850).

Anon., 'Annuity Fund', *New-England Palladium* (Boston, 12 December 1806).

—, *The Bank Note or Lessons for Ladies: A Comedy in Five Acts as Performed at the Boston Theatre* (Boston, 1796).

—, 'Bank Notes Not Money', *Niles' Weekly Register* (31 May 1817).

—, 'Bank Statements', *Boston Commercial Gazette* (3 February 1820).

—, 'Banking – General Remarks', *Niles' Weekly Register* (25 April 1818).

—, 'Banks and Bank Notes', *Niles' Weekly Register* (21 September, 5 October 1816, 21 June 1817).

—, 'Banks in Danger', *Salem Register* (2 April 1807).

—, 'Beauty', *Encyclopedia or a Dictionary of Arts and Science* (Philadelphia, 1798), vol. 5.

—, 'Benevolence', *Something* (25 November 1809).

—, 'Benevolence', *Cabinet; a Repository of Polite Literature* (2 February 1811), pp. 73–5.

—, 'Benevolence of Piety', *Polyanthos* (June 1812), p. 51.

—, 'Benevolence: Or the Good Samaritan', *Massachusetts Magazine* (February 1789), pp. 76–8.

—, *The Changery, an Allegoric Memoir of the Boston Exchange Office: Or the Pernicious Progress of Bank Speculation Unveiled* (Boston, [1805?]).

—, 'Common Sewer of Speculation', *Niles' Weekly Register* (12 December 1818).

—, 'Course of Exchange for Bank Notes and Specie', *Cohen's Lottery Gazette and Register* (21 August 1818), p. 143.

—, 'The Delights of Benevolence', *Massachusetts Magazine* (July 1795), pp. 206–11.

211

—, 'Distinctions between the Beautiful and the Picturesque', *Literary Magazine, and American Register* (June 1806), pp. 439–40.

—, 'Essay on Akenside's *Pleasures of the Imagination*', *Harvard Lyceum*, 1 (23 February 1811), pp. 392–400.

—, 'Essay on Money', *New York Review and Atheneum Magazine*, 1 (September 1825), p. 266.

—, 'Essays on Rhetorick: Sublimity in Writing', *Boston Magazine* (Boston, November/December 1786), pp. 409–17.

—, 'Extract from an Address to the Representatives of the People of Virginia', *American Museum* (July 1787), pp. 34–5.

—, 'Extracts From the Report of the Committee on the Bank of the United States', *Philanthropist*, 9:1 (1819).

—, 'The Faithful Shepherd, A Story Founded on Truth', *Boston Magazine* (May 1784), pp. 265–8.

—, 'Farther Remarks on the Theological Institution in Andover, Occasioned by the Review of its Constitution and Statutes in the *Monthly Anthology*', *Panoplist* (February 1809), pp. 413–25; and (March 1809), pp. 471–81.

—, 'Female Benevolence', *Boston Weekly Magazine* (31 May 1817), p. 134.

—, 'The Genevan Church', *Christian Disciple and Theological Review* (May/June 1821), pp. 214–30.

—, *The Glass: or Speculation, A Poem* (New York, 1791).

—, 'Greenwich Hospital, A True Tale', *Boston Weekly Magazine* (3 April 1824), pp. 10–11.

—, 'Hints on the Nature and Usefulness of Diaries', *Massachusetts Magazine* (May 1795), p. 72.

—, *Intellectual Regale; or Ladies' TEA Tray* (18 July 1815), pp. 537–9.

—, 'Massachusetts Annuity Fund', *Columbian Centinel* (18 March 1807).

—, 'Meditations on the Benevolence of God', *Weekly Monitor* (9 July 1817), pp. 52–4.

—, 'The Middling Interest', *Boston Gazette* (1 April 1805).

—, 'The New STATE BANK', *Columbian Centinel* (31 August 1811).

—, 'On a Taste for the Picturesque', *Lady's Monitor* (20 March 1802), pp. 245–7.

—, 'On a Taste for the Picturesque', *Monthly Magazine, and American Review* (July 1800), pp. 11–14.

—, 'On Charity as a Principle of Consistent Behavior, and Universal Benevolence', *Panoplist* (February 1817), pp. 54–61.

—, 'On Sympathy', *Massachusetts Magazine* (February 1791), p. 105.

—, 'The Paper System' nos 1–7, *Niles' Weekly Register* (25 April–20 June 1818).

—, 'Philosophy of Musical Composition', *Euterpeiad; or Musical Intelligencer, and Ladies Gazette* (June 1823), pp. 27–31.

—, 'Picturesque Voyage round Great Britain', *Athenaeum* (15 August 1818), pp. 361–6.

—, 'The Pleasures of the Imagination', *Boston Literary Magazine* (May 1832), pp. 14–18.

—, 'Political Economy', in *Edinburgh Encyclopedia*, 2nd American edn (New York, 1817), pp. 39–77.

—, 'The Principles of Political Economy' nos I–XXII, *United States Literary Gazette* (October 1825–March 1826).

—, 'Queries and Replies relative to Paper Money', *American Museum* (July 1787), pp. 35–6.

—, Review of Adam Smith's *An Inquiry into the Nature and Causes of Wealth* (French trans., 2nd edn, Paris, 1822), *Boston Journal of Philosophy and the Arts* (July 1824), pp. 65–81.

—, Review of *The Age of Benevolence: A Poem, Gospel Advocate* (November 1822), pp. 353–6.

—, Review of Akenside, *Pleasures of the Imagination, Monthly Anthology*, 3 (July 1806).

—, Review of Alison, *Essays on the Nature and Principles of Taste, Christian Observer* (February 1812), p. 93.

—, 'Review of the Constitution and Associate Statutes of the Theological Seminary in Andover; with a Sketch of its Rise and Progress', *Monthly Anthology* (November 1805).

—, Review of 'Essay on Money', Supplement to the *Encyclopedia Britannica*, vol. 5, part 2 (Edinburgh, 1822), *New York Review and Athenaeum Magazine* (September 1825), pp. 264–83.

—, Review of Nathan Drake, M.D., *Essays, Biographical, Critical, and Historical, Illustrative of the Tattler, Spectator, Guardian, Rambler, Adventurer, and Idler, and of the various Periodical Papers which, in imitation of the Writings of Steele and Addison, have been published between the close of the Eighth volume of the Spectator, and the commencement of the Year 1809, Select Reviews, and Spirit of the Foreign Magazines* (December 1809), pp. 361–5.

—, Review of Richard Payne Knight, 'A Sketch from the Landscape, a Didactic Poem', *American Monthly Review* (July 1795), pp. 232–40.

—, Review of *Self-Control* (Boston and Philadelphia, 1811), *General Repository and Review* (January 1812), pp. 191–2.

—, 'Review of a Sermon Preached 10 January 1810 at the dedication of the Church in Park-Street, Boston', *Monthly Anthology* (February 1810), p. 135.

—, Review of *Summary of the Practical Principles of Political Economy, with Observations on Smith's Wealth of Nations, and Say's Political Economy, North American Review* (October 1826), p. 465.

—, *Review of The True Reasons on which the Election of a Hollis Professor of Divinity in Harvard College was Opposed at the Board of Overseers, Feb, 14, 1805* (Boston, March 1805).

—, Review of Uvedale Price, 'An Essay on the Picturesque, as compared with the sublime and the beautiful: and on the studying of pictures, for the purpose of improving the landscape', *American Monthly Review* (July 1795), pp. 232–40.

—, 'Scripomania', *Universal Asylum and Columbian Magazine* (August 1791), pp. 141–2.

—, 'Self-love … Benevolence', *Boston Spectator; Devoted to Politicks and Belles-Lettres* (19 February 1814), pp. 30–2.

—, 'Sensibility: A Mechanical Virtue', *Massachusetts Magazine* (November 1789), p. 668.

—, 'Sentimental Scenes', *Massachusetts Magazine* (April 1795).

—, 'Singular Instance of Benevolence', *Polyanthos* (September 1814), pp. 292–5.

—, 'Supplement to the Pennsylvania Gazette: Considerations on the Bank of North America', *Pennsylvania Gazette* (7 September 1785).

—, 'Youthful Benevolence', *Panoplist* (October 1806), pp. 223–4.

Baldwin, Laommi, *Thoughts on the Study of Political Economy* (Boston, 1809).

Barbon, Nicholas, *A Discourse on Trade* (London, 1690).

—, *A Discourse Concerning Coining the New Money Lighter in Answer to Mr. Lock's Considerations about Raising the Value of Money* (London, 1696).

Barton, William, *Observations on the Nature and Use of Paper Credit* (Philadelphia, 1781).

—, *The True Interest of the United States and Particularly of Pennsylvania Considered* (Philadelphia, 1786).

Benevolus, 'Thoughts on Benevolence', *Boston Magazine* (January 1786), pp. 26–7.

Blair, Hugh, *Lectures on Rhetoric and Belles Lettres* (Philadelphia, 1790).

Blodget, Samuel, *Economica: A Statistical Manual for the United States of America* (Washington, 1806; Reprint, New York, 1964).

Bollmann, Erick, *Paragraph on Banks* (Philadelphia, 1810).

—, *Plan of an Improved System of the Money-Concerns of the Union* (Philadelphia, 1816).

Channing, William E., 'Likeness to God', in *Unitarian Christianity and Other Essays*, ed. Irving H. Bartlett (New York: Liberal Arts Press, 1957).

—, 'The Moral Argument Against Calvinism' (1820), in *Unitarian Christianity and Other Essays*, ed. Irving H. Bartlett (New York: Liberal Arts Press, 1957).

—, 'Unitarian Christianity: Discourse at the Ordination of the Rev. Jared Sparks, Baltimore, 1819', in *Unitarian Christianity and Other Essays*, ed. Irving H. Bartlett (New York: Liberal Arts Press, 1957).

Colwell, William, 'Banking Speculation: Farmers' Exchange Bank' *Columbian Detector* (9 May 1809).

Cooper, Thomas, *Lectures on the Elements of Political Economy* (1826; New York: Augustus M. Kelley, 1971).

Corneille, 'The Album, No. 1: Novel Reading', *Boston Weekly Magazine* (3 April 1824).

[Cushing, Caleb], 'Miscellanies – The Principles of Political Economy', *United States Literary Gazette* (October 1825–March 1826).

Davies, Benjamin, *The Bank Torpedo* (New York, 1819).

Edinburgh Encyclopedia, 2nd American edn (New York, 1816).

F., 'Novels', *Ladies' Magazine* (August 1828), p. 357.

Franklin, Benjamin, 'Remarks and Facts relative to the American Paper Money' (London, 1764), *American Museum* (July 1787).

Frisbie, Levi, *Inaugural Address Delivered in the Chapel of the University of Cambridge, November 5, 1817* (Cambridge, MA, 1817).

Gallison, J., Review of John Bristed's, *The Resources of the United States of America, or A View of the Agricultural, Commercial, Manufacturing, Financial, Political, Literary, Moral and Religious Capacity and Character of the American People*, North American Review, 21 (December 1818), p. 402.

Gilbert and Dean, *Names of the Banks in Massachusetts, New Hampshire ... Together with the Rates of Exchanging them for Specie* (Boston, 1815).

Gilpin, William, 'An Essay on Picturesque Travel', *New York Magazine* (December 1793), p. 738.

Gossip, No. XIII, 'Ficta Voluptatis causa sint proxima veris', *Boston Weekly Magazine* (22 January 1803), p. 53.

Gray, F. C., Review of Daniel Raymond's *Thoughts on Political Economy, in two parts* (Baltimore, 1820), *North American Review*, 31, n.s. 6 (April 1821).

Griffin, Edward D., *A Sermon Preached Jan. 10, 1810, at the Dedication of the Church in Park Street, Boston* (Boston, 1810).

Haley, 'Benevolence', *Massachusetts Magazine* (April 1796), p. 100.

Harmonicus, *Massachusetts Magazine* (December 1783), p. 65.

Historical Catalogue of the Old South Church (Boston, 1883).

Holley, H., 'On the Pleasure Derived from Witnessing Scenes of Distress', *North American Review* (November 1815), pp. 59–67.

Hume, David, *The Letters of David Hume*, ed. J. Y. T. Greig, 2 vols (Oxford: Clarendon Press, 1932).

—, 'Of Money', in *Writings on Economics*, ed. Eugene Rotwin (Madison: University of Wisconsin Press, 1955).

Hutcheson, Francis, *An Inquiry into the Original of Our Ideas of Beauty and Virtue; In Two Treatises* (1726; New York: Garland, 1971).

Investigator, No. VII, *Massachusetts Magazine* (July 1795), pp. 241–3.

K—, 'Benevolence', *Boston Weekly Magazine* (15 October 1803), p. 206.

Knight, Richard Payne, *An Analytical Inquiry into the Principles of Taste* (London, 1805).

Ladd, Dr, 'Critical Reflections on Style' *American Museum* (June 1787), p. 534.

Lauderdale, James Maitland, Earl of, *An Inquiry into the Nature and Origin of Public Wealth, and into the Means and Causes of its Increase* (Edinburgh and London, 1804).

Law, John, 'Premier memoire sur les banques', in *Oeuvres contenant les principes sur le Numeraire, le Commerce, le Credit et les Banques avec des notes* (Paris, 1790).

Leander, 'On Modern Novels and Their Effects', *Massachusetts Magazine* (November 1791), pp. 662–5.

Locke, John, *An Essay Concerning Human Understanding* (1690), ed. John Yolton (New York: Dutton, 1964).

—, *Two Treatises of Government* (1690), ed. Peter Laslett (Cambridge: Cambridge University Press, 1967).

—, *Further Considerations Concerning the Value of Money* (1695), in *John Locke on Money*, ed. Patrick Hyde Kelly, 2 vols (New York: Oxford University Press, 1991), vol. 2.

—, *Some Considerations of the Consequences of the Lowering of the Interest and Raising the Value of Money* (1696), in *John Locke on Money*, ed. Patrick Hyde Kelly, 2 vols (New York: Oxford University Press, 1991), vol. 1.

—, *Essays on the Law of Nature*, trans. W. von Leyden, corrected reprint of 1954 edn (Oxford: Clarendon Press, 1958).

—, *John Locke on Money*, ed. Patrick Hyde Kelly, 2 vols (New York: Oxford University Press, 1991).

Lowndes, William, *A Report Containing an Essay for the Amendment of the Silver Coins* (London, 1695).

Monzo, 'Benevolence: A Fragment', *Gentlemen and Ladies' Town and Country Magazine* (May 1789), pp. 191–2.

Morse, Jedediah, *The True Reasons on Which the Election of a Hollis Professor of Divinity in Harvard College was Opposed at the Board of Overseers* (Charlestown, 1805), pp. 14–17.

Nestor, 'Thoughts on Paper Money', *American Museum* (July 1787), p. 40.

New Edinburgh Encyclopedia, 2nd American edition (New York, 1817).

Norton, Andrews, Review of *Letters to the Rev. William E. Channing, containing Remarks on his Sermon recently preached at Baltimore. By Moses Stuart* (1819), *Christian Disciple* (1819).

Oresme, Nicole, *Tractatus de Origine, Natura, Jura, et Mutacionibus Monetarum* ([c. 1605]).

Phillips, Willard, *A Manual of Political Economy* (1828; New York: Augustus M. Kelley, 1968).

Pitt, William, *The Bullion Debate: A Serio-Comic Satiric Poem* (London, 1811).

Porter, J., 'Review of Thomas Cooper's *Political Economy*', *North American Review* (Boston, October 1827), p. 416.

Price, Richard, *Observations on the Nature of Civil Liberty, the Principles of Government, and the Justice and Policy of the War with America: To Which is Added, an Appendix, containing a State of the National Debt, an Estimate of the Money Drawn from the Public by the Taxes, and an Account of the National Income and Expenditure since the Last War* (Philadelphia, 1776).

Provident Institution for Savings, *At a Meeting of the Trustees* (31 December 1816).

—, *Act of Incorporation* (Boston, 1817).

—, *Brothers, or Consequences: A Story of What Happens Every Day, With an Account of Savings Banks* (Boston, 1823).

R, 'On Taste', *Monthly Anthology and Boston Review* (8 August 1808).

Raguet, Condy, *An Inquiry into the Causes of the Present State of the Circulating Medium of the United States* (Philadelphia, 1815).

Raymond, Daniel, *The Elements of Political Economy* (1823; New York: Augustus M. Kelley, 1964).

Rees, Abraham (ed.), *The Cyclopaedia; or Universal Dictionary of Arts, Sciences and Literature*, 41 vols (Philadelphia, 1810–24), articles on 'Money', vol. 24, and 'Political Economy', vol. 29.

Reid, Thomas, 'An Essay on Taste', *Massachusetts Magazine* (June 1790).

Remarker, No. 29, *Monthly Anthology and Boston Review* (January 1808).

—, No. 30, *Monthly Anthology and Boston Review* (February 1808).

Reynolds, Joshua, 'On Genius and Taste', *Boston Magazine* (March 1784), pp. 169–71.

S. P., 'Benevolence and Gratitude', *Massachusetts Baptist Missionary Magazine* (June 1814), pp. 42–4.

Shaftesbury, Anthony Ashley Cooper, third Earl of, *Characteristicks of Men, Manners, Opinions, Times*, 3 vols (1711; Farnborough: Gregg, 1968), vol. 2: *An Inquiry Concerning Virtue and Merit*.

Shaw, Joshua, *Picturesque Views of America* (Philadelphia, 1820).

Smith, Adam, *The Theory of Moral Sentiments* (1759; New York: Garland, 1971).

—, *Lectures on Justice, Police, Revenue and Arms* (1763), ed. Edward Cannan (1896; New York: Augustus M. Kelley, 1964).

—, *The Wealth of Nations* (1776; New York: Modern Library, 2000).

Steuart, Sir James, *Inquiry into the Principles of Political Oeconomy* (London, 1767).

Stewart, Dugald, *Elements of the Philosophy of the Human Mind* (London, 1792).

—, *Outlines of Moral Philosophy*, 3rd edn (Edinburgh, 1808).

Stuart, Moses, *Letters to the Reverend William E. Channing Containing Remarks on his Sermon Recently Published at Baltimore* (Andover, 1819).

Sullivan, James, *The Path to Riches* (Boston, 1792).

Swan, James, *An Address to the President, Senate and House of Representatives, of the United States, on The Means of Creating a National Paper by Loan Offices, which shall Replace that of Discredited Banks, and Supersede the Use of Gold and Silver Coin* (Boston, 1819).

TD, 'On British Novels and Romances', *Atheneum; or Spirit of the English Magazines* (15 June 1820), p. 319.

Tracy, Count Destutt, *A Treatise of Political Economy*, trans. by Thomas Jefferson (Georgetown, 1817).

Wallace, Robert, *Characteristics of the Present Political State of Great Britain* (Dublin, 1758; French trans. Le Haye, 1763).

Webster, Aaron, *The Minor Encyclopedia or Cabinet of General Knowledge* (Boston, 1803).

Winthrop, F. W., Review of *Supplement to the Encyclopedia Britannica: Article, 'Beauty'* (Edinburgh, December 1816), *North American Review* (May 1818), pp. 1–25.

Witherspoon, John, *Essay on Money as a Medium of Commerce* (Philadelphia, 1786).

Manuscript and Manuscript Collections

Allston, Washington, Washington Allston volumes, Dana Family Papers, Massachusetts Historical Society.

Callender, Eunice, The Diary of Eunice Callender, May 1808–June 1809 (Boston, 1809), Eunice Callender Papers, Schlesinger Library, Radcliffe Institute, Harvard University.

Channing, William Ellery, William Ellery Channing Papers, Massachusetts Historical Society.

Cogdell, John S., Diary, Courtesy of the Winterthur Library, Joseph Downs Collection of Manuscripts and Printed Ephemera.

Dana Family Papers, Massachusetts Historical Society.

Dawes, M. M., The Diary of M. M. Dawes (Boston), May-Goddard Family Papers, Schlesinger Library, Radcliffe Institute, Harvard University.

Harrison Gray Otis Papers, Massachusetts Historical Society.

Public Records

An Act to Incorporate the President, Trustees and Associates of the Boston Exchange Office, or Association Fund (Boston, 1804).

Boston, Town of, Town of Boston Tax Valuation Books, 1784 to 1822, Rare Book and Manuscript Room, Boston Public Library, Boston, Massachusetts.

Boston Bank Papers, 1796–1826, Massachusetts Historical Society.

Boston Marine Insurance Company Records, 1797–1839, Box 1, Massachusetts Historical Society.

Massachusetts General Court, *The Committee Appointed on the Subject of the Banking System ... An Act Establishing a State Bank* (Boston, 14 January 1808).

—, *Report of the Committee Relative to Penobscot Bank* (Boston, 1811).

—, *Report of the Committee of Both Houses, Appointed to Examine into the doings of the State Bank* (Boston, 1814).

—, *Report of the Committee of Both Houses, on the Hallowell and Augusta Banks* (Boston, 1818).

—, *Acts and Laws of the Commonwealth of Massachusetts* (Boston, 1890).

Massachusetts Mutual Fire Insurance Co., Records of Insurance Companies and Agents, 1781–1909, Baker Library, Harvard University.

Massachusetts Secretary, *A Correct Abstract of All the Statements by the Incorporated Banks in this Commonwealth from 1803 to January 1807* (Boston, 1807).

Massachusetts Senate, *A True Abstract of the Statement of the Several Banks in the Commonwealth of Massachusetts. Rendered in January 1808* (Boston, 1808).

—, *An Act Establishing the State Bank* (Boston, 1810).

—, *A True Abstract of the Statement of the Several Banks in the Commonwealth of Massachusetts. Rendered in January 1811 [to 1819]* (Boston, 1811–19).

—, *Senate Document No. 38, Schedule Exhibiting the Condition of the Banks in Massachusetts for Every Year From 1803 to 1837, Inclusive* (Boston, 1837).

Records of Banks of New England and New York, Boston Bank Papers 1803–1813, Baker Library Collection, Harvard University.

Report of the Committee Appointed by the General Assembly of the State of Rhode Island and Providence Plantations at the February Session, A.D. 1809, to Inquire Into the Situation of the Farmers' Exchange Bank in Glocester (Providence, 1809).

Suffolk County Probate Court Record Books, 1790–1 and 1820–1, Boston Public Library.

Newspapers and Magazines

American Apollo (Boston).

American Monthly Review (New York).

American Museum (Philadelphia).

Athenaeum (Boston).

Boston Daily Advertiser (Boston).

Boston Directory (Boston).

Boston Gazette (Boston).

Boston Magazine (Boston).

Boston Weekly Magazine (Boston).

Boston Patriot (Boston).

Boston Spectator; devoted to Politicks and Belles-Lettres (Boston).

Boston Weekly Magazine (Boston).

Cabinet; a Repository of Polite Literature (Boston).

Christian Disciple and Theological Review (Boston).

Christian Observer (Boston).

Cohen's Lottery Gazette and Register (Baltimore).

Columbian Centinel (Boston).

Columbian Detector (Boston).

Essex Register (Essex).

Euterpiad, or Musical Intelligencer, and Ladies Gazette (Boston).

General Repository and Review (Cambridge, MA).

Gentleman and Lady's Town and Country Magazine (Boston; later *Gentlemen and Ladies'*).

Gospel Advocate (Boston).

Harvard Lyceum (Cambridge, MA).

Independent Chronicle (Boston).

Intellectual Regale, or Ladies' TEA Tray (Philadelphia).

Ladies Magazine (Boston).

Ladies Port Folio (Boston).

Lady's Monitor (New York).

Literary Magazine, and American Register (Philadelphia).

Massachusetts Baptist Missionary Magazine (Boston).

Massachusetts Magazine (Boston).

Monthly Anthology, and Boston Review (Boston).

Monthly Magazine, and American Review (New York).

New England Galaxy (Boston).

New-England Palladium (Boston).

Nightingale, or a Mélange of Literature (Boston).

Niles' Weekly Register (Boston).

Omnium Gatherum (Boston).

Panoplist (Boston).

Philanthropist (Mount Pleasant).

Polyanthos (Boston).

Something (Boston).

Spectator (London).

Universal Asylum and Columbian Magazine (Philadelphia).

United States Literary Gazette (Boston).

Weekly Monitor (Boston).

Library Catalogues

Apprentices' Library, *Catalogue of the Apprentices' Library in Boston: to be loaned gratis, under the superintendence of the Massachusetts Mechanic Association, to the mechanic, and all needy apprentices: with the names of the donors* (Boston, 1820).

Benjamin Guild's Circulating Library, *New Select Catalogue of Benjamin Guild's Circulating Library, containing principally novels, voyages, travels, poetry, periodical publications, and books of entertainment, at the Boston Book-Store, no. 59, Cornhill* (Boston, 1789).

Boston Book-Store, *A Catalogue of Books for Sale or Circulation, by William P. Blake, at the Boston Book-Store, no. 59, Cornhill. Consisting of the most approved authors, in history, voyages, travels, lives, memoirs, antiquities, philosophy, novels, divinity, law, physic, surgery, chemistry, geography, husbandry, navigation, arts, sciences, architecture, miscellanies, poetry, plays, &c&c&c.* (Boston, 1793, 1796, 1798, 1800).

Boston Library, *A Catalogue of Books in the Boston Library. March 1, 1800* (Boston, 1800).

Boston Union Circulating Library, *Catalogue of the Boston Union Circulating Library and Reading Room* (Boston, 1815).

Charlestown Circulating Library, *Catalogue of the Charlestown Circulating Library* (Charlestown 1815).

Mein's Circulating Library, *A Catalogue of Mein's Circulating Library; consisting of above twelve hundred volumes, in most branches of polite literature, arts and sciences* (Boston, 1765).

New Circulating Library, *A Catalogue of the New Circulating Library kept at no. 82, Newbury Street: to which is prefixed, the conditions of said library* (Boston, 1804).

Pelham's Circulating Library, *Catalogue of Pelham's Circulating Library, no 59, Cornhill: consisting of a chosen assortment of books in the various branches of literature* (Boston, 1801).

Suffolk Circulating Library, *Catalogue of the Suffolk Circulating Library, corner of Court and Brattle Streets, Boston: containing History – Biography – Voyages – Travels – Miscellanies – Magazine – Reviews – Novels – Tales – Romances and plays – alphabetically arranged* (Boston, 1822).

Union Circulating Library, *Catalogue of the Union Circulating Library, No. 3, School-Street* (Boston, 1806, 1810).

Secondary Sources

Abrams, M. H., *The Mirror and the Lamp: Romantic Theory and the Critical Tradition* (Oxford: Oxford University Press, 1953).

Appleby, Joyce Oldham, 'Locke, Liberalism and the Natural Law of Money', *Past and Present*, 71 (May 1976), pp. 43–69.

—, *Economic Thought and Ideology in Seventeenth-Century England* (Princeton: Princeton University Press, 1978).

—, *Capitalism and a New Social Order: The Republican Vision of the 1790s* (New York: New York University Press, 1984).

—, *Inheriting the Revolution: The First Generation of Americans* (Cambridge, MA: Harvard University Press, 2000).

—, 'The Vexed Story of Capitalism told by American Historians', *Journal of the Early Republic*, 21 (Spring 2001), pp. 1–18.

Appleton, Nathan, *Currency and Banking* (Boston, 1857, 1841).

Bailey, Dudley P., Jr, 'History of Massachusetts Savings Banks', *Banker's Magazine* (June 1876), pp. 963–74.

Barker-Benfield, G. J., *The Culture of Sensibility: Sex and Society in Eighteenth Century Britain* (Chicago: University of Chicago Press, 1992).

Bermingham, Ann, *Landscape and Ideology: The English Rustic Tradition, 1740–1860* (Berkeley: University of California Press, 1986).

Berthold, Dennis, 'Charles Brockden Brown, "Edgar Huntly", and the Origins of the American Picturesque', *William and Mary Quarterly*, 3rd series, 41:1 (January 1984), pp. 62–84.

Bjelajac, David, 'The Boston Elite's Resistance to Washington Allston's *Elijah in the Desert*', in David C. Miller (ed.), *American Iconology* (New Haven: Yale University Press, 1993), pp. 39–57.

Bodenhorn, Howard, *State Banking in Early America: A New Economic History* (New York: Oxford University Press, 2003).

Bolton, Charles K., 'Circulating Libraries in Boston, 1765–1865', *Proceedings of the Colonial Society of Massachusetts* (February 1907).

Bradford, George P., 'Philosophic Thought in Boston', in Justin Winsor (ed.), *The Memorial History of Boston*, 4 vols (Boston, 1881), vol. 4, pp. 295–330.

Braudel, Fernand, *Civilization and Capitalism, 15th–18th Century, Volume 1, The Structures of Everyday Life: The Limits of the Possible*, trans. Sian Reynolds (London: Harper & Row, 1981).

Bredvold, Louis I., *The Natural History of Sensibility* (Detroit: Wayne State University Press, 1962).

Breitenbach, William, 'The Consistent Calvinism of the New Divinity Movement', *William and Mary Quarterly*, 3rd series, 41:2 (April 1984), pp. 241–64.

Brewer, John, *Pleasures of the Imagination* (New York: Farrar Strauss Giroux, 1997).

Buckle, Stephen, *Natural Law and the Theory of Property: Grotius to Hume* (Oxford: Clarendon Press, 1991).

Buell, Lawrence J., 'Unitarian Aesthetics and Emerson's Poet-Priest', *American Quarterly*, 20:1 (Spring 1968), pp. 3–20.

—, *New England Literary Culture: From Revolution Through Renaissance* (New York: Cambridge University Press, 1986).

Burgess, Miranda Jane, 'The Work of Romance: The British Novel and Political Discourse' (PhD Dissertation, Boston University, 1995).

Caffentzis, Constantine George, *Clipped Coins, Abused Words and Civil Government: John Locke's Philosophy of Money* (New York: Autonomedia, 1989).

Camfield, Gregg, 'The Moral Aesthetics of Sensibility: A Missing Key to Uncle Tom's Cabin', *Nineteenth-Century Literature*, 43:3 (December 1988), pp. 319–45.

Campbell, Colin, *The Romantic Ethic and the Spirit of Modern Consumerism* (Oxford: Basil Blackwell, 1987).

Carafiol, Peter, *Transcendent Reason: James Marsh and the Forms of Romantic Thought* (Tallahassee: University Presses of Florida, 1982).

Carey, Daniel, 'Hutcheson's Moral Sense and the Problems of Innateness', *Journal of the History of Philosophy* (January 2000), pp. 103–10.

Channing, William E., *Unitarian Christianity and Other Essays*, ed. Irving H. Bartlett (New York: Liberal Arts Press, 1957).

Channing, William Henry, *The Life of William Ellery Channing* (Boston, 1880).

Charvat, William, *The Origins of American Critical Thought, 1810–1835* (Philadelphia: University of Pennsylvania Press, 1936; New York, A. S. Barnes, 1961).

Checkland, S. G., *Scottish Banking: A History, 1695–1973* (Glasgow and London: Collins, 1975).

Cohen, Ralph (ed.), *Studies in Eighteenth-Century British Art and Aesthetics* (Berkeley: University of California Press, 1985).

Colley, Linda, 'The Sea Around Us', *New York Review of Books*, 22 June 2006, pp. 43–5.

Conforti, Joseph A., 'Samuel Hopkins and the New Divinity: Theology, Ethics, and Social Reform in Eighteenth-Century New England', *William and Mary Quarterly*, 3rd series, 34:4 (October 1977), pp. 572–89.

Crane, R. S., 'Suggestions Toward a Genealogy of the "Man of Feeling"', *ELH*, 1:3 (December 1934), pp. 205–30.

Crocker, Matthew, *The Magic of the Many: Josiah Quincy and the Rise of Mass Politics in Boston, 1800–1830* (Amherst: University of Massachusetts Press, 1999).

Crowley, John E., *The Privileges of Independence: Neomercantilism and the American Revolution* (Baltimore: Johns Hopkins University Press, 1993).

—, *The Invention of Comfort: Sensibilities and Design in Early Modern Britain and America* (Baltimore: Johns Hopkins University Press, 2001).

Dall, Caroline, *The Romance of the Association; or, One Last Glimpse of Charlotte Temple and Eliza Wharton* (Cambridge, MA, 1875).

Davidson, Cathy N., Revolution and the Word: The Rise of the Novel in America (Oxford: Oxford University Press, 1986).

—, 'Introduction', in Hannah W. Foster, *The Coquette* (New York: Oxford University Press, 1986), pp. vii–xx.

—, 'The Life and Times of Charlotte Temple', in Cathy N. Davidson (ed.), *Reading in America* (Baltimore: Johns Hopkins University Press, 1989), pp. 157–79.

Davis, Edward B., 'Christianity and Early Modern Science: The Foster Thesis Revisited', in David G. Livingstone, D. G. Hart and Mark A. Noll (eds), *Evangelicals and Science in Historical Perspective* (Oxford: Oxford University Press, 1999), pp. 75–99.

Davis, Joseph Stancliffe, *Essays in the Earlier History of American Corporations* (Cambridge, MA: Harvard University Press, 1917).

De Roover, Raymond, 'Scholastic Economics: Survival and Lasting Influence from the Sixteenth Century to Adam Smith', Quarterly Journal of Economics, 69:2 (May 1955), pp. 161–90.

De Vries, Jan, *The Economy of Europe in an Age of Crisis, 1600–1750* (Cambridge: Cambridge University Press, 1976).

Diamond, Peter J., 'Witherspoon, William Smith and the Scottish Philosophy in Revolutionary America', in Richard B. Sher and Jeffrey R. Smitten (eds), *Scotland and America in the Age of Enlightenment* (Princeton: Princeton University Press, 1990), pp. 1–32.

Dinkin, Robert J., 'Seating the Meeting House in Early Massachusetts', *New England Quarterly*, 43:3 (1970), pp. 450–64.

Dorfman, Joseph, 'Introduction', in Thomas Cooper, *Lectures on the Elements of Political Economy* (1826; New York: Augustus M. Kelley, 1971).

—, *The Economic Mind in American Civilization* (New York: Viking Press, 1946–59).

Douglas, Ann, *The Feminization of American Culture* (New York: Knopf, 1977).

Dowling, John, 'Capricho as Style in Life, Literature, and Art From Zamora to Goya', *Eighteenth-Century Studies*, 10:4 (Summer 1977), pp. 413–33.

—, 'The Crisis of the Spanish Enlightenment: Capricho 43 and Goya's Second Portrait of Jovellanos', *Eighteenth-Century Studies*, 18:3 (Spring 1985), pp. 331–59.

Dunn, John, 'From Applied Theology to Social Analysis: The Break Between John Locke and the Scottish Enlightenment', in Istvan Hont and Michael Ignatieff (eds), *Wealth and Virtue: The Shaping of Political Economy in the Scottish Enlightenment* (Cambridge: Cambridge University Press, 1983), pp. 119–36.

—, *Locke* (New York: Oxford University Press, 1984).

—, "'Bright Enough for All Our Purposes', John Locke's Conception of a Civilized Society', *Notes and Records of the Royal Society of London*, 43:2, Science and Civilization Under William and Mary (July 1989), pp. 133–53.

Eagleton, Terry, *The Ideology of the Aesthetic* (London: Basil Blackwell, 1990).

Elliott, J. H., 'Atlantic History: A Circumnavigation', in David Armitage and Michael J. Braddick (eds), *The British Atlantic World, 1500–1800* (New York: Palgrave Macmillan, 2002), pp. 233–4.

Ellis, Markman, *The Politics of Sensibility* (Cambridge: Cambridge University Press, 1996).

Ellison, Julie, 'Cato's Tears', *ELH*, 63:3 (Fall 1996), pp. 571–601.

Engell, James, *The Creative Imagination: Enlightenment to Romanticism* (Cambridge, MA: Harvard University Press, 1981).

Everett, Alexander H., 'History of Intellectual Philosophy', in Perry Miller (ed.), *The Transcendentalists* (Cambridge, MA: Harvard University Press, 1950), pp. 26–33.

Fales, Dean, *American Painted Furniture 1660–1880* (New York: Dutton, 1972).

Field, Peter S., *The Crisis of the Standing Order: Clerical Intellectuals and Cultural Authority in Massachusetts, 1780–1833* (Amherst: University of Massachusetts Press, 1998).

Fiering, Norman S., 'Irresistible Compassion: An Aspect of Eighteenth-Century Sympathy and Humanitarianism', *Journal of the History of Ideas*, 37:2 (April–June 1976), pp. 195–218.

—, 'The Transatlantic Republic of Letters: A Note on the Circulation of Learned Periodicals to Early Eighteenth-Century America', *William and Mary Quarterly*, 3rd series, 33:4 (October 1976), pp. 642–60.

Finkelstein, Andrea, *Harmony and the Balance: An Intellectual History of Seventeenth-Century English Economic Thought* (Ann Arbor: University of Michigan Press, 2000).

—, 'Nicholas Barbon and the Quality of Infinity', *History of Political Economy*, 32:1 (Spring 2000), pp. 83–102.

Foster, M. B., 'The Christian Doctrine of Creation and the Rise of Modern Natural Science', *Mind*, 43 (1934), pp. 446–68.

—, 'Christian Theology and Modern Science of Nature', *Mind*, 44 (1935), pp. 439–66; and 45 (1936), pp. 1–27.

Gaustad, Edwin S., 'The Theological Effects of the Great Awakening in New England', *Mississippi Valley Historical Review*, 40:4 (March 1954), pp. 681–706.

German, James D., 'The Social Utility of Wicked Self-Love: Calvinism, Capitalism, and Public Policy in Revolutionary New England', *Journal of American History*, 82:3 (December 1995), pp. 965–98.

Goldie, Mark, 'Review of *Locke's Education for Liberty*', *Journal of Modern History*, 58:1 (March 1986), pp. 300–1.

Goodman, Paul, *The Democratic-Republicans of Massachusetts: Politics in a Young Republic* (Cambridge, MA: Harvard University Press, 1964).

—, 'Ethics and Enterprise: The Values of a Boston Elite, 1800–1860', *American Quarterly*, 18:3 (Autumn 1966), pp. 437–51.

Graebner, Norman A., 'New England and the World, 1783–1791', in Conrad Edick Wright, *Massachusetts and the New Nation* (Boston: Massachusetts Historical Society, 1992), pp. 1–35.

Gras, N. S. B., *The Massachusetts First National Bank of Boston, 1784–1934* (Cambridge, MA: Harvard University Press, 1934).

Griswold, Charles L., Jr, *Adam Smith and the Virtues of the Enlightenment* (Cambridge: Cambridge University Press, 1999).

Guggenheim, Thomas, *Preclassical Monetary Theories* (New York: Pinter, 1989).

Haakonssen, Knud, *The Science of a Legislator: The Natural Jurisprudence of David Hume and Adam Smith* (New York: Cambridge University Press, 1981).

—, *Natural Law and Moral Philosophy: From Grotius to the Scottish Enlightenment* (Cambridge: Cambridge University Press, 1996).

Hafertepe, Kenneth Charles, 'The Enlightened Sensibility: Scottish Philosophy in American Art and Architecture' (PhD Dissertation, University of Texas at Austin, 1986).

Haltunnen, Karen, 'Humanitarianism and the Pornography of Pain in Anglo-American Culture', *American Historical Review*, 100:2 (April 1995), pp. 303–34.

Hammond, Bray, *Banks and Politics in America: From the Revolution to the Civil War* (Princeton: Princeton University Press, 1957, 1985).

Hamowy, Ronald, *The Scottish Enlightenment and the Theory of Spontaneous Order* (Carbondale: Southern Illinois University Press, 1987).

Hancey, James O., 'John Locke and the Law of Nature', *Political Theory*, 4:4 (November 1976), pp. 439–54.

Harkin, Maureen, 'Mackenzie's Man of Feeling: Embalming Sensibility', *ELH*, 61:2 (Summer 1994).

Haskell, Thomas L., 'Capitalism and the Origins of the Humanitarian Sensibility, Part 1', *American Historical Review*, 90:2 (April 1985), pp. 339–61.

Heinzelman, Kurt, *The Economics of the Imagination* (Amherst: University of Massachusetts, 1980).

Hipple, Walter John, Jr, *The Beautiful, the Sublime, and the Picturesque in Eighteenth-Century British Aesthetic Theory* (Carbondale: Southern Illinois University Press, 1957).

Hirschman, Albert O., *The Passions and the Interests: Political Arguments for Capitalism Before its Triumph* (Princeton: Princeton University Press, 1977).

Hochstrasser, T. J., 'Early Modern Natural Law Theories and Their Contexts', *Historical Journal*, 38:2 (June 1995), pp. 487–90.

—, *Natural Law Theories in the Early Enlightenment* (Cambridge: Cambridge University Press, 2000).

Holbo, Christine, 'Imagination, Commerce, and the Politics of Associationism in Crevecoeur's *Letters from an American Farmer*', *Early American Literature*, 32:1 (1997), pp. 20–65.

Horsefield, J. Keith, *British Monetary Experiments, 1650–1710* (Cambridge, MA: Harvard University Press, 1960).

Howe, Daniel Walker, *The Unitarian Conscience* (Cambridge, MA: Harvard University Press, 1970).

—, 'European Sources of Political Ideas in Jeffersonian America', *Reviews in American History*, 10:4, The Promise of American History: Progress and Prospects (December 1982), pp. 28–44.

—, 'The Cambridge Platonists of Old England and the Cambridge Platonists of New England', in Conrad Edick Wright (ed.), *American Unitarianism, 1805–1865* (Boston: Northeastern University Press 1989), pp. 87–120.

—, *Making the American Self* (Cambridge, MA: Harvard University Press, 1997).

Hunter, Doreen, 'America's First Romantics: Richard Henry Dana, Sr. and Washington Allston', *New England Quarterly*, 45:1 (March 1972), pp. 3–30.

Hunter, Phyllis Whitman, 'Ship of Wealth: Massachusetts Merchants, Foreign Goods, and the Transformation of Anglo-America, 1670–1760' (PhD Dissertation, William and Mary College, VA, 1996).

Hutchison, Terence, *Before Adam Smith: The Emergence of Political Economy, 1662–1776* (London: Basil Blackwell, 1988).

Jackson, J. B., *The Necessity for Ruins* (Amherst: University of Massachusetts, 1980).

Jenks, William L., 'The First Bank in Michigan', *Michigan Historical Magazine*, 1 (July 1917), pp. 41–62.

Jennings, Robert M., Donald F. Swanson and Andrew P. Trout, 'Alexander Hamilton's Tontine Proposal', *William and Mary Quarterly*, 3rd series, 45:1 (January 1988), pp. 107–15.

Johnson, Kathleen Eagan, 'Painted Furniture in Female Academies', Winterthur Museum (Term Paper, Artifacts in American History, Winterthur Program in Early American Culture, n.d.).

Jones, Chris, *Radical Sensibility: Literature and Ideas in the 1790s* (London: Routledge, 1993).

Kamensky, Jane, *The Exchange Artist: A Story of Paper, Bricks, and Ash in Early National America* (New York: Viking/ Penguin, in press).

Kaufmann, David, *The Business of Common Life: Novels and Classical Economics between Revolution and Reform* (Baltimore: Johns Hopkins University Press, 1995).

Kelly, Patrick Hyde, 'Introduction', in *John Locke on Money*, ed. Patrick Hyde Kelly, 2 vols (Oxford: Oxford University Press, 1991), vol. 1, pp. 1–121.

Kidder, Henry P., and Francis H. Peabody, 'Finance in Boston', in Justin Winsor (ed.), *The Memorial History of Boston*, 4 vols (Boston, 1881), vol. 4, pp. 151–78.

Kivy, Peter, 'The "Sense" of Beauty and the Sense of "Art": Hutcheson's Place in the History and Practice of Aesthetics', *Journal of Aesthetics and Art Criticism*, 53:4 (Fall 1995), pp. 349–57.

Kramnick, Isaac, 'Republican Revisionism Revisited', *American Historical Review*, 87:3 (June 1982), pp. 629–64.

Lamoreaux, Naomi, *Insider Lending: Banks, Personal Connections and Economic Development in Industrial New England* (New York: Cambridge University Press, 1994).

Laslett, Peter, 'John Locke, the Great Recoinage, and the Origins of the Board of Trade: 1695–1698', *William and Mary Quarterly*, 3rd series, 14:3 (July 1957), pp. 370–402.

Lerner, Ralph, 'Commerce and Character: The Anglo-American as a New-Model Man', *William and Mary Quarterly*, 3rd series, 36:1 (January 1979), pp. 3–26.

Letwin, William, *The Origins of Scientific Economics* (London: Methuen, 1963).

Levy, David, 'Adam Smith's "Natural Law" and Contractual Society', *Journal of the History of Ideas*, 39:4 (October–December 1978), pp. 665–74.

Li, Ming-Hsun, *The Great Recoinage of 1696–1699* (London: Weidenfeld & Nicholson, 1963).

Livingstone, David N., D. G. Hart and Mark A. Noll (eds), *Evangelicals and Science in Historical Perspective* (New York: Oxford University Press, 1999).

Loshe, Lillie Deming, *The Early American Novel* (New York: Ungar, 1907).

Lundbery, Kenneth V., 'Daniel Raymond: A Note', in Daniel Raymond, *The Elements of Political Economy* (1823; New York: Augustus M. Kelley, 1964).

Maier, Pauline, 'The Revolutionary Origins of the American Corporation', *William and Mary Quarterly*, 3rd series, 50:1, Law and Society in Early America (June 1993), pp. 51–84.

Marshall, David, *The Figure of Theatre: Shaftesbury, Defoe, Adam Smith, and George Eliot* (New York: Columbia University Press, 1986).

Martin, Joseph G., *A Century of Finance: Martin's History of the Boston Stock and Money Markets, One Hundred Years, From January 1798 to 1898* (Boston, 1898).

Martin, Terence, *The Instructed Vision: Scottish Common Sense Philosophy and the Origins of American Fiction* (Indiana: Indiana University Press, 1961).

Matson, Cathy, 'American Political Economy in the Constitutional Decade', in *The United States Constitution: The First Two Hundred Years* (New York: Manchester University Press, 1989), pp. 16–35.

Mattick, Paul, Jr (ed.), *Eighteenth-Century Aesthetics and the Reconstruction of Art* (Cambridge: Cambridge University Press, 1993).

McCloskey, Deirdre N., '*Bourgeois Virtue* and the History of P and S', *Journal of Economic History*, 58:2 (June 1998), pp. 297–317.

McKeon, Michael, *The Origins of the English Novel, 1660–1740* (Baltimore: Johns Hopkins University Press, 1987).

McMahon, A. Philip, *Preface to an American Philosophy of Art* (Chicago: University of Chicago Press, 1945).

Meek, Ronald L., 'The Scottish Contribution to Marxist Sociology', *Economics and Ideology and Other Essays* (London: Chapman & Hall, 1967), pp. 34–50.

Miller, David (ed.), *American Iconology: New Approaches to Nineteenth Century Art and Literature* (New Haven: Yale University Press, 1993).

Morgan, John, 'The Puritan Thesis Revisited', in David G. Livingstone, D. G. Hart and Mark A. Noll (eds), *Evangelicals and Science in Historical Perspective* (Oxford: Oxford University Press, 1999), pp. 43–74.

Morison, Samuel Eliot, *The Maritime History of Massachusetts* (Boston and New York: Houghton Mifflin Company, 1921).

Mortensen, Preben, 'Francis Hutcheson and the Problem of Conspicuous Consumption', *Journal of Aesthetic and Art Criticism*, 53:2 (Spring 1995), pp. 155–65.

Mott, Frank Luther, *A History of American Magazines* (Cambridge, MA: Harvard University Press, 1939).

Mulcaire, Terry, 'Public Credit; or, the Feminization of Virtue in the Marketplace', *PMLA*, 114:5 (October 1999), pp. 1029–42.

Mulford, Carla (ed.), *The Power of Sympathy and the Coquette* (New York: Penguin, 1996).

Mullan, John, *Sentiment and Sociability* (Oxford: Oxford University Press, 1988).

Munn, Charles W., *The Scottish Provincial Banking Companies, 1747–1864* (Edinburgh: Donald, 1981).

Myers, Kenneth John, 'On the Cultural Construction of Landscape Experience: Contact to 1830', in David Miller (ed.), *American Iconology: New Approaches to Nineteenth Century Art and Literature* (New Haven: Yale University Press, 1993), pp. 58–80.

Newell, Margaret Ellen, *From Dependency to Independence: Economic Revolution in Colonial New England* (Ithaca: Cornell University Press, 1998).

Novak, Barbara, *American Painting of the Nineteenth Century* (New York: Vendome, 1969).

Nygreen, Edward J., *Views and Visions: American Landscapes Before 1830* (Washington: Corcoran Gallery, 1986).

Paracelsus, *Paracelsus: Selected Writings*, ed. Jolande Jacobi (London: Routledge & Kegan Paul, 1951).

Paulson, Ronald, *Breaking and Remaking: Aesthetic Practice in England, 1700–1820* (Brunswick: Rutgers University Press, 1989).

Perkins, Edwin J., *American Public Finance and Financial Services, 1700–1815* (Columbus: Ohio State University Press, 1994).

Pierce, Richard D. (ed.), *The Records of the First Church in Boston* (Boston: Publications of the Colonial Society of Massachusetts, 1961).

Pitcher, E. W., 'Fiction in the *Boston Magazine* (1783–1786): A Checklist with Notes and Sources', *William and Mary Quarterly*, 3rd series, 37:3 (July 1980), pp. 473–83.

Pocock, J. G. A., *The Machiavellian Moment: Florentine Political Thought in the Atlantic Republic Tradition* (Princeton: Princeton University Press, 1975).

—, 'Cambridge Paradigms and Scotch Philosophers: A Study of the Relations between the Civic Humanist and Civil Jurisprudential Interpretation of Eighteenth Century Thought', in Istvan Hont and Michael Ignatieff (eds), *Wealth and Virtue: The Shaping of Political Economy in the Scottish Enlightenment* (Cambridge: Cambridge University Press, 1983), pp. 235–53.

—, 'Virtues, Rights and Manners: A Model for Historians of Political Thought', in *Virtue, Commerce and History* (Cambridge: Cambridge University Press, 1985), pp. 37–50.

—, 'The Mobility of Property and the Rise of Eighteenth Century Sociology', in *Virtue, Commerce and History* (Cambridge: Cambridge University Press, 1985), pp. 103–25.

Quimby, Lee, 'Thomas Jefferson, the Virtue of Aesthetics and the Aesthetics of Virtue', *American Historical Review*, 87:2 (April 1982), pp. 337–57.

Rather, Susan, 'Stuart and Reynolds: A Portrait of Change', *Eighteenth-Century Studies*, 27:1 (Autumn 1993), pp. 61–84.

Redlich, Fritz, *The Molding of American Banking: Men and Ideas* (New York: Johnson Reprint Corporation, 1968).

Reiss, Timothy J., and Roger H. Hinderliter, 'Money and Value in the Sixteenth Century: The Monete Cudende Ratio of Nicholas Copernicus', *Journal of the History of Ideas*, 40:2 (April–June 1979), pp. 293–313.

Rendall, Jane, *The Origins of the Scottish Enlightenment* (London: Macmillan, 1978).

Riesman, Janet, 'The Origins of American Political Economy, 1690–1781' (PhD Dissertation, Brown University, 1983).

—, 'Money, Credit and the Federalist Political Economy', in Richard Beeman and Edward Carter II (eds), *Beyond Confederation: Origins of the Constitution and the American National Identity* (Chapel Hill: University of North Carolina Press, 1987), pp. 128–61.

Rose, Ann C., 'Social Sources of Denominationalism Reconsidered: Post-Revolutionary Boston as a Case Study', *American Quarterly*, 38:2 (Summer 1986), pp. 243–64.

Rothenberg, Winnifred, *From Market-Places to a Market Economy: The Transformation of Rural Massachusetts, 1750–1850* (Chicago: Chicago University Press, 1992).

Rothschild, Emma, *Economic Sentiments: Adam Smith, Condorcet and the Enlightenment* (Cambridge, MA: Harvard University Press, 2001).

Sakamoto, Tatsuya, 'Hume's Political Economy as a System of Manners', in Tatsuya Sakamoto and Hideo Tanaka (eds), *The Rise of Political Economy in the Scottish Enlightenment* (London and New York: Routledge, 2003), pp. 86–102.

Schabas, Margaret, 'David Hume on Experimental Natural Philosophy, Money and Fluids', *History of Political Economy*, 33:3 (2001), pp. 411–35.

Schouls, Peter A., *Reasoned Freedom: John Locke and the Enlightenment* (Ithaca: Cornell University Press, 1992).

Schumpeter, Joseph A., *History of Economic Analysis* (New York: Oxford University Press, 1954).

Shackle, G. L. S., *Epistemics and Economics* (Cambridge: Cambridge University Press, 1972).

Shell, Marc, *Money, Language and Thought: Literary and Philosophical Economies from the Medieval to the Modern Era* (Berkeley: University of California Press, 1982).

Shields, David, *Civil Tongues and Polite Letters in British America* (Chapel Hill: University of North Carolina Press, 1997).

Skinner, Gillian, *Sensibility and Economics in the Novel, 1740–1800: The Price of a Tear* (New York: St Martin's Press, 1999).

Sohn-Rethel, Alfred, *Intellectual and Manual Labour: A Critique of Epistemology* (New York: Macmillan, 1978).

Stark, W., *The Ideal Foundations of Economic Thought* (London: Routledge & Kegan Paul Limited, 1943, 1948).

Stern, Julia A., *The Plight of Feeling: Sympathy and Dissent in the Early American Novel* (Chicago: University of Chicago Press, 1997).

Stolnitz, Jerome, 'Beauty: Some Stages in the History of an Idea', *Journal of the History of Ideas*, 22:2 (April–June 1961), pp. 185–204.

Swanson, Donald F., and Andrew P. Trout, 'Alexander Hamilton, "the Celebrated Mr. Neckar", and Public Credit', *William and Mary Quarterly*, 3rd series, 47:3 (July 1990), pp. 422–30.

Tarcov, Nathan, *Locke's Education for Liberty* (Chicago: University of Chicago Press, 1984).

Taylor, Charles, *Sources of the Self: The Making of the Modern Identity* (Cambridge, MA: Harvard University Press, 1989).

Teichgraeber, Richard F., III, *Free Trade and Moral Philosophy: Rethinking the Sources of Adam Smith's Wealth of Nations* (Durham, NC: Duke University Press, 1986).

Thompson, James, *Models of Value: Eighteenth-Century Political Economy and the Novel* (Durham, NC: Duke University Press, 1996).

Toman, Rolf (ed.), *Neoclassicism and Romanticism: Architecture, Sculpture, Painting, Drawing, 1750–1848* (London: Konemann, 2002).

Tompkins, Jane, *Sensational Designs: The Cultural Work of American Fiction, 1790–1860* (Oxford: Oxford University Press, 1985).

Townsend, Dabney, 'From Shaftesbury to Kant: The Development of the Concept of Aesthetic Experience', *Journal of the History of Ideas*, 48:2 (April–June 1987), pp. 287–305.

Tully, James, *A Discourse on Property: John Locke and his Adversaries* (Cambridge: Cambridge University Press, 1980).

Van Fenstermaker, J., *The Development of American Commercial Banking: 1782–1837* (Kent: Kent State Bureau of Economic and Business Research, 1965).

—, 'The Statistics of American Commercial Banking, 1782–1818', *Journal of Economic History*, 25:3 (September 1965), pp. 400–13.

Van Fenstermaker, J., John E. Filer and Robert Stanley Herren, 'Money Statistics of New England, 1785–1837', *Journal of Economic History*, 44:2, The Tasks of Economic History (June 1984), pp. 441–53.

Vickers, Douglas, *Studies in the Theory of Money, 1690–1776* (Philadelphia: Chilton, 1959).

Wallach, Alan, 'Making a Picture of the View from Mount Holyoke', in David Miller (ed.), *American Iconology: New Approaches to Nineteenth Century Art and Literature* (New Haven: Yale University Press, 1993), pp. 81–92.

Walsh, Evelyn Marie, 'Effects of the Revolution upon the Town of Boston: Social, Economic, and Cultural' (PhD Dissertation, Brown University, 1964).

Ware, William, *Lectures on the Works and Genius of Washington Allston* (Boston, 1852).

Warner, Michael, *The Letters of the Republic* (Cambridge, MA: Harvard University Press, 1990).

Watt, Ian, *The Rise of the Novel: Studies in Defoe, Richardson and Fielding* (Berkeley: University of California Press, 1962).

Weir, David R., 'Tontines, Public Finance, and Revolution in France and England, 1688–1789', *Journal of Economic History*, 49:1 (March 1989), pp. 95–124.

Wennerlind, Carl, 'The Link Between David Hume's *Treatise of Human Nature* and his Fiduciary Theory of Money', *History of Political Economy*, 33:1 (2001), pp. 139–60.

White, Alan R., *The Language of Imagination* (London: Basil Blackwell, 1990).

White, Lawrence, *Free Banking in Britain* (Cambridge: Cambridge University Press, 1984).

Wilson, Robert J. III, *The Benevolent Deity: Ebenezer Gay and the Rise of Rational Religion in New England, 1696–1787* (Philadelphia: University of Pennsylvania Press, 1984).

Wolf, Bryan Jay, *Romantic Re-Vision: Culture & Consciousness in Nineteenth Century American Painting and Literature* (Chicago: University of Chicago Press, 1982).

Wood, Gordon S., 'The American Love Boat', Review of Andrew Burstein's *Sentimental Democracy: The Evolution of America's Romantic Self-Image* (New York: Hill and Wang, 1999), *New York Review of Books* (7 October 1999), p. 41.

Wright, Richard, *The Wealth of Nations Rediscovered* (Cambridge: Cambridge University Press, 2002).

Wright, Robert E., 'Banking and Politics in New York' (PhD Dissertation, SUNY Buffalo, 1996).

Appendix: Tables for Charts 1–9

Table 1: Select Boston Banks' Liabilities and
Specie Totals and Ratio, 1803–19.*

	Mass Liabilities	Mass Specie	Union Liabilities	Union Specie	Boston Liabilities	Boston Specie
June 1803	673200	253400	1190656	308269		
Jan. 1804	422900	229400	1231148	160127	532006	181226
June 1804	291800	126300	607430	135509	454906	141021
Jan. 1805	186000	90500	402679	105700	353538	153299
June 1805	212100	95500	364449	60870	363364	170056
Jan. 1806	282028	109005	567009	88307	696645	150367
June 1806	362964	83746	786195	176624	741926	131308
Jan. 1807	242157	59229	613315	67841	691421	98620
Jan. 1811	621077	173803	725496	148549	867639	156977
June 1812	2101826	1189901	1119813	473083	1143369	621640
Feb. 1813	2387579	1852057	1253961	642490	1318866	1005655
Jan. 1814	3086956	2114165	1172375	657796	1356947	1182572
June 1814	2625160	1959406	1056669	636789	1293620	1270731
Jan. 1815	972346	763682	537862	202786	778307	691729
Jan. 1817	806336	279158	513121	123485	834248	291639
June 1817	833659	263120	499659	147283	841932	165581
Jan. 1819	549331	117021	420130	81329	395799	61611

	Mass Liab/Specie Ratio	Union Liab/ Specie Ratio	Boston Liab/ Specie Ratio
June 1803	2.66	3.86	
Jan. 1804	1.84	7.68	2.94
June 1804	2.30	4.48	3.22
Jan. 1805	2.05	3.80	2.30
June 1805	2.22	5.98	2.13

* Massachusetts Secretary, *A Correct Abstract of all the Statements ... 1803 to January 1807*; Massachusetts Senate, *A True Abstract ... January 1808*; Massachusetts Senate, *A True Abstract ... January 1811 [to 1819]*.

	Mass Liab/Specie Ratio	Union Liab/ Specie Ratio	Boston Liab/ Specie Ratio
Jan. 1806	2.59	6.42	4.63
June 1806	4.33	4.45	5.65
Jan. 1807	4.08	9.04	7.00
Jan. 1811	3.57	4.88	5.52
June 1812	1.76	2.37	1.84
Feb. 1813	1.29	1.95	1.31
Jan. 1814	1.46	1.78	1.14
June 1814	1.34	1.66	1.01
Jan. 1815	1.27	2.65	1.13
Jan. 1817	2.89	4.16	2.86
June 1817	3.17	3.39	5.08
Jan. 1819	4.69	5.16	6.42

Table 2: Debts Due to Town and Country Banks, 1803–22.*

Date	Region					
	Boston (town)			Country		
	debts due banks	on interest	not on interest	debts due banks	on interest	not on interest
June 1803	2600763			1256728		
June 1804	3620587			2466987		
June 1805	3264258			3033923		
June 1806	3951690			3106476		
June 1807	3757848			3132280		
June 1808	4600125	3104382	1495743	2832575	1956451	876124
June 1809	4922483	3434462	1488021	2875041	1698394	1176647
June 1810	8689237	2355653	6333584	2990101	1941257	1048844
June 1811	7033655	5155186	1878469	3068619	2015873	1052746
June 1812	7499068	2446562	5052506	2759576	1829025	930551
June 1813	5355776	3852935	1502841	1868634	1248175	620459
June 1814	10922197	9281236	1640958	2532096	1538785	993311
June 1815	10857900			2877202		
June 1816	10612021			3094781		
June 1817	9388952			3258137		
June 1818	8844874			3738785		
June 1819	8821254			4110589		
June 1820	9312055			4217605		
June 1821	8893228			4126891		
June 1822	9695184			4875837		

* Massachusetts Secretary, *A Correct Abstract of all the Statements ... 1803 to January 1807*; Massachusetts Senate, *A True Abstract ... January 1808*; Massachusetts Senate, *A True Abstract ... January 1811 [to 1819]*.

Table 3: Select Boston Bank Stock Prices,
Percentage Increase, Par=$100, 1799–1822.*

Boston Banks 1799–1822	Boston	Massachusetts	Union	United States	M and M	New England	State	Suffolk
1799-H			125	125				
1799-L			118	116				
1800-H			128	137				
1800-L			119	121				
1801-H			136	144				
1801-L			130	130				
1802-H			152	154				
1802-L			135	140				
1803-H	119	150	150	150				
1803-L	110	132	120	144				
1804-H	115	135	132	146				
1804-L	109	130	126	141				
1805-H	112	130	129	143				
1805-L	102	122	118	125				
1806-H	116	124	118	137				
1806-L	104	120	112	128				
1807-H	114	124	116	137				
1807-L	109	113	109	115				
1808-H	115	125	115	128				
1808-L	110	115	110	118				
1809-H	119	128	118	130				
1809-L	116	122	114	127				
1810-H	120	128	119	130				
1810-L	117	125	116	113				
1811-H	120	130	120	114				
1811-L	97	117	100	88				
1812-H	115	118	112	99			107	
1812-L	97	108	97	93			100	
1813-H	116	118	114			107	110	
1813-L	108	111	108			100	107	
1814-H	109	111	108		108	111	110	
1814-L	89	98	91		97	99	65	
1815-H	100	106	100		104	112	100	
1815-L	93	100	85		90	105	84	
1816-H	96	101	90		99	110	92	
1816-L	90	94	83		88	99	80	
1817-H	112	106	106	135	104	115	114	

* Martin, *A Century of Finance*, p. 94. Chart 3 and Table 3 are based on Martin's price data.

Boston Banks 1799–1822	Boston	Massachusetts	Union	United States	M and M	New England	State	Suffolk
1817-L	99	96	90	133	92	103	93	
1818-H	113	107	107	152	105	115		106
1818-L	101	101	103	110	100	106		100
1819-H	107	103	105	108	105	113		107
1819-L	100	100	102	91	100	106		103
1820-H	112	107	107	105	109	113		111
1820-L	105	101	103	93	102	108		105
1821-H	112	115	110	119	115	117		115
1821-L	109	102	105	102	109	110		109
1822-H	110	115	110	115	115	118		114
1822-L	104	100	100	102	100	110		104

Table 4: Town and Country Data, 1803–22.*

Date	Town of Boston				
	Capital stock paid in	Deposits	Bills in circulation	Liabilities	Specie
June 1803	1600000	1179116	714840	1893956	561669
June 1804	3400000	835841	518295	1354136	402830
June 1805	3400000	669519	250394	919913	326426
June 1806	3400000	1586569	304516	1891085	391678
June 1807	3400000	1303375	243518	1546893	225690
June 1808	3800000	2022031	259878	2281909	632137
June 1809	3800000	1549753	646221	2195974	399184
June 1810	4600000	1707713	906578	2614291	700606
June 1811	4600000	1847747	1059313	2907060	830829
June 1812	5800000	4146031	1079748	5225779	2882116
June 1813	7000000	5472348	1375380	6847728	4569575
June 1814	8725000	7363867	1745752	9109619	5466659
June 1815	9100000	3090770	1548193	4638963	2232353
June 1816	9100000	1674115	1142307	2816422	816027
June 1817	6800000	2989812	1220251	4210063	1304374
June 1818	7049425	2311005	1142116	3453121	597088
June 1819	7350000	2058287	1067682	3125969	740216
June 1820	7350000	2599025	1272226	3871251	790068
June 1821	6550000	4661901	1329411	5991312	2277909
June 1822	7421125	2611572	1191971	3803543	432615

Date	Country				
	Capital stock paid in	Deposits	Bills in circulation	Liabilities	Specie
June 1803	625262	343155	850349	1193504	518259
June 1804	1612887	286278	1177006	1752078	575072
June 1805	2060000	351710	1303430	1655140	521572
June 1806	2085000	449921	1309168	1759089	567716
June 1807	2160000	410593	1238259	1648852	489093
June 1808	2160000	526686	778164	1304850	383707
June 1809	2160000	765034	688727	1453761	422758
June 1810	2085000	754164	1191913	1946077	647116
June 1811	2085000	537974	1296258	1834232	682171
June 1812	2160000	588294	1082610	1670904	799579
June 1813	1895000	1434246	811457	2245703	1211223
June 1814	2325000	1837852	1176859	3014711	1479883
June 1815	2362000	966624	1192318	2245703	1231888
June 1816	2375000	459163	992383	1451546	444182

* Massachusetts Senate, *Senate Document No. 38*; Van Fenstermaker et al., 'Money Statistics of New England'; Van Fenstermaker, 'The Statistics of American Commercial Banking'.

Date	Capital stock paid in	Deposits	Country Bills in circulation	Liabilities	Specie
June 1817	2498050	530981	1275109	1806090	546079
June 1818	2699850	594793	1538361	2133154	532510
June 1819	3024750	516959	1396375	1913334	458672
June 1820	3250000	576977	1342508	1919485	490783
June 1821	3250000	786707	1681351	2468058	770919
June 1822	3400000	624256	1940581	2564837	513651

Date	Capital stock paid in	Deposits	Total = Town + Country Bills in circulation	Liabilities	Specie
June 1803	2225262	1522271	1565189	2645117	1079928
June 1804	5012887	1122119	1695301	2673203	977902
June 1805	5460000	1021229	1553824	2575053	847998
June 1806	5485000	2036490	1613684	3650174	959394
June 1807	5560000	1713968	1481777	3195745	714783
June 1808	5960000	2546717	1038042	3584759	1015843
June 1809	5960000	2314788	1334948	3649736	821942
June 1810	6685000	2461877	2098491	4560368	1347723
June 1811	6685000	3385721	2355571	5741292	1513001
June 1812	7960000	4734826	2162358	6897184	3681696
June 1813	8895000	6903593	2186837	9090430	5780798
June 1814	11050000	9201718	2922611	12124329	6946543
June 1815	11462000	4057395	2740511	6797906	646241
June 1816	11475000	2133279	2134690	4267969	1260210
June 1817	9298050	3520794	2495460	6016254	1577454
June 1818	9749275	2905797	2680477	5586274	1129598
June 1819	10374750	2574347	2464057	5038404	1198889
June 1820	10600000	3176003	2614734	5790737	1280852
June 1821	9800000	5448608	3010762	8459370	3048829
June 1822	10821125	3235828	3132552	6368380	946267

Table 5: Assessed Personal Property Ward-by-Ward, 1795–1821.*

	Year						
	1795	1796	1797	1798	1799	1800	1801
Ward 1	30850	45200	46100	48150	58000	88700	97650
Ward 2	51050	63000	59150	63200	73250	55850	64000
Ward 3	74950	87250	89400	89000	93050	94600	91150
Ward 4	55650	73900	65550	80700	94650	89050	90900
Ward 5	82550	100350	110450	110000	106700	116400	117200
Ward 6	194750	224650	204400	229350	194000	231150	220000
Ward 7	399950	390550	373950	415550	445600	539750	421850
Ward 8	292400	359650	289750	336900	289700	286350	320850
Ward 9	640900	658250	600000	654600	576650	614050	669550
Ward 10	355600	397150	430600	520600	577650	614650	655950
Ward 11	388500	524600	459150	555550	624000	651600	727700
Ward 12	392650	463700	411800	550100	632950	710200	725550

	1802	1803	1804	1805	1806	1807	1808
Ward 1		178050	197200	183100	263200	278700	219300
Ward 2	114650	117350	128850	111250	229700	221100	178000
Ward 3		204850	184550	160300	357400	337100	281300
Ward 4	194850	219300	211000	216500	408700	988500	899900
Ward 5	234900	176800	165250	370100	733100	740700	735400
Ward 6	440650	475900	418400	1044500		301000	282900
Ward 7	1101500	1127150	1045850	972500	1274700	1386600	1458800
Ward 8	679000	880750	812500	1431500	755400	955700	932700
Ward 9	1335700	1382350	1432300	1401800	829500	904100	891700
Ward 10	1496100	1362300	1434700	696700	1070100	968800	1070800
Ward 11	819250	688050	641200	1044650	561100	506100	490300
Ward 12	1032550	971900	992350		497200	465600	430800

	1809	1810	1811	1812	1813	1814	1815
Ward 1	214400	211900	159200	128100	116200	95300	97100
Ward 2	188500	174300	191800	136800	135200	12300	112500
Ward 3	283200	272800	280300	231800	213300	200200	202800
Ward 4	843900	803900	817300	893100	853700	773900	830800
Ward 5	765300	741300	627500	485800	489800	544600	542300
Ward 6	371400	372600	357400	355900	329100	306400	259800
Ward 7	1627500	1651600	1613700	1345200	1422500	1362000	1322800
Ward 8	889400	768800	750000	922300	900700	834200	827600
Ward 9	912700	1000600	1093400	951400	1043200	1081600	922500
Ward 10	1215700	1244800	1475100	1409400	1490800	1433900	1351600
Ward 11	516900	573700	582500	576500	591200	494400	484500
Ward 12	484700	456600	441100	345900	297400	333400	369400

*   *Town of Boston Tax Valuation Books, 1784 to 1822.*

	1816	1817	1818	1819	1820	1821
Ward 1	111200	124800	109000	93600	94700	103400
Ward 2	115800	98900	103200	88900	97300	99200
Ward 3	186300	187100	184000	199100	183000	213800
Ward 4	862200	970900	1002500	852600	767700	452600
Ward 5	556100	598200	642100	498300	480500	555200
Ward 6	270000	265100	274000	290300	300600	312700
Ward 7	1519700	1536800	1570100	1692500	1732400	2305900
Ward 8	804400	1103300	1257400	1296900	1247300	1281500
Ward 9	1054100	961900	958300	944100	944900	1098300
Ward 10	1388700	1450800	1424600	1370700	1430300	1456200
Ward 11	452500	465900	457900	538100	576300	682500
Ward 12	392400	423000	456600	426600	446100	474500

Year

Table 6: Assessed Property, Town of Boston, 1795–1821.*

Year	Polls	Real Estate	Personal Estate
1795	3162	2240100	2959800
1796	3432	2781700	3388250
1797	3531	2913050	3140300
1798	4074	3116350	3653700
1799	4389	3124800	3766200
1800	4483	3450500	4101350
1801	4772	3493359	4202200
1802	4768	5164300	7449150
1803	5739	6172100	7784750
1804	5428	6876700	7664150
1805	6481	7551100	7811400
1806	4166	7690650	6980100
1807	6915	9399300	8053500
1808	7148	9547000	7871900
1809	7410	9856000	8313600
1810	7764	10177200	8272900
1811	8053	10552000	8389300
1812	6845	9696900	7782200
1813	6726	9057000	7882900
1814	6636	8962700	7472200
1815	6457	9132800	7323700
1816	7720	10456100	7713400
1817	7491	10821800	8186700
1818	7699	11160900	8439700
1819	8030	11397900	8291700
1820	7810	10843500	8301100
1821	8646	11060200	9035800

* *Town of Boston Tax Valuation Books, 1784 to 1822.*

Table 7: Ward 9 Assessed Personal and Real Property, 1795–1821.*

Year	Polls	Real Estate	Personal Estate
1795	214	288300	640900
1796	185	331700	658250
1797	197	324150	600000
1798	281	631600	654600
1799	272	349100	576650
1800	217	380850	614050
1801	245	406650	669550
1802	274	537050	1335700
1803	363	646950	1382350
1804	280	786950	1432300
1805	435	973150	1431500
1806	484	802650	829500
1807	520	1020500	904100
1808	549	966700	932700
1809	642	1019200	912700
1810	739	1129500	1000600
1811	847	1237900	1093400
1812	755	1168500	951400
1813	718	1094500	1043200
1814	684	1072000	1081600
1815	625	1045000	922500
1816	814	1163300	1054100
1817	740	1150500	961900
1818	743	1286600	958300
1819	754	1323100	944100
1820	716	1243400	944900
1821	824	1278100	1098300

* *Town of Boston Tax Valuation Books, 1784 to 1822.*

Table 8: Ward 10 Assessed Personal and Real Property, 1795–1821.*

Year	Polls	Real Estate	Personal Estate
1795	291	284000	355600
1796	319	325550	397150
1797	324	324150	600000
1798	441	361600	654600
1799	430	382050	577650
1800	435	419300	614650
1801	420	433700	655950
1802	627	831350	1496100
1803	640	931350	1362300
1804	558	1041600	1434700
1805	585	1116200	1401800
1806	373	916600	1070100
1807	423	976000	968800
1808	408	1023100	1070800
1809	468	1061400	1215700
1810	513	1064900	1244800
1811	496	1046900	1475100
1812	405	1033400	1409400
1813	425	994300	1490800
1814	423	975800	1433900
1815	402	1034300	1351600
1816	448	1247700	1388700
1817	397	1273800	1450800
1818	396	1240200	1424600
1819	400	1250100	1370700
1820	389	1149600	1430300
1821	411	1226300	1456200

* *Town of Boston Tax Valuation Books, 1784 to 1822.*

Table 9: Ward 12 Assessed Personal and Real Property, 1800–21.*

Year	Polls	Real Estate	Personal Estate
1795	633	363350	392650
1796	688	425050	463700
1797	659	425350	411800
1798	624	503300	550100
1799	1078	542800	632950
1800	1154	601300	710200
1801	1282	634450	725550
1802	1114	936550	1032550
1803	1152	1016950	971900
1804	1119	1337500	992350
1805	1242	1407800	1044650
1806	752	760650	497200
1807	729	763700	465600
1808	780	851600	430800
1809	876	851900	484700
1810	889	876300	456600
1811	855	878600	441100
1812	783	825000	345900
1813	693	713500	297400
1814	728	708900	333400
1815	690	745700	369400
1816	896	903600	392400
1817	880	879400	423000
1818	877	895700	456600
1819	919	954200	426600
1820	931	914000	446100
1821	1048	891000	474500

*   *Town of Boston Tax Valuation Books, 1784 to 1822.*

INDEX